The Right of Innocent Passage and the Evolution of the International Law of the Sea

The Current Regime of 'Free' Navigation in Coastal Waters of Third States

A publication of the Graduate Institute of
International Studies, Geneva

The Right of Innocent Passage and the Evolution of the International Law of the Sea

The Current Regime of 'Free' Navigation in Coastal Waters of Third States

Francis Ngantcha

Pinter Publishers
London and New York

First published in Great Britain in 1990 by
Pinter Publishers Limited
25 Floral Street, London WC2E 9DS

British Library Cataloguing in Publication Data

A CIP catalogue record for this book is available from the British Library
ISBN 0-86187-851-5

Library of Congress Cataloging-in-Publication Data

Ngantcha, Francis.
The right of innocent passage and the evolution of the international law of the sea: the current regime of 'free' navigation in coastal waters of third states/Francis Ngantcha.
p. cm.
'This work was initially a Ph.D. thesis submitted and defended at the Graduate Institute of International Studies of the University of Geneva, Switzerland, in 1986'—Acknowledgement.
Includes bibliographical references (p.).
ISBN 0-86187-851-5
1. Maritime law. 2. Territorial waters. I. Title.
JX4411.N53 1990
341.7'566–dc20

90–31910
CIP

Typeset by Florencetype Ltd, Kewstoke, Avon
Printed and bound in Great Britain by Biddles Ltd.

For Papa Monie Ngantcha, my mother, my wife,
brothers and sisters and
Charlotte Ngantcha

I am master of the earth but the law
is the mistress of the sea

Emperor Antoninus

Contents

Abbreviations

AFDI	Annuaire français de droit international
AJIL	The American Journal of International Law
BYBIL	British Year Book of International Law
ILC *Yearbook*	Yearbook of the International Law Commission
ICJ *Reports*	International Court of Justice, Reports of Judgments, Advisory Opinions and Orders
ICLQ	The International and Comparative Law Quarterly
IDI *Annuaire*	Annuaire de l'Institut de droit international
L O N Doc.	Documents of the League of Nations
ADI *Recueil*	Recueil des cours de l'Académie de droit international de La Haye
(First) UNCLOS	United Nations Conference on the Law of the Sea (1958)
Third UNCLOS	Third United Nations Conference on the Law of Sea
1982 Convention	The United Nations Convention on the Law of the Sea

Acknowledgements

This work was initially a Ph.D. thesis submitted and defended at the Graduate Institute of International Studies of the University of Geneva, Switzerland, in 1986. Hence a lot of people have to be thanked for contributing, directly or indirectly, to its final completion. First thanks go to my supervisor and both the academic and administrative staff of the Graduate Institute.

Professor Lucius Caflisch went beyond his supervisory role and, despite his administrative and other obligations, acted as *the* major source of inspiration all through the hardships of an exercise of this nature. His effort was corroborated by Professors George Abi-Saab and Philippe Cahier. To all these gentlemen I express my sincere thanks and extend to them my perpetual bond of friendship.

The personnel of the administrative corps of the Graduate Institute and of the Library of the United Nations in Geneva who also contributed their quota to this work are many to cite by names. I would like to salute all of them through Mme Simone Bourquin and M. André Lapper.

I would never forget, of course, the fountain of my interest in the Law of the Sea—Ambassador Paul Bamela Engo, former Chairman of one of the three Committees of the Third United Nations Conference on the Law of the Sea (1973–82). I hope he will enjoy reading this book.

My last, but not the least, words of appreciation go to my family. The always readily available long-distant exhortation from my mother, Mama Elizabeth Yinga, and my brother, Mr Emmanuel Ngantcha, was comforting. Claudine, obviously overshadowed everybody else with her type of assistance—the indispensable emotional and psychological support from a beloved wife.

Francis T. Ngantcha
Geneva, Switzerland
September 1989

General introduction

Despite the signing of the United Nations Convention on the Law of the Sea in 1982, the presence of foreign vessels in coastal seas of third states remains subject to legal polemics. This has been surprisingly common in the 1980s where despite the increase in utilization of the oceans and coastal seas as global highways for navigation and shipping[1] in a beneficial interdependent maritime economy, strategic military and scientific equations have been introduced into these zones by the superpowers.

On 13 March 1986, two American naval vessels, a cruiser and a destroyer, equipped with sensors and listening devices, entered the Black Sea via the Turkish Straits, in order to exercise what the American naval authorities called their right of innocent passage in the territorial waters of the Soviet Union. The Soviet authorities placed its Black Sea air and naval forces on combat readiness and in its official note of protest characterized the American action as provocative and a manifest violation of their territorial rights.[2]

Shortly after this incident, some units of the United States naval forces of the Sixth Fleet in the Mediterranean sailed into the Gulf of Sirte south of latitude 32°30′, a zone claimed by the Libyan Arab Jamahiriya as internal waters.[3] This was purported to be in keeping with the Declaration made in July 1985 by the United States delegation to the United Nations to the effect that: '[she] rejects as an unlawful interference with the freedoms of navigation and overflight and related high seas freedoms, the Libyan claim to prohibit navigation . . . in the Gulf of Sirte'[4]

The Law of the Sea has traditionally been aimed at protecting the international community's interests over the inexhaustible uses of ocean space. To this end, the main pillar of that law has been the freedom of the sea—with the implication that seagoing vehicles and other similar structures may freely roam the oceans. When much of the ocean space was considered 'high seas' and the governing rule *res communis*, this tenet was unquestionable.

The 'territorialization' of the ocean space, i.e. its division into zones of coastal State sovereignty and/or jurisdiction, has put a stop to the 'old' system of 'free' global maritime communication and transportation. Consequently, the international networks of trade and commerce, naval mobility, overflight, etc. have come to depend upon the national maritime spaces of third States for purposes of passage.

Various regimes have been proposed, particularly within the forum of the Third United Nations Conference on the Law of the Sea, with the main purpose of protecting the rights of passage of vessels of third States in such 'territorialized' coastal waters. Among these rights are the right of innocent passage in the territorial sea, in archipelagic waters and sometimes in internal waters; the right of transit passage in international straits; and the right of archipelagic sealanes passage in archipelagic sealanes. Unlike the right of innocent passage, the last two rights are the products of intensive negotiations in the Third United Nations Conference on the Law of the Sea.

However dissimilar these other rights are to the right of innocent passage, they can be considered offshoots of the latter. Prior to the 1982 United Nations Convention on the Law of the Sea, the Geneva Conventions of 1958 were the governing law, acknowledging only that right for navigation in portions of waters subject to coastal State sovereignty. Beyond these waters, the rule of freedom of navigation applied.

The waters placed under coastal State sovereignty are made up of internal waters, the territorial seas and archipelagic waters. Within these zones, the coastal State generally exercises full sovereignty subject to the right of innocent passage. The exercise of full sovereignty on the one hand and the exercise of the right of innocent passage on the other invites the simultaneous projection of two sets of competing jurisdictions—those of individual coastal States and those of the international community *via* the flag State. One of the major goals of the Law of the Sea has been to strike a balance between the two.

The right of innocent passage is deeply rooted in the practice of States and universally recognized as one of the main rules of customary international law. Thus, independently of any convention, the right of innocent passage can be said to stand on its own merit. It is said to limit the sovereignty of States over their coastal waters.

However, in recognition of the sovereignty exercised by States over their coastal waters, it is also generally accepted that the right of innocent passage is confined to maritime surface navigation conducted for inoffensive and exclusively peaceful purposes. Secondly, the exercise of that right prima facie excludes overflight and submerged navigation. And, finally, it has been argued that appropriate prior notification and/or authorization of the coastal State is necessary to give certain foreign vessels such as warships the right to exercise innocent passage. That having been said, the codification of the right of innocent passage has inevitably been aimed at defining with greater precision that right and at delimiting the scope of coastal State sovereignty over its exercise. Key issues in this respect are the regulatory power of the coastal State in relation to passage and the innocent character of such passage.

While coastal States are not to enact measures that virtually nullify or hamper the right of innocent passage, third States exercising that right are in turn not to construe it subjectively or to interpret it in a capricious or impetuous way. The delicate balance between the security and other interests of the coastal State, and the interest of the international community in free and unimpeded navigation in coastal waters, is therefore the backbone of the right of innocent passage.

The Third United Nations Conference on the Law of the Sea, with its issue-aggregate or package-deal considerations, used the rights-of-passage issue as a trump card in many respects.

The exercise of these rights in coastal waters was obtained in exchange for a grant to the coastal States of a 12-nautical-mile territorial sea, 'limited' sovereignty and economic jurisdiction in other portions of coastal waters, and a consent regime for marine scientific research. Thus a detailed analysis of the right of innocent passage will highlight prevailing trends in international relations (and their effects on the contemporary international order)—the bending and forging of rules to serve political ends. This is especially so with the 1982 Convention, the product of the Third United Nations Conference on the Law of the Sea. The 1982 Convention reproduces verbatim parts of the 1958 Geneva Convention, adds innovations in many instances and contradicts some national laws. International navigational issues, independently of any doctrinal developments, have evolved into a 'comprehensive conventional arrangement of several interacting, contradicting and overlapping regulatory regimes'.

This bring us to the final point, which concerns the sovereignty recognized and attributed to States over their coastal waters. Sovereignty is still considered as a fundamental principle of positive international law, despite various opinions to the contrary. By virtue of the double recognition of the coastal States' exclusive rights in the coastal waters and the international community's inclusive right of passage in these waters, could it be said that these two rights coexist in equality or that there is an inherent hierarchy among them?

To address the various issues identified above, we shall conduct our analysis by attempting to answer the following questions:

- What is the right of innocent passage?
- Why does it exist?
- Where is it exercised?
- Who exercises it?
- And who decides whether its exercise or the refusal to allow its exercise is abusive?

With these questions in mind, we shall, in the chapters that follow, attempt to analyse the origin, nature and scope of the right of innocent passage, starting with an introductory chapter on the status of coastal waters. This will involve an evolutionary recapitulation of the legal status of the adjacent coastal seas in early State practice, bilateral and multilateral treaties, etc., and its successive accommodation with the rights-of-passage regimes.

In Chapter 2, we shall focus our investigation on the right of innocent passage as the principal derogation made by customary international law to the exercise of coastal State sovereignty. To this end, we shall scrutinize the debates preceding the adoption of provisions on the meaning of the right of innocent passage, and identify the special characteristics differentiating that right from other sea passage regimes. In this way, it is hoped that, as the nature, importance and interests at stake over coastal waters vary considerably, objective, stable and common rules will emerge for a uniform pattern of conduct in determining what does or does not constitute the exercise of the right of innocent passage.

Chapter 3 will be concerned with innocent passage in certain coastal zones. This will involve, where appropriate, a determination of the ideas which justified the exercise of that right pursuant to the special legal status accorded to certain coastal zones other than the territorial sea *stricto sensu*. It should be emphasized, of course, that the principle traditionally was concerned with navigation in the territorial sea generally and dealt neither with straits, nor 'internal waters', nor archipelagic waters.

Chapters 4 and 5 will consider the relationship between different categories of sea-going vessels and the degree of their entitlement to the exercise of the right of innocent passage. Here we shall attempt to analyse the 'powers of interference' of the coastal State with regard to foreign merchant ships and foreign official ships, particularly warships.

These two chapters, the backbone of the book, will show that despite the various treaty provisions, by virtue of their all-powerful 'sovereignty', coastal States can frustrate the exercise of the 'independent' right of innocent passage by ships regardless of ownership and/or nationality.

To add to this examination of the right of innocent passage in connection with coastal State sovereignty, Chapter 6 will examine the rights and obligations of both the coastal State and the flag State in the exercise of that right, and Chapter 7 will focus on the mandatory or optional nature of the disputes settlement mechanism regarding the issues of non-innocent passage or of refusal of innocent passage by the coastal State.

Finally, the concluding chapter will evaluate in the light of contemporary law and practice the place of the right of innocent passage in coastal waters acknowledged to be under the sovereignty of the coastal State. In this way, the book could also be looked upon as a contribution to the international law of territorial sovereignty.

Throughout this book, we shall attempt, wherever appropriate, to examine customary international law and the municipal laws of some States, and to examine relevant case law, so as to grasp properly the policy intentions underlying the debates preceding the adoption of the only two sets of conventions that relate exclusively to the Law of the Sea: the 1958 Geneva Conventions and the 1982 United Nations Convention on the Law of the Sea. In this way, we hope to clarify the various interests which divided the negotiators and to decipher the rationale behind the specific provisions adopted.

We have adopted the 1930 Hague Codification Conference as a watershed, and the 1982 Convention as the present codified international law on innocent passage. It would be an error to regard the latter as having settled all issues involving international navigation in coastal waters. As will be seen, coastal States, and particularly the major maritime powers, have in many ways successfully managed to avoid the inclusion in the final text of any provisions expressly contrary to their interests in this area. Ambiguous clauses were the price paid for agreement in many circumstances. This uncertainty casts its shadow on the right of innocent passage in the face of a strong, full-fledged sovereignty of the coastal State in its coastal waters. Although the right of innocent passage in coastal waters has never been a scholarly *terra incognita*, its changing meaning and significance remain a subject of academic as well as practical interest. For, according to conventional wisdom, 'la mer est juridiquement toujours "autre chose" que la terre; le navire est juridiquement toujours "autre chose" qu'un simple objet permettant à des êtres humains d'agir dans le milieu maritime.'[5]

Notes

1. Moore, J.N., 'Regime of Straits and the Third United Nations Conference on the Law of the Sea', *AJIL*, vol. 74, 1980, pp. 77–121, at p. 119.
2. For further details see Butler, W.E., 'Innocent Passage and the 1982 Convention: The Influence of Soviet Law and Policy', *AJIL*, vol. 81, 1987, pp. 331–47, at pp. 343ff.

On 12 February 1988, two United States warships and two Soviet frigates 'collided' in Soviet territorial waters in the Black Sea. The Soviet Union issued another formal protest of the American 'presence'.

3. More facts can be distilled from the following volumes of *Keesing's Contemporary Archives*: 1981, vol. 27, pp. 31181–3; 1986, vol. 32, pp. 34454–7. In 1987, a *note* circulated to all members of the United Nations referring to the accord entitled 'Agreement on the historical waters of the Republic of Vietnam and the Republic of Kampuchea' signed 7 July 1982. It was stated expressly: '. . . the United States views the historic claim to the waters in question as without foundation and reserves its rights and those of its nationals in this regard.' Per notes by governments—*Law of the Sea Bulletin*, No. 10, November 1987, p. 23.
4. *Law of the Sea Bulletin*, No. 6, October 1985, p. 40.
5. Per Riphagen, W., in *Perspectives du droit de la mer à l'issue de la 3e Conférence des Nations Unies*. Société française pour le droit international, Colloque de Rouen, Paris, Pedone, 1984, p. 201. Another philosophy upholds that portions of the seas 'colour' a particular vessel in a certain 'legal light', op. cit., note 2, p. 340.

Chapter 1

Legal status of adjacent coastal waters and the regime of passage (evolutionary perspective)

1. Introduction

There are today no more doubts that the cherished Grotian concept of the freedom of the seas does not apply to all the areas of the globe that belong to the sea in the geographical sense.[1] A coastal State is entitled, by virtue of its sovereignty over the land territory, to exercise a similar[2] prerogative over a marginal area of the sea adjacent to its coast.

In its Article 2(1), the United Nations Convention on the Law of the Sea (1982 Convention)[3] states the following fundamental principle: 'The sovereignty of a coastal State extends, beyond its land territory and internal waters and, in the case of an archipelagic State, its archipelagic waters, to an adjacent belt of sea, described as the territorial sea'. This provision by and large reproduces Article 1 of the 1958 Convention on the Territorial Sea and the Contiguous Zone,[4] which itself was based on Article 1 of the draft of the International Law Commission.

The International Law Commission stated in its commentary on the draft of this Article, in its report to the General Assembly, that

> the rights of the coastal State over the territorial sea do not differ in nature from the rights of sovereignty which the State exercises over other parts of its territory . . . It is also the principle underlying a number of multilateral conventions—such as the Air Navigation Convention of 1919 and the International Civil Aviation Convention of 1944—which treat the territorial sea in the same way as other parts of State territory.[5]

Similar statements had been made in the 1920s and 1930s. At The Hague Codification Conference of 1930, held under the auspices of the League of Nations, it was declared, in an observation relating to an identical article on the same subject-matter, that

> the idea . . . sought . . . by stating that the belt of territorial sea forms part of the territory of the State is that the power exercised by the State over this belt is in its nature in no way different from the power which the State exercises over the land domain. This is also the reason why the term "sovereignty" has been retained, a term which better than any other describes the juridical nature of this power.[6]

However, Article 2 of the 1982 Convention on the Law of the Sea goes on to declare, in its paragraph 3, that '. . . the sovereignty over the territorial sea is exercised subject to this Convention and to other rules of international law'.

This paragraph, like the first one discussed above, is a verbatim reproduction of paragraph 2 of Article 1 of the 1958 Geneva Convention on the Territorial Sea and the Contiguous Zone. Similar provisions are found in the 1956 Draft Articles of the International Law Commission and in the adopted Articles contained in the Final Act of The Hague Codification Conference of 1930.

Two questions of international law arise in connection with this expressed limitation of sovereignty over coastal waters. The first is whether sovereignty, wherever exercised, may be subject to the rules of international law. The second is whether both the special limitation ('subject to this Convention') and the general limitation ('other rules of international law') are not superfluous. These questions become all the more pertinent when reference is made to a statement made by Max Huber in the *Island of Palmas* arbitration:

> International law, the structure of which is not based on any super-State organisation, cannot be presumed to reduce a right such as territorial sovereignty, with which almost all international relations are bound up, to the category of an abstract right, without concrete manifestations.[7]

As a response to the first question, it is indisputable today that sovereignty, wherever exercised, is limited by the rules of international law.[8] Thus, in the same *Island of Palmas* arbitration, Max Huber went on to declare:

> Territorial sovereignty, as has already been said, involves the exclusive right to display the activities of a State. This right has a corollary duty: the obligation to protect within the territory the rights of other States, in particular their right to integrity and inviolability in peace and in war, together with the rights which each State may claim for its nationals in foreign territory. Without manifesting its territorial sovereignty in a manner corresponding to circumstances, the State cannot fulfil this duty. Territorial sovereignty cannot limit itself to its negative side, i.e. to excluding the activities of other States; for it serves to divide between nations the space upon which human activities are employed, in order to assure them at all points the minimum of protection of which international law is the guardian.[9]

By expressly limiting the sovereignty of States in their coastal waters, despite the inherent limitations of the exercise of sovereignty anywhere, the Hague Codification Conference, which first considered international draft articles on this matter, justified its position as follows, thus answering the second question:

> Obviously, sovereignty over the territorial sea, like sovereignty over the domain on land, can only be exercised subject to the conditions laid down by international law. As the limitations which international law imposes on the power of the State in respect of the latter's sovereignty over the territorial sea are greater than those it imposes in respect of the domain on land, it has not been thought superfluous to make special mention of these limitations in the text of the article itself.

As to the issue of having a special limitation and a general limitation, the 1930 Codification Conference further commented: 'These limitations are to be sought in the first place in the present Convention; as, however, the Convention cannot hope to exhaust the matter, it has been thought necessary to refer also to other rules of international law.[10]

A logical question that follows from the above is: What are the limitations restricting coastal State sovereignty on the coastal waters? At first glance, it appears that the limitations are so many that the Convention cannot exhaust all of them; hence the call for residual assistance from 'other rules of international law'. When the question of identifying some of these limitations came up in the debates of the International Law Commission in the 1950s, only one which could fall into the category of restrictions to coastal State sovereignty both under the future Convention and under general international law could be identified.

In paragraphs 4 and 5 of its commentary on draft Article 1 the International Law Commission stated:

> Some of the limitations imposed by international law on the exercise of sovereignty in the territorial sea are set forth in the present articles which cannot, however, be regarded as exhaustive. Incidents in the territorial sea raising legal questions are also governed by the general rules of international law, and these cannot be specially codified in the present draft for the purposes of their application to the territorial sea. That is why 'other rules of international law' are mentioned in addition to the provisions contained in the present articles.

To illustrate some other uncodifiable limitations, the commentary of the Commission went on to state:

> It may happen that, by reason of some special relationship, geographical or other, between two States, rights in the territorial sea of one of them are granted to the other in excess of the rights recognised in the present draft. It is not the Commissions's intention to limit in any way any more extensive right of passage or other right enjoyed by States by custom or treaty.[11]

At the debates in the International Law Commission, the following opinions were expressed on what could be some possible limitations to coastal State sovereignty in the territorial sea. Contradicting those who saw the reference to 'other rules of international law' as unnecessary, Lauterpacht considered that allowance had to be made for the possibility of an involuntary omission. In addition, he said that there were certain general rules of international law which were applicable in the matter, as indeed to other topics of international law, such as the principle prohibiting the abuse of rights, and generally the law of State responsibility.[12] For George Scelle, the matter was much simpler: 'The sovereignty exercised over the territorial sea was not of the same nature as that exercised over the mainland. It was in fact completely different from it, as was shown by the right of innocent passage, the right of pursuit . . .'[13] Zourek thought that only the right of innocent passage represented a limitation on the exercise of sovereignty over territorial waters; thus, the Commission's mandate was limited to studying the conditions under which that right was to be exercisable.[14] Sharing this same opinion when the topic was first presented to the Commission in 1952, Amado, another member, had earlier stated the cardinal principle that the only important additional condition to which sovereignty over the territorial sea was subject, as compared to sovereignty over the land domain, was, as everyone knew and recognized, the right of innocent passage.[15]

When all factors are considered in the light of the above, it may be said that the only substantial and practical limitation on State sovereignty in the coastal waters which differentiates that sovereignty from sovereignty over the land domain is the right of innocent passage by foreign ships. Any other limitation of sovereignty is actually a derivative or consequence of the above right of innocent passage. This, therefore, means that the residual rights within the territorial sea belong to the coastal State.

A substantial portion of conventions and drafts on the Law of the Sea deal with the right of innocent passage in a comprehensive manner. However, that right is a classical element of customary international law, as pointed out by Jessup in 1927: 'As a general principle, the right of innocent passage requires no supporting argument or citation of authority; it is firmly established in international law.'[16]

In the view of many authors, the existence of this restriction on coastal State sovereignty is no longer in dispute. However, the scope of the right of innocent passage, and the solution of consequent issues of maritime jurisdiction to which that right gives rise, depend on a correct historical and evolutionary appreciation of the nature of coastal waters. This is so for several reasons. Primarily, the juridical regime of these waters has had to adapt to present-day realities. Whereas the customary regime of coastal waters was dictated by centuries of State practice based essentially on unilateral action, today multilateral fora try to forge rules in the face of diametrically opposing interests of States. Of course there is no doubt that any innocent use of straits, archipelagos or canals is not easily acquiesced to by small States in the vicinity of such geographical features.

In the present chapter, an attempt will therefore be made to analyse the juridical nature of coastal waters in the light of their special geographical configuration, with a view to identifying, where appropriate, the types of passage regimes applicable. The discussion will portray some of the unique components of the right of innocent passage which necessitated the application of different passage regimes to different types of coastal waters. This survey of the legal status of the various types of coastal waters in the light of passage regimes will be effected in a historical and analytical manner, so as to show the 'growth' of the right of innocent passage in the continued global search for a balance between State sovereignty in coastal seas and the exceptions to that sovereignty.

2. The notion of territorial sea

The 1982 United Nations Convention on the Law of the Sea, expressing present-day positive international law, affirms the sovereignty[17] of the coastal State in its territorial sea.[18] That this recognition was not an easy achievement could be perceived from the debates on what terminology was most appropriate to describe these coastal waters.[19] However, the concept of sovereignty is too nebulous and elastic to identify with maximum precision the nature of the rights exercised in coastal waters. Depending on the constitutional make-up of coastal States, these rights could differ from one country to another.[20]

Although international law guarantees sovereignty over coastal waters, it is another matter whether the coastal State automatically incorporates these waters within the national boundary.[21] Thus, in the words of O'Connell, '[t]he function of international law is not to invest States with legal regimes but to secure recognition of regimes contrived by action of individual members of the community of nations'.[22] But then the International Court of Justice had held, regarding the continental shelf,

> [t]hat the rights of the coastal State in respect of the area of continental shelf that constitutes a natural prolongation of its land territory into and under the sea exist *ipso facto* and *ab initio*, by virtue of its sovereignty . . . In order to exercise it, no special legal process has to be gone through, nor have any special legal acts to be performed.[23]

Thus, one wonders why the water column superjacent to space over which the coastal State has sovereignty should revert to it only by express proclamation. In spite of these shortcomings, 'la souveraineté reste aujourd'hui encore la pierre angulaire de l'ordre juridique international', and '[p]our le droit international classique, la souveraineté est dite "territoriale", parce qu'elle désigne avant tout un pouvoir politique (comportant une puissance de contrainte) s'exerçant de façon exclusive sur un territoire déterminé'.[24]

Below an evaluation will be made of the origins, rationale, nature and extent of the territorial sea, in order to elucidate the contemporary practice relating to the classical exception limiting coastal State sovereignty in coastal waters.

(a) Origins and rationale for a territorial sea

The idea that a coastal State could exercise some authority beyond its land territory in the adjacent seas is thought to pre-date the concept of freedom of the seas. According to some authors,[25] this idea took root around the fourteenth century, when law was interpreted, not created; discovered, not made; and when 'the classical Roman Law indicated the growth of the belief that the Emperor, King, or "State" possess some kind of inchoate property rights in the sea adjacent to the territories of the same.[26] Of course the notion of sovereignty in these waters was then a moot question since the concept of the personality of a nation-State, as understood today, was non-existent. Nonetheless, despite the Treaty of Westphalia (1648) establishing the contemporary notion of the nation-State, the concept of the territorial sea as an accepted principle of international law only crystallized in the 1958 Geneva Conference on the Law of the Sea.

Without attempting to recite the complete history of the evolution of coastal State claims to adjacent seas,[27] we intend to emphasize the role played by the concept of innocent passage within the framework of such claims to the sea.

It should be recalled at this stage that the doctrine of the freedom of the seas was based on the proposition that, being a space of free communication, inappropriable by the laws of nature, the sea was a *res communis par excellence*. Historically, the modern doctrine of the freedom of the seas could be traced to the defeat of the Spanish Armada in 1588 and the firm attitude of the English monarch at the time, Queen Elizabeth I of England.[28]

Hugo Grotius (1583–1645), considered the 'father' of the Law of the Sea, was among those who articulated the doctrine and ultimately enabled it to crystallize into rules of international law around the end of the eighteenth century, despite occasional opposition.[29]

Opposing the concept of the freedom of the seas was the age-old belief that the sea was susceptible to appropriation by individual coastal States. As we saw earlier, this tendency was encouraged by the interpretations of Roman Law and goes back at least to the Middle Ages.[30] Classical Roman Law recognized and perpetuated the belief that there existed a special interest of a monarch in the neighbouring waters and over the sea at large for the suppression of piracy and the consequent protection of sea traffic, etc. It is a historical fact that the maritime nations of Europe at the time—Spain, Portugal, Venice, Denmark and England—were in favour of an appropriation or at least the exercise of exclusive rights over large expanses of the sea.[31] Combating piracy was among the most important justification of these claims.

One nineteenth-century publicist sees the desire to fight against piracy as being at the origin of the notion of territorial sea:

> Pour se défendre des pirates, les caravelles marchandes payaient des taxes aux Etats maritimes qui faisaient la police des eaux. Venise en percevait dans l'Adriatique, Gênes dans la Méditerranée, l'Angleterre dans la mer du Nord, la Manche et l'Océan jusqu'au Golfe de Biscaye. Puis, peu à peu, des protestations s'élevèrent contre l'abus de ces taxes fiscales. La domination des mers par les Princes fut niée. C'est alors que se forma la notion de la mer territoriale.[32]

The above justification fell into obslescence when it became possible to go beyond the seas of Europe to conquer territories and spread Christianity. In consideration of all these factors, and in an extreme application of the idea of appropriability of the sea, the Pope partitioned the oceans of the world and the land space therein between Spain and Portugal in 1493.[33] Under this act, Spain claimed the exclusive right of navigation in the western portion of the Atlantic, in the Gulf of Mexico and in the Pacific. Portugal assumed a similar right in the Atlantic south of Morocco and in the Indian Ocean.[34] As could be expected, this extravagant display of sovereignty at sea by two nations could not go unchallenged.

The strongest objections came from England and Holland. The Spanish monopoly of commerce in the West Indies was challenged by British Tudor policies, and Elizabeth I affirmed the freedom of the seas in answer to a Spanish protest arising from the expedition of Sir Francis Drake.[35]

However, this policy was dictated by, and changed on account of, self-interest. Preoccupied by the rise of Holland as a maritime and trading power, England began to lay claim to the seas surrounding the British Isles.[36] In the seventeenth century, when English pretensions to sovereignty over the seas were at their height, many British scholars such as Coke, Selden and Prynne, maintained that to be on the four seas as well as within them was to be within the realm and the jurisdiction of the Admiralty.[37]

The most serious attempt to define the seas of England as being under British sovereignty was made in 1635. The jurist John Selden (1584–1654), whose work

Mare Clausum was first published in that year, asserted that the sea of England was 'that which flows between England and the opposite shores and ports.[38] He described the British Sea (*Oceanus Britannicus*) as being divided into four parts corresponding to the four quarters of the world. Selden's thesis was based on two main propositions: (1) contrary to the assertion of Grotius, the sea is not common to all by the laws of nature and hence is capable of appropriation by States; and (2) the King of Britain is sovereign over the seas surrounding his realm, and these seas are perpetual attributes of his sovereignty.[39] The sovereignty exercised by Britain included exclusive fishing rights, prohibition of acts of war and the obligation of foreign ships to extend a submissive salute to British vessels by hauling down their flag and striking their top-sail.

Towards the end of the eighteenth century, when British naval supremacy came to be recognized by the Dutch, British claims to the sea based on the doctine of *Mare Clausum* lost their importance.

For the Dutch, the main proponent of their thesis was Hugo Grotius (1583–1645). Grotius's *Mare Liberum*, which had formed the twelfth chapter of *De jure praedae* (1604), was the fruit of a legal consultation.[40] *Mare Liberum* was written in defence of Dutch interests in international trade and intercourse in the East Indies.[41] As stated earlier, Grotius's main contention was that the sea could not be appropriated. He thus helped popularize the principle of freedom of the seas, which received universal acceptance in the nineteenth century. The Industrial Revolution, the search for new markets and sources of raw materials, and the national rivalries among the European maritime powers added to the futility of one power endeavouring to maintain a lasting and exclusive dominion over the seas.

However, even the advocates of the doctrine of the freedom of the seas did not carry their proposition to its extreme conclusion, namely, that no part whatsoever of the sea was susceptible of being placed under coastal State jurisdiction. Such a conclusion would have been a practical absurdity, for States have a vital interest in the protection of their laws, their security and, possibly, their neutrality within a strip of the seas adjacent to their coasts.[42]

The idea of coastal State jurisdiction over adjacent waters of a relatively modest breadth (reasonable application of the *Mare Clausum* principle) could be based on effective domination, as is the case of land territory.[43] It was held that a legally recognized proprietary right in portions of the sea must be rooted on land, and that it was the *duty* of the coastal sovereign to punish offences committed at sea and to suppress piracy. The origin of this type of coastal State jurisdiction can be traced back to Azo, Bartolus, Baldus and Gentilis.

Azo, a disciple of the Glossators, first made the point that a private right over the seas may be granted in two ways; by the bestowal of a privilege or by long-standing custom acknowledged by the monarch.[44] Bartolus considered that the question of property rights in the sea touched an issue of first importance to the development of a theory of territorial waters. He held that a State owned islands located near its coasts and, consequently, as territorial sovereign, exercised exclusive jurisdiction over the intervening space. He even held that islands at a distance of one hundred miles belonged to the adjacent territory and that, within this distance, a State exercised its exclusive jurisdiction.[45]

Baldus, a pupil of Bartolus, helped to incorporate his teacher's theory into feudal law. In the feudal system, the king was the ultimate owner of all land in his realm. This included adjacent seas, which were considered a judicial district in which the civil law of the State possessing the corresponding land territory was to be applied.[46]

The final step was taken in the latter part of the sixteenth century by Gentilis. Alberico Gentili (1552–1608), who regarded his doctrine as part of the law of nations, was the first scholar to use the label '*territorium*' for the adjacent sea.[47] Coastal waters are an integral part of the territory of the State whose shores they wash.[48]

In conclusion, therefore, within a historical context the notion of territorial sea could be traced to the Glossators who as a group presented the primitive doctrine of the power of the monarch over offences committed at sea. Then followed Azo, Bartolus, Baldus and Gentilis. Azo recognized the authority of the monarch to limit the communal character of the sea; Bartolus asserted the right of the monarch to exclusive jurisdiction over the adjacent sea to the extent of one hundred miles; Baldus incorporated the doctrine into feudal law, calling the adjacent sea a judicial district. Finally, Gentilis brought the work to completion by categorically stating that the territorial rights of sovereignty which are vested in the head of State extend over the sea adjacent to his land territory.[49] These various formulations of the concept of coastal State rights in adjacent waters took place within three centuries: from the early part of the thirteenth to the latter part of the sixteenth centuries, a period which saw the height and ruin of feudalism and the rise of the modern State.[50]

These doctrines, formulated in order to grant coastal States 'sovereignty' over coastal waters within reasonable limits, met with very limited objections. As we saw earlier, the rationale for this lack of protest can be traced to the thirteenth century, when the practice of suppressing piracy and the exercise of some jurisdiction over other offences committed at sea crystallized.[51] Even supporters of the doctrine of the freedom of the seas, who strongly advocated free maritime communication by virtue of natural law and who saw the sea as a *res communis* belonging to all nations, stopped short of asserting that no part whatever of the sea was susceptible of being placed under coastal State jurisdiction.[52] Such a conclusion would have been obviously contrary to specific and vital interests.

Among the numerous justifications advanced for coastal State sovereignty in adjacent waters, one must mention security, the welfare of the coastal population, the protection of local laws, and the protection of neutrality in case of conflict. Philip Marshall Brown, an eminent authority on the subject, asserted in an editorial comment that: 'It is to be regarded as a question of the primordial right of every nation to exercise a "protective jurisdiction" over its coastal waters in matters affecting its own safety and welfare.'[53]

Although eminent authors of the late nineteenth century differed on the appropriate scientific and legal terminology to be used to describe the nature of the right enjoyed by a State over the territorial sea (ownership, sovereignty, dominium, imperium, servitude, etc.), and although differences persisted up to the twentieth century, they all agreed that the coastal State was to play a pre-eminent role in these waters.

Even the most articulate proponent of the freedom of the seas, Hugo Grotius, stated in Chapter III of his great work *De jure belli ac pacis* that sovereignty can be acquired over a part of the sea:

> It has . . . been a fairly easy matter to extend sovereignty only over a part of the sea without involving the right of ownership; and I do not think that any hindrance is put in the way of this by the universal customary law of which I have spoken. It seems clear, moreover, that sovereignty over a part of the sea is acquired in the same way as sovereignty elsewhere, that is, as we have explained above, through the instrumentality of persons and of territory. It is gained through the instrumentality of persons if, for example, a fleet, which is an army afloat, is stationed at some point of the sea; by means of territory, in so far as those who sail over the part of the sea along the coast may be constrained from the land no less than if they should be upon the land itself.[54]

From the eighteenth century onwards, many authors emphasized the security implications, for coastal States, of a freedom of the seas doctrine that would be applicable up to their shores. Consequently, to some authors the territorial sea was a prolongation of the territory of the State.[55] For others, the territorial sea was to be thus defined:

> Coastal sea is the name given to all that portion of the ocean that bathes the coasts of a State, and over which the latter exercises its sovereignty to the exclusion of all others . . . The greatest interest of preservation and defence, as well as the protection of mercantile and fiscal interests, is the origin of this prolongation of the national territory, to which is also given the name of territorial sea.[56]

The twentieth-century commentators who assert the vital necessity of coastal State sovereignty over coastal waters include Gidel,[57] Colombos,[58] O'Connell,[59] and Anzilotti. Anzilotti took the view that, whatever be the breadth of the territorial sea, it forms part of the territory of the State which exercises its power over it in the same manner and with the same title as over all other portions of the territory.[60]

Summing up the general trends on the relevance and rationale of coastal State prerogatives in coastal waters, an eminent statesman and jurist, Elihu Root, while acknowledging his sympathy for the freedom of the seas, recognized that:

> These vague and unfounded claims [of the seventeenth and eighteenth centuries] disappeared entirely, and there was nothing of them left . . . But the new principle of freedom, when it approached the shore, met with another principle, the principle of protection, not a residuum of the old claim, but a new independent basis and reason for modification, near the shore, of the principle of freedom. The sovereign of the land washed by the sea asserted a new right to protect his subjects and citizens against attack, against invasion, against interference and injury, to protect them against attack threatening their peace, to protect their revenues, to protect their health, to protect their industries. This is the basis and the sole basis on which is established the territorial zone that is recognized in the international law of today.[61]

However, despite the above-mentioned rationale for the existence of a territorial sea, a minority of writers had earlier denied the territorial character of that maritime belt.[62] Most of those holding this view were of the French school.[63] For these authors, as far as the security of the coastal State was concerned, only certain powers of control, jurisdiction, police, and the like could be conceded to the coastal State, and not sovereignty.

Nevertheless, the majority view favouring coastal States sovereignty in coastal waters has consistently been upheld in many international conventions dealing with issues related to those waters,[64] with the result of creating greater substantive new rights for coastal States in most instances and, consequently, broad derogations from the principle of the freedom of the high seas.

(b) Nature and extent of the territorial sea

Although the trend favouring the existence of a territorial sea prevailed in the end, the breadth of that sea was only agreed upon in the United Nations Convention on the Law of the Sea of 1982. The main obstacle to reaching agreement has always been the link made by most States between the legal status of the territorial sea and the issue of its maximum permissible outer limit.[65] Speaking of the extension of coastal State jurisdiction into the adjacent seas, an author asserts that: 'the seaward limits to which jurisdiction was exercised varied according to the particular purpose involved; these included the protection of neutrality, fisheries, and customs and sanitary laws'.[66]

As we saw earlier, the prime basis of coastal State claims to a territorial sea was the principle of protection. Logically the extent of that sea was supposed to depend on the power of the coastal State to exercise control from her shores. This idea was popularized in the eighteenth century by the Dutch jurist Cornelius van Bynkershoek who translated it into his famous maxim: '*Potestatem terrae finiri, ubi finitur armorum vis*'.[67] According to this author, the territorial dominion of a State extended as far as projectiles fired from cannons on the shore could reach. Thus was conceived the 'cannon-shot' rule, at least as generally understood in many circles today. In terms of distance in numbers, the figure of one marine league or three nautical miles is generally associated with that rule.

The zone in question, however, was not thought of as a belt of uniform breadth following the coastline of a State, but as covering only those waters which fell within the range of guns effectively placed on the coast.[68] As expected, the cannon range varied through the years[69] and thus varied from the three-mile measure. Nonetheless, this criterion was accepted by the major maritime powers, especially Great Britain and the United States, as part of a rule of international law setting a convenient compromise between the conflicting interests of coastal States and the international community.[70]

In any event, the three-mile rule was not universally accepted as the limit of territorial waters in international law. Some writers and States forged other methods of delimiting the jurisdictional zones a State might claim in the interest of its security.[71] Eventually, State practice amalgamated these different methods at the close of the nineteenth century with the following results:

(1) Coastal State jurisdiction extended to a continuous belt of coastal waters, the uniform breadth of which was generally set at three nautical miles.
(2) The various functional zones (security, neutrality, fishing, smuggling, etc.) gradually coalesced into one single multi-jurisdictional zone placed under the territorial sovereignty of the coastal State.
(3) Foreign vessels retained a right of innocent passage through the waters of the new single zone.[72]

Despite strong support given to the three-mile maxim by a majority of States and by the major maritime powers at the Hague Codification Conference in 1930, it was not accepted as a rule setting the breadth of the tereritorial sea.[73] The ensuing uncertainty characterized the discussions in the International Law Commission between 1950 and 1956. In its 1956 report to the General Assembly of the United Nations, the Commission noted in a commentary on this issue that it was an 'incontrovertible fact' that there was no uniformity as regards the three-mile limit of territorial sea; that 'the extension by a State of its territorial sea to a breadth between three and twelve miles was not characterized by the Commission as a breach of international law'; and that 'international law did not justify an extension of territorial sea beyond twelve miles'.[74]

Whatever was thought of the three-mile maxim as a rule of general international law until 1960, the momentum for the extension of national jurisdiction beyond that limit gained ground. Thus, before the opening of the Third United Nations Conference on the Law of the Sea, the number of States claiming a 12-mile territorial sea had increased from 13 in 1960 to 52 in 1973. Another 15 States claimed territorial waters ranging from 18 to 200 miles, while 25 States, including most of the maritime powers, dogmatically clung to the largely discredited three-mile formula. It is interesting to note that the Soviet Union had consistently advocated a 12-mile territorial sea.[75] As noted earlier, the 1982 United Nations Convention on the Law of the Sea has adopted the 12-mile limit as the maximum breadth of the territorial sea. But what is the true nature of this territorial sea *qua* territory of the coastal State today?

Calling the sea 'territory' is etymologically incorrect. Nevertheless, in international law, the term 'territory' has a well-defined connotation. It is being used here to describe the marginal sea, principally because in that sea coastal States may claim similar prerogatives as they do on their land territory. However, these prerogatives have had to be exercised taking into account the objective differences that exist between land and maritime spaces.

Prior to the 1958 Convention and particularly the 1982 UN Convention, both of which tried to reconcile the freedom of communications with the security needs of coastal States, two extreme positions had emerged.

At one extreme was the Grotian position. Grotius distinguished between the concepts of *dominium* and *imperium* as they related to the prerogatives of the coastal State in the adjacent seas. The sea being incapable of occupation, and occupation being a *sine qua non* of ownership, *dominium*, i.e. ownership of property, sovereignty could never be claimed by the coastal State.[76]

Accordingly, the coastal State would be left with *imperium*. *Imperium* only permits the exercise of maritime jurisdiction connected specifically with protection against piracy and prize-making.

At the other extreme was the position that the adjacent seas formed an integral part of the coastal State. For those holding this view, the coastal waters was a submerged space of the coastal State 'incidentally' covered by water. This was in direct opposition to Grotius's thinking.

Besides being for or against Grotius's views, legal theorists later on imagined peculiar combinations of both. Nevertheless, up to the twentieth century, some writers preferred the Grotius's *imperium* theory and spared no effort to look for justifications to comfort their views. Among them were distinguished members of the French School such as Lapradelle,[77], Fauchille[78] and Scele.[79] The most articulate and original theory was that expressed by Lapradelle.

Lapradelle expounded the idea of the unity of the seas. His point of departure was that any right of sovereignty results from the ability to take into possession the object in question.[80] According to Lapradelle, the whole sea should substantially be governed by the same rules and belong to one and the same international person: the community of States ('la société des Etats'). If coastal State regulations merely modified the regime of the sea, without depriving it of the quality of *res communis*, the indispensable unity of the ocean would in his opinion be maintained. The coastal State, he added, was neither the owner nor the sovereign of the territorial sea, and did not have the right to impose on the true sovereign, the community of States, restrictions based on the necessity of its own protection. To this end, he went on, the coastal State possessed, 'par la nature des lieux, à raison de sa qualité de riverain, des servitudes côtières destinées à garantir ses intérêts'. In other words, a coastal State should have over the immediate sea a right of its own which is not that of sovereignty, but a servitude established for its benefit:

> La mer littorale étant frappée d'un simple faisceau de servitudes, l'Etat côtier ne doit avoir sur elle que les droits que la nécessité exige . . . Ses droits se borneront aux [triples rapports] suivants:
>
> (a) Il aura le pouvoir d'interdire la guerre navale aux approches de sa côte pour éviter à son rivage le coup de la bataille.
> (b) Il aura le droit d'imposer aux vaisseaux, dans le voisinage du littoral, une surveillance douanière pour se défendre contre les facilités qu'une frontière de mer donne à la contrebande.
> (c) Il aura le pouvoir de tenir à distance les navires d'origine ou d'état suspects pour se protéger contre l'invasion des épidémies.[81]

Consequently, the three limitations imposed on other States when approaching foreign coastal waters pertained to military, customs and sanitary matters.

To complete the logical consequences which flow from his analysis and which directly concern our study as regards the rights of the international community in the coastal zone, Lapradelle stated:

> Comme la mer territoriale n'est pas incluse dans les frontières de l'Etat riverain, il en résulte d'abord qu'elle ne peut ni faire des nationaux *jure soli*, ni donner compétence aux tribunaux et aux lois du riverain tant au point de vue civil qu'au point de vue pénal: il s'ensuit, d'autre part, pour la même raison,

> que l'Etat côtier ne peut empêcher les Etats étrangers de faire passer, même en temps de guerre, leurs navires de commerce et leurs vaisseaux de guerre par la mer territoriale . . . il ne pourra pas réclamer, en matière de pêche, un droit privilégié.[82]

And, illustrating the above views with arguments of a practical nature, he said:

> Sur le territoire ferme, il n'est pas permis d'entrer sans l'assentiment de l'Etat territorial à un étranger, et plus particulièrement à une unité militaire étrangère. Au contraire, dans la mer qu'on appelle la mer territoriale, il n'est pas permis de refuser l'entrée. L'Etat côtier ne peut pas fermer sa mer dite territoriale comme il fermerait son territoire ferme ou plus simplement ses ports.[83]

Lapradelle's theory exerted a marked influence on scores of other jurists, who adopted it wholesale.[84]

However, another authoritative member of the Faculty of Law of Paris, Paul Fauchille, although supporting the essential conclusions arrived at by Lapradelle, rejected the basic premises of the 'servitudes' theory. Instead he adopted the principle of self-preservation, reasoning in the following manner:

> La conservation de soi-même constitue un droit fondamental des Etats: elle est même pour eux un devoir. Un Etat est dès lors autorisé à prendre toutes les mesures destinées à assurer son existence, à se défendre contre tous les actes pouvant porter atteinte aux éléments de celle-ci, c'est-à-dire à son territoire, à sa population, à sa richesse matérielle. Son droit d'action et son droit de défense à cet égard ne peuvent pas toutefois être exercés directement sur le domaine d'un autre Etat car ils méconnaîtraient alors les droits de ce dernier. Mais ils peuvent être pratiqués par l'Etat en dehors de ses frontières et aussi sur des choses qui, comme la mer, n'appartiennent à personne, à condition bien entendu qu'ils respectent le droit de conservation égal des Etats tiers . . . Telle étant la raison d'être des droits de l'Etat sur la mer littorale, il va de soi qu'il doit y posséder tous les droits nécessaires à la sauvegarde des éléments de son existence, mais qu'il ne doit pouvoir y exercer que les seuls droits indispensables à cette sauvegarde et seulement dans les limites réclamées par elle: en dehors de là, la mer côtière doit, comme la haute mer, demeurer pleinement ouverte à l'usage de tous.[85]

To support his views, Fauchille quoted a work by Imbart-Latour published in 1889, particularly a passage where this author stated:

> La mer territoriale ne peut être assimilée au territoire, et l'Etat ne peut exercer sur elle que les droits relatifs à la défense et à la sécurité de ses côtes, à la garantie de ses intérêts commerciaux et fiscaux, à la protection des intérêts des habitants du littoral.[86]

Philip Marshall Brown, an American scholar of the 1920s, who apparently did not examine the matter too deeply, gave preference to Fauchille's analysis when he said:

> the problem of the marginal sea is to be viewed neither as one of ownership, of sovereignty, of *dominium*, or *imperium*, of servitudes . . . It is to be regarded as a question of the primordial right of every nation to exercise a 'protective jurisdiction' over its coastal waters in matters affecting its own safety and welfare.[87]

Espousing the view of the French school that the territorial sea is to be regarded as a portion of the high seas, and despite growing contrary views, Georges Scelle, speaking as a member of the International Law Commission in 1954, stated:

> la mer territoriale est une partie du territoire . . . elle constitue un domaine de souveraineté de l'Etat. C'est un cas-type selon nous, de *méconnaissance* de la réalité des faits matériels, de fiction juridique et de technique vicieuse du droit . . . On peut seulement souhaiter, sans trop se faire d'illusions, que cela change.[88]

The views of the French school were contradicted by those who saw the territorial sea as an integral part of the territory of the coastal State. The 'territorialists', as some authors call this group, condemned any liberal approach to the legal status of the territorial sea. Paradoxically, this theory, too, was chiefly based on the requirements of national protection and the welfare of the littoral population (which the French school also invoked). But these requirements were considered to be of paramount importance, outweighing the advantages of considering the coastal zone as forming part of the high seas.

In other words, the main difference between two schools was one of emphasis. Nevertheless, as circumstances changed and State practice evolved, the views of the territorialists gained the upper hand. For, in the words of one author,

> State action in this field is guided by pragmatism rather than by strict adherence to any specific legal principle, so that in any given situation State authorities would generally be expected to be more concerned with the enforcement of their claims to exercise exclusive jurisdiction for whatever purpose rather than with the characterisation of every individual claim either as one flowing from its territorial sovereignty over a maritime belt of adjacent seas assimilated to their land territory, or as a claim to jurisdiction only for a specialised purpose.[89]

The earliest support for the 'territorialist' approach is traceable to the origins of the notion of territorial waters. As we noted earlier, in the thirteenth century, a theory was developed according to which the territorial sovereign was entitled to extend his sovereignty over the coastal waters surrounding his territory.[90]

Many later authors attempted to look for new principles to justify coastal States claiming the territorial sea as their territory and subject to their sovereignty. Among these authors, Georg Friedrich von Martens is one of the most prominent. He viewed the territorial sea as being a prolongation of the territory of the State rather than a prolongation of the high seas.[91]

In a present-day setting, the weight of opinion, possibly influenced by the various official and non-official codification attempts, considers the territorial sea to be, by and large, an integral part of the coastal State. Among the numerous authorities, one may cite: Jessup,[92] Oppenheim,[93] Colombos,[94] O'Connell,[95] Brownlie[96] and Gidel. The latter expressed the following view:

> La mer territoriale n'est que du territoire submergé; celui-ci ne diffère du territoire ordinaire qu'en ce qu'un certain volume d'eau s'intercale en chaque point de ce territoire entre le sol lui-même et l'air qui normalement le surplombe immédiatement. La différence est d'ordre physique; elle n'entrîne aucune différence juridique essentielle.[97]

In response to the arguments put forward by Lapradelle and mentioned earlier, relating to the fundamental differences between the exercise of certain rights on land territory and in the territorial sea, an Italian internationalist, Baldoni, is credited with having provided the first original argument in favour of the assimilation of the territorial sea to land territory. Baldoni based his argument on certain rules of international law in other fields, particularly on the rule that a State may not, unless reasonable notice is given, close its frontiers to the citizens of other States without committing an international wrong. Nor may a State subject aliens, once admitted to its territory, to a particularly disadvantageous legal regime. These are general rules limiting sovereignty in respect of land territory, and the rules limiting sovereignty over maritime territory are really no more than specific applications of the same principles of international law. The restrictions imposed by international law on the sovereignty over territorial sea do not, therefore, possess some special character which would distinguish a State's maritime domain from its land territory. The legal status of the territorial sea is indeed no more than the legal status of the State itself, and the supposed differences between land and territorial sea really derive from the ambiguity characterizing the nature of 'territory'.[98]

To dispel that ambiguity, most classics in international law define territory very broadly. Thus Oppenheim asserts that 'State territory is that definite portion of the surface of the globe which is subject to the sovereignty of the State'.[99]

Besides the views elaborated above, there have been also official and non-official codification efforts to reconcile the claims of the opposing schools.

These efforts at codification have all come closer to promoting the ideas of the territorialists than to condemning the excesses that might result from coastal State sovereignty over territorial waters. An analysis of the sets of draft articles prepared prior to the 1930 Hague Codification Conference is revealing in this regard. Under the aegis of the American Institute of International Law, Bustamante y Sirven compiled a list of the most important of these drafts elaborated between 1861 and 1930.[100] All the draft proposals on the status of littoral waters placed these waters under the territorial sovereignty of the coastal State.

A first pertinent draft was that presented by the Austrian writer Alphonse de Domin Petrushevecz: 'The maritime territory of every State extends to . . . parts of the sea that are within such distance of the coast as may be reached by cannon-shot fired from the coast'.[101]

In a draft published by Internoscia (USA) in the form of a Code of International Law, one finds the following phrase: 'Littoral seas, that is to say those which wash the shores of a State, are considered to be the property of that State and, as an extension of its territory, they are under its dependence'.[102]

A 1894 Resolution of the Institute of International Law in turn provided: 'The State has *a* right of sovereignty over a zone of the sea washing the coast . . . This zone bears the name of territorial sea'.[103]

It must be stressed, of course, that by stating that the 'the State has a right of sovereignty', instead of using the shorter phrase 'has sovereignty', the Institute's draft tried to restrict the ambit of coastal States' rights in these waters. In 1895, the Institute Rules of 1894 were adopted by the International Law Association with virtually no substantive modification.

The Institute's views were to change some years later to take into account scientific discoveries threatening the coastal State.[104] A new draft was elaborated by Sir Thomas Barclay, whose idea it had always been to emphasize coastal State supremacy in the territorial waters. At its Lausanne session in 1927, the Institute of International Law adopted the new draft, Article 1 of which provided that: 'Les Etats ont la souveraineté sur une zone de la mer qui baigne leurs côtes . . . Cette zone porte le nom de mer territoriale.' [105]

In addition to these collective and individual initiatives, a certain number of national bodies, too, adopted draft proposals recognizing sovereignty over the territorial waters to the coastal State. In this regard, the American Institute of International Law,[106] the Harvard Law School[107] and the Japanese Association of International Law[108] may be mentioned.

In an effort to codify parts of international law, the Assembly of the League of Nations, in 1924, appointed a Committee of Experts, notably to prepare the codification of the regime of the territorial sea. A first draft, which was later amended and submitted to governments for comment, notably provided:

> A State shall have an unlimited right of dominion over the zone which washes its coast, in so far as, under general international law, the rights of common user of the international community or the special rights of any State do not interfere with such right of dominion. The right of dominion shall include rights over the air above the said sea and the soil and subsoil beneath it.[109]

Summarizing the reactions of governments to that text, it was acknowledged by the League of Nations Preparatory Committee for the forthcoming 1930 Codification Conference that:

> The replies show that the governments agree in considering that a State has sovereignty over a belt of sea around its coast. The only reservations expressed appear to be due to the desire not to pronounce upon the theoretical aspect of a question of terminology, or the anxiety not to leave out the fact that in exercising such sovereignty, the coastal State must respect the restrictions which result from international law.[110]

Strengthened by these reactions, the Preparatory Committee requested the Council of the League of Nations to communicate to governments a set of articles on the legal status of the territorial sea. These articles were provisionally approved, with a view to their possible incorporation in a general convention on the territorial sea. The relevant article, which was inserted in all subsequent Law of the Sea conventions, but for some minor additions and alterations of phrasing, read:

> The territory of a State includes a belt of sea described in this Convention as the territorial sea. Sovereignty over this belt is exercised subject to the conditions prescribed by the present Convention and other rules of international Law.[111]

Although it does accommodate the views of the French school to some extent, the above wording undoubtedly gives greater weight to the thesis of the 'territorialists'.

Referring to the very delicate balance achieved by the above formulation, one writer asserts:

> that while there was a majority, but not a unanimous opinion in favour of the coastal State's exercising sovereignty over the territorial sea, the expression 'sovereignty' could accommodate a variety of views, ranging from inclusion of the territorial sea within national boundaries to an extra-territorial exercise of powers, which, because of their compendious nature, did not require specific enumeration. That the expression disguised profound doctrinal divergences and embodied only a superficial agreement is obvious.[112]

To say that the term 'sovereignty' can accommodate a variety of views and therefore is 'elastic' is in principle incorrect. 'Sovereignty is supreme authority, an authority which is independent of any other earthly authority.'[113] Indeed,

> [l]a souveraineté de l'Etat, c'est le droit pour l'Etat-personne de décider lui-même: *a*) quelle est la règle de droit, *b*) d'apprécier lui-même la valeur des situations juridiques où il est impliqué (par conséquent de n'accepter d'autre juge que soi-même); *c*) enfin, de repousser toute action exécutive extérieure tendant à obliger à respecter la règle de droit ou la sentence judiciaire; c'est le droit de se faire justice à soi-même. Autant dire que l'Etat n'est soumis au Droit que d'une façon purement 'potestative'; qu'il n'y a pas pour lui d'obligations juridiques préétablies.[114]

Consequently, any condition in a convention or even in international law generally, relating to a sovereign territory, must in strict law be accepted by the State exercising sovereignty over that territory. No obligation can be forced upon a 'sovereign' State by either the international community or by international law, except under a situation of compact or as a result of the outcome of a war. Otherwise, such an obligation is always ineffective and may be ignored.

However, in order to ensure the development of international law unhindered by the 'whims and caprices' of State governments, some legal scholars criticize the rigidity of the conception of sovereignty as defined above. They contend that the idea of sovereignty understood in its absolute sense does not square with modern international law, which is no longer a simple defence against wars and conquests, but above all an organization of economic and social relations. According to these authors, one is moving

> vers une situation nouvelle: celle d'un exercice, concerté ou commun, de la souveraineté, se substituant au traditionnel exercice solitaire sans qu'elle ait

véritablement changé de mains ou ait été amoindrie . . . La souveraineté pourrait-elle survivre à une telle évolution? La question est posée. La réponse risque de se faire attendre encore longtemps.[115]

International communications, particularly transportation in the territorial sea, straits, channels, archipelagic waters, and even in international rivers and by railway, illustrate that when 'reasonableness' is the watchword, the principle of sovereignty of the State over its territory is not inconsistent with the right of passage over this territory by other States. Obviously such a conception is beneficial to all. One legal scholar who defended the thesis of the French school adumbrated earlier, de Lapradelle, even asserted that a general *jus communicationis* for the international community exists and that the prohibition of free passage (particularly in the seas) by any State is repugnant to the fundamental and essential requirements of international trade and communication.[116]

The conditions attached to the recognition of coastal State sovereignty over the territorial sea in international conventions actually address this issue of communications. It is of course with a view to reconciling freedom of the seas with sovereignty over territorial waters that the notion of the right of innocent passage was formulated as a direct component of *jus communicationis*.

It may be said in conclusion, regarding the nature of the territorial sea, that coastal State sovereignty over these waters is unavoidable owing to the mutual dependency between land and waters, subject only to a right of third States and their ships to use such waters innocently. However, in some sea and ocean formations, this right can be dangerous for the coastal States. This is the case when the geographical configuration is such that the security and territorial integrity of the coastal State can be easily jeopardized. Such configurations are international straits.

3. Status of international straits and the right of passage

International straits are natural waterways used for international navigation between two bodies of land which may be continental land masses, a continental land mass and an island, or even two islands, irrespective of the size, width and length of the waterway.[117] Since these straits are physically part of the oceans, they may comprise internal waters, territorial seas, exclusive economic zones and even areas of high seas. This being the case, third States would appear to enjoy a right of innocent passage in the portion which belongs to the territorial sea and the freedom of navigation in the other portions of the strait. This is the situation which seems to prevail in straits which, throughout their length, are wider than 24 nautical miles and therefore encompass an area of exclusive economic zone. Where, however, the breadth of the international strait is less than 24 nautical miles at some point within its length, a special passage regime appears necessary.

Before examing the latter situation any further, two clarifications are necessary.

First, the navigational use of some international straits is regulated wholly or partly by treaty provisions.[118] These provisions are not affected by the existing Law of the Sea conventions.[119] Artificial waterways connecting portions of the open sea belong generally to the same category. In these cases, their navigational use is inevitably governed by special treaties. These types of straits and man-made waterways, which are regulated not by the Law of the Sea conventions but by independent instruments, are outside the scope of this dissertation.

Second, it should be noted that where the breadth of an international strait is 24 miles or less, as is the case in most instances, the waters, air space, and seabed are subject to the sovereignty of the State or States bordering the strait.[120] And, as is the case for the territorial sea, the sovereignty of the riparian State is exercised subject to the rules of international law.[121]

Even prior to the 1958 Convention, the regime of passage in international straits was assumed in State practice to differ from the regime of innocent passage prevailing in 'ordinary' territorial waters.[122]

However, the importance of straits for the freedom of communications was so much stressed by some nineteenth-century commentators that El-Baradei was able to cite one of them as having voiced the opinion that straits linking two parts of the high seas should be treated as part of the high seas they connect.[123]

By including this area in the high seas, the high seas freedoms of communication could be stretched to their maximum limit, so as to cover the submerged movement of submarines and overflight. By contrast, reference to the concept of innocent passage precludes such forms of passage in territorial waters in general and, thus, through territorial waters in straits.

Unlike the territorial sea, if a strait were closed to navigation, the freedom of communication could be seriously disrupted because of the absence of alternative passage. But more so than in the 'ordinary' territorial sea, the security and environmental interests of the coastal State could easily be threatened in straits.

Efforts to draft a convention applicable to all straits and ensuring freedom of navigation were begun in the 1920s. It was agreed that straits should not be closed, but that, on account of the security interests of coastal States, they should be considered as forming part of the territorial sea of the coastal States, navigation being limited to passage which is innocent.[124]

Innocent passage as the appropriate passage regime in some international straits was affirmed authoritatively by the International Court of Justice in the *Corfu Channel* case of 1949. Although the judgment dealt mainly with warships, its operative part could apply to all ships navigating through straits. The pertinent part of the judgment reads:

> It is, in the opinion of the Court, generally recognized and in accordance with international custom that States in time of peace have a right to send their warships through straits used for international navigation between two parts of the high seas without the previous authorization of a coastal State, provided that passage is *innocent*.[125]

However, the specificity of this 'innocent' passage in straits, as contrasted to passage in the territorial sea, was also emphasized by the Court when it added: 'Unless otherwise prescribed in an international convention, there is no right for a coastal State to prohibit such passage through straits in time of peace.' [126]

The first general treaty covering this issue—the 1958 Convention on the Territorial Sea and the Contiguous Zone—very carefully follows the words used by the Court. Without directly stating that innocent passage is the regime applicable in international straits, that Convention provides:

> Except in international straits, the coastal State may, without discrimination amongst foreign ships, suspend temporarily in specified areas of its territorial sea the innocent passage of foreign ships if such suspension is essential for the protection of its security.

Furthermore,

> [t]here shall be no suspension of the innocent passage of foreign ships through straits which are used for international navigation between one part of the high seas and another part of the high seas or the territorial sea of a foreign State.[127]

As we shall see in the next chapter, the regime of innocent passage in straits leaves wide discretion to the coastal State in determining what is and what is not innocent passage.[128] Moreover, submarines are required to navigate on the surface and show their flag,[129] and there is no right of overflight.[130]

These restrictions were relatively unimportant as long as the breadth of the territorial sea was limited to three nautical miles. Most international straits were wide enough to have a strip of high seas running in their middle, where freedom of navigation could be exercised. When a 12-mile territorial sea was pushed by many States in the 1960s, about 94 international straits were about to fall under riparian control.[131] The maritime powers saw this as a threat to the right of their aircraft and submarines to traverse such straits. Accordingly, they decided to advocate, in the Third United Nations Conference on the Law of the Sea, a new right of passage through straits and one that would be more extensive than that of innocent passage.

In an effort to balance the diverging interests of riparian and maritime States, the 1982 Convention establishes two types of rights of passage in international straits—transit passage and innocent passage.

Transit passage will be dealt with in the next chapter. Suffice it to say here that that regime applies to straits 'between one part of the high seas or an exclusive economic zone and another part of the high seas or an exclusive economic zone'.[132] In such straits, 'all' ships and aircraft have the right of 'transit passage',[133] which is defined to mean '. . . the exercise . . . of the freedom of navigation and overflight solely for the purpose of continuous and expeditious transit'.[134]

A particular regime of innocent passage, that of non-suspendable innocent passage, applies to straits used for international navigation and connecting a part of the high sea or an exclusive economic zone with the territorial sea, or to straits specifically excluded by the Convention from the regime of transit passage (such as straits formed by the mainland and an island if there exists, around the island, a high sea or exclusive economic zone route of similar convenience).[135] But for the fact that passage is non-suspendable in these categories of straits, all the other conditions to which the exercise of the right of innocent passage is subjected in ordinary territorial waters remain applicable. Consequently, this regime of innocent passage governing certain categories of straits includes neither a right of overflight for aircraft nor a right of submerged passage for submarines.[136] One may ask whether this regime also applies to archipelagic waters. Archipelagic waters are often crossed by sealanes having the same characteristics as international straits. Most of these lanes fall within the territorial control of the archipelagic State.

4. Archipelagic waters as a legal concept and the appropriate passage regimes

The archipelago concept is founded on the straight baseline method. Where a group of islands is perceived as a geographical, economic and political unit,[137] its territorial sea is measured from straight archipelagic baselines drawn around the outer perimeter of the said islands forming the group.

By using straight archipelagic baselines, instead of the customary low-water mark on shore, to measure the territorial waters of groups of islands forming archipelagos, an expanded area of territorial or internal waters is created, with the consequence that the surface of international waters will be reduced. For, unlike the low-water mark method, pursuant to which lines are drawn along the coasts of each island taken separately, straight archipelagic baselines are a series of imaginary lines drawn on water between 'appropriate' salient points on the islands.[138]

The straight-baseline method, when applied to groups of islands or archipelagos under the same sovereign, adds to the preservation of unity and of the intimate relationship between the natural elements of the archipelago.[139]

But inevitably, this same method encloses vast expanses of what belonged to the high seas, particularly for mid-ocean archipelagos; in most cases, some international straits are enclosed as well. This poses the problem of the rights to be retained by the international community with respect to navigation, overflight, etc., on the basis of the principle of the freedom of the seas.

Despite resistance to the use of straight baselines (outside the context of 'historic rights') for delimiting the territorial sea, the International Court of Justice, in the *Fisheries* case,[140] emphasized the need for greater flexibility and included this method among the general rules of international law governing maritime limits.

In the *Fisheries* case, the dispute involved a Norwegian Decree of 1935 purporting to measure Norway's territorial sea from straight baselines connecting salient points of a deeply indented coast and islands, islets and reefs off the mainland.[141] The main objection of the United Kingdom was that international law did not permit a State arbitrarily to select baselines for measuring its territorial sea and that Norway's baselines were in conflict with what was then regarded as the accepted customary rule, namely, that the baseline should follow the low-water mark along the coast or the proper closing line for bays. In one of its most often cited statements, the Court held:

> the delimitation of sea areas has always an international aspect, it cannot be dependent merely upon the will of the coastal State as expressed in its municipal law. Although it is true that the act of delimitation is necessarily

> a unilateral act because only the coastal State is competent to undertake it, the validity of the delimitation with regard to other States depends upon international law.[142]

However, as far as the method envisaged in the Norwegian Decree of 1935 was concerned, the Court boldly stated that:

> the system of delimitation applied in 1935, a system characterised by the use of straight lines, does not infringe the general law; it is an adaptation rendered necessary by local conditions.[143]

In its judgment, the Court departed radically from the rules accepted by the 1930 Hague Codification Conference, where straight baselines were objected to as encouraging the treatment of island groups as units, with the undesirable consequence of treating the waters enclosed as internal, thus reducing the freedom of navigation.[144] In 1930, the fact that these waters served for international navigation was decisive for excluding the use of straight baselines to delimit the territorial sea; in the *Fisheries* case, the intimate link between the sea areas concerned and the land was given priority by allowing the use of straight baselines.

As far as foreign navigation in areas enclosed by straight baselines was concerned, Norway made it clear that, although it regarded these areas as internal waters on the basis of historic title, there was going to be no interference with international navigation.[145] However, this guarantee was not thought sufficient in other situations and areas. Thus, when the subject of archipelagos came up at the 1958 Geneva Conference, instead of reflecting the findings of the Court, contrary to what occurred for the Court's findings in the *Corfu Channel* case, the findings were not embodied in the relevant Convention.

Speaking of the freedom of the seas, with obvious reference to the 1951 judgment of the Court, the delegate of a maritime nation in the Conference, presumably expressing the opinion of other maritime nations, considered any attempts to use straight baselines for archipelagos as an infringement of that freedom.[146] And, in a press release issued during the Conference, the United States delegation asserted that:

> If you lump islands into an archipelago and utilize a straight baseline system connecting the outermost points of such islands, and then draw a 12 mile area around the entire archipelago, you unilaterally attempt to convert into territorial waters or possibly even internal waters, vast areas of the high seas formerly freely used for centuries by the ships of all countries.[147]

In an effort to reduce such fears, some delegations prepared draft proposals which, among other safeguards of the right of international navigation, reserved the right of innocent passage in areas enclosed by such baselines.[148] Apparently the idea to use the concept of innocent passage for such enclosed areas came from a study on archipelagos that had been submitted at the beginning of the 1958 Conference. The Evensen proposal, as the document was called, revealed a determined effort to provide a compromise solution to the question of island groups, particularly as far as international navigation was concerned. Evensen suggested that in the case of an outlying archipelago belonging to a single State and 'which may reasonably be considered as a whole, the extent of the territorial sea shall be measured from the outermost points of the outermost islands and islets of the archipelago',[149] thus accepting the application of the straight baselines. On the passage regime to be applicable in those circumstances, Evensen concluded:

> the waters between and inside the islands and islets of the above-mentioned type of archipelago must be considered as internal waters. But, where the waters of such an archipelago form a strait, it is in conformity with the prevailing rules of international law that such a strait cannot be closed to [the innocent passage of foreign ships]. Whether a water passage is to be considered a strait or not must be decided in each specific case.[150]

As stated earlier, the idea of 'archipelagic waters' as a legal concept, assorted with the appropriate passage regime, was summarily touched upon and promptly 'forgotten' in the 1958 Geneva Conference. However, in the post-1958 years, through a determined and concerted effort on the part of archipelagic States,[151] these issues were forcefully revived, and a new regime was eventually negotiated under the auspices of the Third United Nations Conference on the Law of the Sea.

One of the first major achievements of the archipelagic States was the adoption, by the Seabed Committee called upon to prepare the Third United Nations Law of the Sea Conference, of a report which, *inter alia*, contained the following statement on the issue of archipelagos:

> the preservation of the political and economic unity of an archipelagic State and the protection of its security, the preservation of its marine environment and the exploitation of its marine resources justified the inclusion of the waters inside an archipelago under the sovereignty of the archipelagic State or the granting of a special status to such waters.[152]

In a separate but contemporaneous document, these same archipelagic States formulated three principles which, among other points, touched on the status of enclosed waters and the appropriate passage regime.

On this last point the document asserted as a third principle that the

> innocent passage of foreign vessels through the waters of the archipelagic State shall be allowed in accordance with its national legislation, having regard to the existing rules of international law. Such passage shall be through sealanes as may be designated for that purpose by the archipelagic State.[153]

In a further elaboration of this last point, in subsequent Draft Articles on Archipelagos prepared by the interested States, the traditional dichotomy of internal and territorial waters was rejected in favour of the concept of archipelagic waters. The Draft Articles emphasized that the archipelagic State should hold more powers over these waters than over the territorial sea, yet less than over internal waters. In these waters, as in the territorial sea, a right of innocent passage was conceded, but this right was to be subject to very extensive coastal State control.[154]

Summing up the originality of the concept of archipelagic waters, the delegation of an archipelagic State, in an attempt to promote the Draft, pointed out that:

> the sponsors had introduced a new concept, according to which the waters inside the baselines would be known as 'archipelagic waters', or 'waters of the archipelagic State', having an attribute of internal waters—namely sovereignty over the waters and their resources—and an attribute of territorial seas—the recognition of innocent passage through sealanes. Unlike the concept of 'inland waters', the concept of archipelagic waters admitted the existence of innocent passage. Unlike the concept of 'territorial sea', it admitted innocent passage only through sealanes, and not through the whole body of archipelagic waters.[155]

It is interesting to note that the Draft Articles of the archipelagic States carefully abstained from mentioning international straits and conceivably included these areas within archipelagic waters among the 'sealanes'. The reasoning was, as subsequently pointed out by a writer, that '[t]he concept of sealanes is essentially a functional notion relating to the special utility of a particular sea area as distinct from the geographic concept of strait'.[156]

Subsequent negotiating sessions within the Third United Nations Conference on the Law of the Sea showed that the major maritime States were not convinced by these proposals. Instead, they submitted a counter-draft which, in all sessions where the issue of archipelagos was discussed, had a common theme: *transit passage* through waters used as routes for international navigations, accompanied by a right of *innocent passage* in the other parts of archipelagic waters.[157]

The compromise solution adopted at the end of the Third United Nations Conference and included in the 1982 United Nations Convention on the Law of the Sea encompasses two types of passage regimes in archipelagic waters. In contrast to the revised Draft submitted by the archipelagic States and outlined above, the attributions of the archipelagic State are considerably reduced.

Under Article 52 of the 1982 Convention, there is a right of innocent passage for all ships through archipelagic waters, similar to the right exercised in the territorial sea proper. Whereas the revised Draft of the archipelagic States limited this right to specific 'routes customarily used for international navigation', Article 52 refers to archipelagic waters generally. This does not mean, however, that foreign ships can 'roam' at will in archipelagic waters. By virtue of Article 22(1) of the Convention, read in conjunction with Article 52(1),

> [the archipelagic State] may where necessary require foreign ships exercising the right of innocent passage through its [archipelagic waters] to use such sealanes and traffic separation schemes as it may designate or prescribe for the regulation of the passage of ships.

The second type of passage is the archipelagic sealanes passage provided for in Article 53 of the 1982 Convention. According to that Article, an archipelagic State may designate sealanes and air routes in 'conformity with generally accepted international regulations' for the 'continuous and expeditious passage of foreign ships and aircraft through or over its archipelagic waters and the adjacent *territorial sea*'. The sealanes are required to be either of a certain minimum width (expressed in the Convention by means of maximum distances measured from the axis of the lane), or at a certain distance from the nearest points on islands bordering the sealane. In the next chapter, this point will be considered in greater detail, so as to highlight the specificity of the navigational regime in archipelagic waters.

5. Conclusion

An attempt has thus far been made to show how various maritime areas came to be deprived of their high seas status and were subjected to the sovereignty of the coastal State. When these areas had formed part of the high seas, the freedom of navigation had been quite comprehensive. When they became the object of creeping coastal State jurisdiction, the situation changed.

As we shall see, despite the sovereignty the coastal State might possess over waters beyond the low-water line or straight baselines, that State will have no exclusive navigational rights in such waters, nor the right to impede the navigation of ships of other States, except under certain conditions. Wherever the sovereignty of the coastal State has had to co-exist with the high seas freedom of navigation, the minimum legal guarantee for foreign vessels to use such waters for purposes of passage independently of any treaty regime has been provided through the customary right of innocent passage.

In the next chapter, this right will be analysed in the framework of international customary law, focusing on the various fora in which the idea was conceptualized. Once a proper definition is obtained, an attempt will be made to distinguish innocent passage from the other passage regimes that have been referred to in this chapter.

Notes

1. 'In addition, this principle [Grotius's] had its ups and downs; it did not crystallize into rules of international law until the end of the eighteenth century, and even then it continued to be opposed occasionally. In fact, there seems to have been no period in history during which the freedom of the seas went entirely unchallenged.' Caflisch, L.C., 'The Doctrine of "Mare Clausum" and the Third UNCLOS', *International Relations in a Changing World*, Geneva, IUHEI, Leiden, Sijthoff, 1977, pp. 197–228, at p. 198.
2. There was a suggestion made by one member of the International Law Commission in 1952 that it should be explicitly stated in an article that 'sovereignty over this belt be exercised by the coastal State'. This suggestion was rejected by 7 votes to 5, with 2 abstentions. ILC, *Yearbook* 1952, vol. I, p. 151.
3. United Nations Convention on the Law of the Sea (1982), New York, United Nations, 1983 (hereinafter cited as the 1982 Convention).
4. UN Doc. A/Conf. 13/L.52–L.55 (hereinafter cited as the 1958 Convention).
5. Report of the International Law Commission to the General Assembly, Doc. A/3159, Article 1, commentary, para. 1, ILC, *Yearbook* 1956, vol. II, p. 265.

6. The Hague Conference for the Codification of International Law, March–April 1930, LON Doc. C.230.M.117.1930.V, p. 6.
7. The *Island of Palmas* arbitration, United Nations, *Reports of International Arbitral Awards*, vol. II, pp. 829–71, at p. 839.
8. 'In fact, through the entire branch of international law related to State territory and territorial sovereignty there runs as a constant theme: the phenomenon of limitation of sovereignty in various spheres and directions.' Lauterpacht, H., 'Sovereignty over Submarine Areas', *BYBIL*, vol. 27, pp. 376–433, at p. 391.
9. The *Island of Palmas* arbitration, op. cit., note 7, at p. 839.
10. LON Doc. C.230.M.117.1930.V, p. 6; Final Act of the Conference for the Codification of International Law, Doc. C.251.M.145.1930.V, p. 126.
11. op. cit., note 5, p. 265.
12. ILC, *Yearbook* 1954, vol. I, p. 59.
13. ibid., p. 60.
14. ibid., p. 60.
15. ILC, *Yearbook* 1952, vol. I, p. 150.
16. Jessup, P.C., *The Law of Territorial Waters and Maritime Jurisdiction*, New York, Jennings and Co., 1927, p. 120.
17. In the context of our study, sovereignty is defined as the freedom to perform governmental acts to the exclusion of all other authority, subject to such limitations as are self-imposed or imposed by international law. For an elaborate definition of the word 'sovereignty', see the collective works of M. Bettati, R. de Bottini, R.-J. Dupuy, P. Isoart, J. Rideau, J.-P. Sortais, J. Touscoz, A.H. Zarb, *La Souveraineté au XXe siècle*, Paris, Armand Colin, 1971, at pp. 14ff.
18. 1982 Convention, Article 2.
19. This terminology included: coastal waters, littoral sea, marginal waters, maritime belt, etc. The 1930 Hague Codification Conference endorsed the categorization of the maritime space into four zones: internal waters, territorial sea, contiguous zone and high seas. cf. Acts of the Conference for the Codification of International Law, Vol. III: Summary Records of the Second Committee—Territorial Waters, LON Doc. C.351 (b) M. 145(b). V, p. 32. In the International Law Commission, in 1954, some members felt that although in 1930 the term 'territorial sea' had been retained for the zone which now bears that name, an appropriate translation of the concept into other languages called for the use of the expression 'territorial waters'. It was only by a vote of 12 to 7 that the Commission retained the term 'territorial sea', as found in the subsequent treaty provisions.
20. cf. Sommers, E., 'The Division of Powers in Maritime Areas', *Revue belge de droit international*, vol. 17, 1983, pp. 323–47.
21. The Republic of Lebanon is alleged not to have ever declared a territorial sea. Does this mean that it may refuse the benefits and burdens inherent in the concept, though geographically it is a coastal State? 'To every State whose land territory is at any place washed by the sea, international law attaches a corresponding portion of maritime territory consisting of what the law calls territorial waters (and in some cases national waters in addition). International Law does not say to a State: "You are entitled to claim territorial waters if you want them". No maritime State can refuse them. International law imposes upon a maritime State certain obligations and confers upon it certain rights arising out of the sovereignty which it exercises over its maritime territory. The possession of this territory is not optional, not dependent upon the will of the State, but compulsory.' Dissenting opinion of Sir Arnold NcNair in the *Fisheries* case (*United Kingdom* v. *Norway*), ICJ *Reports* 1951, p. 116, at p. 160.
22. O'Connell, D.P., 'The Juridical Nature of the Territorial Sea', *BYBIL*, vol. XLV, 1971, pp. 303–83, at p. 304.

23. *North Sea Continental Shelf* cases, ICJ *Reports* 1969, p. 3 at p. 22.
24. Virally, M., 'Une pierre d'angle qui résiste au temps: avatars et pérennité de l'idée de souveraineté', op. cit., note 1, pp. 179–95, at pp. 180, 186.
25. cf. Fenn, P.T., Jr., 'Origins of the Theory of Territorial Waters', *AJIL*, vol. 20, 1926, pp. 465–82, at p. 467; Florsheim, 'Territorial Sea, 3000-Year Old Question', *J. Air L.Com.*, vol. 36, 1970, pp. 73–100; Bustamante y Sirven, A.S. de, *The Territorial Sea*, New York, Oxford University Press, 1930, pp. 5ff.; Fulton, T.W., *The Sovereignty of the Sea*, Edinburgh and London, William Blackwood and Sons, 1911, pp. 134 and 538–9; Gidel, G.C., 'La mer territoriale et la zone contiguë', *RCADI*, vol. 48, 1934–II, pp. 137–277, at p. 140; Oudendijk, J.K., *Status and Extent of Adjacent Waters: A Historical Orientation*, Leiden, Sijthoff, 1970, p. 10; O'Connell, op. cit., note 22, p. 304.
26. Fenn, op. cit., note 25, p. 467.
27. Among the writings comprehensively dealing with the issue in a historical manner, the following may be cited: O'Connell, op. cit., note 22, pp. 305ff.; Colombos, C.J., *The International Law of the Sea*, 5th ed, Longmans, 1962; Lucchini, L. and Voelckel, M., *Les Etats et la mer: Le nationalisme maritime*. La Documentation française, Notes et études documentaires No. 4451–4452; McDougal, M.S. and Burke, W.T., *The Public Order of the Oceans: A Contemporary International Law of the Sea*, New Haven, Yale University Press, 1962, pp. 174–304; Hall, W.E., *A Treatise on International Law*, 8th ed, Oxford, Clarendon Press, 1924, pp. 178–99; Fauchille, P., *Traité de droit international public*, vol. I, Part II, Paris, Rousseau and Co., éditeurs, 1925, pp. 126–72; Gidel, G., *Le droit international de la mer: Le tempts de paix*, Paris, Sirey, 1932–4, vol. I, Paris, pp. 123–200; Fulton, op. cit., note 25, pp. 1ff.; Jessup, op. cit., note 16; Bustamante y Sirven, op. cit., note 25; Masterson, W.E., *Jurisdiction in Marginal Waters with Special Reference to Smuggling*, New York, The Macmillan Co., 1929; Potter, P.B., *The Freedom of the Seas in History, Law and Politics*, London, Longmans, Green and Co., 1924; Ngantcha, F., *International Seabed Authority (A study of a proposal for the implementation of the Common Heritage Concept)*, Memoire, IRIC, University of Yuolandé, Cameroon, 1980.
28. Gidel, op. cit., note 27, pp. 133–6.
29. There were national laws, such as the British Hovering Acts of the eighteenth and nineteenth centuries and the United States customs legislation, which extended British and American jurisdiction far beyond their respective coasts.
30. Gidel, op. cit., note 27, pp. 128–33.
31. Fulton, op. cit., note 25, p. 4.
32. Lapradelle, A.G. de, 'Le droit de l'Etat sur la mer territoriale', *Revue générale de droit international public*, vol. 5, 1898, pp. 264–84 and 309–47, at p. 268.
33. Bull '*Inter Caetera*' issued by Pope Alexander VI on 4 May 1493, confirmed and modified by the Treaty of Tordesillas concluded between Spain and Portugal on 7 June 1494. These instruments are reproduced in *Annals of International Studies*, vol. 4, 1973, pp. 309–35. For an exhaustive description of these early claims, cf. Fulton, op. cit., note 25, pp. 537ff.; Colombos, op. cit., note 27, pp. 44ff.; O'Connell, *The International Law of the Sea*, Oxford, Clarendon Press, 1982, vol. 1, pp. 1ff.
34. Fulton, op. cit., note 25, p. 5.
35. For more details, see ibid., pp. 86ff.
36. Gidel, op. cit., note 27, pp. 151–60, 171–94.
37. Fulton, op. cit., note 25, p. 17.
38. *Mare Clausum*, lib. ii, c.xiii, translated by M. Nedham, London, W. du Gard, 1652; facsimile reproduced by Arno Press, New York, 1972.
39. Caflisch, op. cit., note 1, p. 200.
40. Grotius's theory is largely an extrapolation of the ideas of the Spanish jurist Vazquez,

who is quoted at length in *De Jure Praedae Commentarius*, cap. XII (translation of the original manuscript of 1604 by L. Williams, *The Classics of International Law*, Scott, J.B. (ed.), Oxford, Clarendon Press, 1950, No. 22/1, pp. 249–53. Similar ideas had been expressed in 1557 by Franciscus de Vitoria, *De Indiis et Iure Belli Relectiones*, section III (translation by J.P. Bate, *The Classics of International Law*, Scott, J.B. and Nys, E. (eds), Carnegie Institution, Washington, 1917, No. 7, particularly p. 152, where it is asserted as Proof 10: 'By natural law running water and the sea are common to all, so are rivers and harbors, and by the Law of nations ships from all parts may be moored there').

41. For a summary, see Caflisch, op. cit., note 1, p. 199.
42. ibid., p. 201.
43. On the criteria of effective domination and of discovery in connection with the acquisition of land territory between the sixteenth and nineteenth centuries, see the arbitral award of M. Huber, of April 1928, in the *Island of Palmas* case, cited in note 7, at pp. 834–46.
44. Fenn, op. cit., note 25, p. 466.
45. ibid., p. 476.
46. ibid., p. 481.
47. *De jure belli libri tres* (1612), lib. III, cap. XVII (translation of the 1612 edition by Rolfe, J.C., *The Classics of International Law*, No. 16/2, Scott, J.B. (ed.), Oxford, Clarendon Press, 1933, p. 384: 'The Argives once expostulated with the Athenians, because the Athenians had allowed the Spartans, who were enemies of the Argives, to pass over their sea . . . the remonstrance was justified, since the sea is a portion of the land . . . as our jurists admit. The adjacent part of a sea belongs to one dominion, and the term "territory" (*territorium*) is used both of land and water.'
48. Fenn, op. cit., note 25, p. 481.
49. ibid., p. 481.
50. ibid., p. 482.
51. ibid., p. 465.
52. Caflisch, op. cit., note 1, p. 201.
53. Brown, P.M., 'The Marginal Sea' (editorial comment), *AJIL*, vol. 17, 1926, pp. 89–95, at p. 94.
54. *De Jure Belli ac Pacis Libri Tres* (1646) lib. 2, cap. 3 (translation of the edition of 1646 by Francis W. Kelsey, *The Classics of International Law*, Scott, J.B. (ed.), vol. II, Carnegie Endowment for International Law, Washington, Clarendon Press, Oxford, 1925, pp. 212–14). However, by the same token, with reference to innocent passatge, Grotius asserted: 'It is certain that one who has occupied a part of the sea cannot hinder navigation which is without weapons and of innocent intent, when such a passage cannot be prevented by land, where it is generally less necessary and more productive of damage.' Ibid, p. 212.
55. Martens, G.F. von, 'Le Tribunal d'arbitrage de Paris et la mer territoriale', *Revue générale de droit international public*, vol. 1, 1894, pp. 32–43, at p. 39.
56. Planas-Suarez, Simon, *Tratado de Derecho International Publico*, Madrid, 1916, vol. 1, p. 173, quoted in Bustamante y Sirven, op. cit., note 25, p. 25.
57. Gidel, op. cit., note 27, vol. III, pp. 45ff.
58. Colombos, op. cit., note 27, pp. 82ff.
59. O'Connell, op. cit., note 33, pp. 59ff.
60. Anzilotti, D., *Corso di diritto internationale*, Roma, 1922, vol. 1., p. 182, quoted in Bustamante y Sirven, op. cit., note 25, pp. 27–8.
61. Statement of Elihu Root in the *North Atlantic Coast Fisheries Arbitration*, Oral Argument, Part II (1910), p. 1214, quoted by Jessup, op. cit., note 16, p. 5; also found in Scott, J.B. (ed.), *The Hague Court Reports*, New York, Oxford University

Press, 1916, pp. 141–225.

62. Their arguments were ably stated by Lapradelle, A.G. de, *La Mer*, Paris, Editions Internationales, 1934, pp. 203–12. In an article written in 1898, Lapradelle regrettably acknowledged that: '. . . cette vieille conception de la mer territoriale comme une réalité distincte, sous la souveraineté de l'Etat côtier . . . trop longtemps la théorie des droits du riverain en a été la prisonnière . . . Ce qui a contribué à la puissance de cette formule, c'est son caractère hautement doctrinal. Dans un droit un peu libre, à textes rares, à conceptions larges comme est le droit des gens, les vues théoriques sont tentées de jouer un rôle excessif. Ainsi s'est créée, au mépris des exigences de la pratique, contre le droit et contre la nature, cette idée que l'Etat côtier est souverain de la mer teritoriale, comme s'il existait une mer territoriale dans le régime physique des mers, et comme s'il était possible d'exercer l'empire sur elle dans le régime juridique de la souveraineté. Mais contre ce système, ses conséquences protestent. En niant la mer territoriale comme mer distincte, en reconnaissant, non pas une souveraineté caractérisée, mais de simples servitudes côtières à l'Etat riverain, nous n'avons pas malheureusement d'autorités à invoquer . . .' op. cit., note 32, p. 347.
63. At the 1954 meeting of the International Law Commission, George Scelle still put forward that view. See ILC *Reports* 1954, vol 1, pp. 59ff.
64. Among these instruments, one may mention: the Air Navigation Convention of 1919, whose Article 1 defines State territory as including adjacent territorial waters; the Convention on International Civil Aviation of 7 December 1944 (Article 2); the 1958 Convention on the Territorial Sea and the Contiguous Zone (Article 1); and the 1982 United Nations Convention on the Law of the Sea (Article 2).
65. On the close relationship between these two questions, as viewed at the 1930 Conference, see Raestad, 'Le problème des eaux territoriales à la Conférence pour la codification du droit international', *Revue du droit international*, vol. 7, 1931, pp. 107–46, at p. 110.
66. Extavour, W.C., *The Exclusive Economic Zone*, Leiden, Sijthoff, 1981, p. 13, expressing a nineteenth-century conception expounded by Lapradelle, op. cit., note 32, p. 339.
67. 'Wherefore on the whole it seems a better rule that the control of the land [*over the sea*] extends as far as cannon will carry; for that is as far as we seem to have both command and possession . . . the control from the land ends where the power of men's weapons ends: for it is this . . . that guarantees possession.' *De dominio maris dissertatio* (1744), cap. II (translation of the 1744 edition by Magoffin, R. van D., *The Classics of International Law*, No. 11, Scott, J.B. (ed.), New York, Oxford University Press, 1923, pp. 41–5, at p. 44).
68. For details, see Walker, W.L., 'Territorial Waters: The Cannon-Shot Rule', *BYBIL*, vol. 22, 1945, pp. 210–31, at p. 215; Swarztrauber, S.A., *The Three-Mile Limit of Territorial Seas*, Annapolis, Md., Naval Institute Press, 1972, p. 27. Oudendijk, op. cit., note 25, pp. 55–7.
69. Swarztrauber, op. cit., note 68, pp. 34–5, citing several manuals of artillery.
70. Jessup, op. cit., note 16, p. 7.
71. For a good summary of the two other methods, see Caflisch, op. cit., note 1, pp. 202–4. For details, consult Jessup, op. cit., note 16, at pp. 77ff., 66; but cf. Fulton, op. cit., note 25, pp. 576–603.
72. Caflisch, loc. cit., pp. 203–4.
73. McDougal and Burke, op. cit., note 27, pp. 522ff.
74. ILC, *Yearbook* 1956, vol. II, p. 265.
75. According to the Soviet doctrine of international law, 'the issue of the breadth of the territorial sea had been determined by each coastal State in accordance with

geographical considerations . . .' and the USSR 'applied the twelve-mile-limit; that breadth had been determined by Russia half a century ago'. Krylov in ILC, *Yearbook* 1955, vol. 1, p. 156.

76. Imbart-Latour describes *imperium* as 'le droit de commandement . . . la souveraineté . . . le pouvoir conféré à un Etat pour garantir sa liberté et son indépendance et assurer sa sécurité'; 'dominium', on the other hand, is 'un droit de propriété', cf. *La Mer territoriale au point de vue théorique et pratique*, Paris, G. Pedone-Lauriel, 1889, p. 8. For further clarifications, see Fauchille, op. cit., note 27, vol. I, Part II, pp. 133ff.
77. Lapradelle, op. cit., note 62, pp. 201–12; Lapradelle, op. cit., note 32, pp. 5–63.
78. Fauchille, op. cit., note 27, vol. I, Part II, pp. 131ff. For critical comments on the views of Lapradelle and Fauchille, cf. Gidel, op. cit., note 27, vol I, pp. 199–200.
79. Scelle, G., *Manuel de droit international public*, Paris, Domat-Montchrestien, 1948, pp. 418ff.
80. Lapradelle, op. cit., note 62, p. 206.
81. See Fauchille, op. cit., note 77, vol. I, Part II, p. 146.
82. ibid.
83. Lapradelle, op. cit., note 59, p. 203.
84. Among these was Masterson, op. cit., note 26, p. 400.
85. Fauchille, op. cit., note 27, vol. I, Part II, pp. 147 and 148.
86. Imbart-Latour, op. cit., note 76, pp. 14 and 306.
87. Brown, loc. cit., note 53.
88. Scelle, op. cit., note 79, pp. 421 and 422.
89. Extavour, op. cit., note 63, p. 23.
90. Fenn, op. cit., note 25, pp. 470 and 471.
91. Martens, op. cit., note 55, at p. 39.
92. Jessup, op. cit., note 16, particularly p. XXIV.
93. Oppenheim, L., *International Law*, vol. 1: *Peace*, 8th ed (ed. H. Lauterpacht), London, Longmans, 1955, p. 487.
94. Colombos, op. cit., note 27, p. 78.
95. O'Connell, op. cit., note 33, vol. I, pp. 59ff.
96. Brownlie, I., *Principles of Public International Law*, 3rd ed, Oxford, Clarendon Press, 1979, pp. 183ff.
97. Gidel, op. cit., note 27, vol. III, p. 169.
98. Baldoni, *Il Mare Territoriale nel Diritto Internazionale Commune* (1934), quoted from O'Connell, op. cit., note 33, vol. I, p. 79.
99. Oppenheim, op. cit., note 93, p. 451.
100. Bustamante y Sirven, op. cit., note 25, pp. 35–78.
101. ibid., p. 38.
102. ibid., p. 39.
103. ibid., p. 45.
104. They included the invention of the airplane at the beginning of the century, and the use of submarines and bombs during the First World War.
105. IDI, *Annuaire* 1927, vol. I, p. 73 (Article 1). However, the Institute went on to specify, in the same provision, that 'par l'expression: "Les Etats ont la souveraineté", il faut entendre, non qu'ils ont sur la mer territoriale un droit de propriété, mais que leur puissance s'étend à toute cette région'.
106. *AJIL*, vol. 20, 1926, Special Supplement, p. 318.
107. *AJIL*, vol. 23, 1929, Special Supplement, p. 243 (Article 13).
108. ibid., p. 376.
109. Bustamante y Sirven, op. cit., note 25, p. 63.
110. LON Doc. C.74.M.39.
111. LON Doc. C.230.M.117.1930. V, p. 6 (Annex I).

112. O'Connell, op. cit., note 33, vol. I, pp. 77–8.
113. Oppenheim, op. cit., note 93, pp. 118–19.
114. Scelle, op. cit., note 79. p. 98.
115. Virally, op. cit., note 24, pp. 193 and 194.
116. Lapradelle, op. cit., note 62, pp. 137ff.
117. McNees, R.B., 'Freedom of Transit through International Straits', *Journal of Maritime Law and Commerce*, vol. 6, 1974/1975, pp. 175–211, at p. 191.
118. An example of such a treaty regime is the 1936 Montreux Convention relating to the Turkish Straits. A case of partial treaty regulation is the regime of the Baltic Straits resulting from the Sound Treaties of 1857. These treaties do not deal with the passage of warships, nor with overflight, thus implicitly allowing Danish municipal law to apply. cf. Alexandersson, G., *The Baltic Straits*, The Hague, Nijhoff, pp. 63ff.
119. 1982 Convention, Article 35(c).
120. ibid., Article 34(1).
121. ibid., Article 39(2).
122. Brüel, E., *International Straits*, London, Sweet and Maxwell, 1947, vol. 1, p. 101.
123. 'Straits which connect two parts of the high seas are considered—irrespective of their width, and of the territorial sovereignty—as part of the high seas and therefore free for the international community.' K. Gareis, *Institutionen des Völkerrechts*, 2nd ed, 1901. Translated by El-Baradei, M., 'The Egyptian-Israel Peace Treaty and Access to the Gulf of Aqaba: A New Legal Regime', *AJIL*, vol. 76, 1982, pp. 532–54, at p. 535. In other words, according to that author, such straits would not be regarded as straits in a legal sense, and their waters would be subject to neither transit passage nor innocent passage.
124. See, for example, the Harvard Research in International Law, Territorial Waters, Articles 8–12, *AJIL*., vol. 23, 1929, Special Supplement, pp. 280–8; Schücking, 'Le développement du Pacte de la Société des Nations', ADI, *Recueil*, vol. 20, 1927–V, pp. 353–458, at pp. 353ff.
125. The *Corfu Channel* case (United Kingdom v. Albania), ICJ *Reports* 1949, p. 4, at p. 28.
126. ibid.
127. 1958 Convention, Article 16(3) and (4).
128. ibid., Article 16.
129. ibid., Article 14(6).
130. Aircraft are implicitly excluded from exercising the right of innocent passage by virtue of the definition given to the word 'passage' which, under Article 14(2), is 'navigation through the territorial sea for the purpose either of traversing that sea without entering internal waters, or of proceeding to internal waters, or of making for the high seas from internal waters'. Independently of the 1958 Convention, the 1944 Chicago Convention on International Civil Aviation is explicit on that point as regards State aircraft, see its Articles 2 and 3(c). For details, see Chapter 2, section 3(c) below.
131. McNees, op. cit., note 117, at p. 185.
132. 1982 Convention, Article 37. The exclusive economic zone is an area beyond and adjacent to the territorial sea which cannot extend beyond 200 nautical miles from the baselines from which the territorial sea is measured. In this zone, the coastal State may exercise sovereign rights over the living and non-living resources therein, and jurisdiction over marine scientific research, etc. Other States, however, continue to enjoy the freedoms of overflight and navigation, as well as the freedom to lay cables and pipelines. See Articles 55–75.
133. 1982 Convention, Article 38(1).
134. ibid., Article 38(2).
135. ibid., Article 45(1) (b).

136. ibid., Article 45(1).
137. Rodgers, P.E.J., *Midocean Archipelagos and International Law*, New York, Vantage Press, 1981, p. XVIII.
138. ibid.
139. UN Doc. A/CONF.13/39 (First) UNCLOS, Official Records, vol. III, p. 49.
140. The *Fisheries* case (United Kingdom v. Norway), ICJ *Reports* 1951, p. 116.
141. For a thorough treatment of the facts and law of this dispute, see Waldock, C.H.M., 'The Anglo-Norwegian Fisheries Case', *BYBIL*, vol. 28, 1951, pp. 114–71.
142. ICJ *Reports* 1951, p. 130.
143. ibid., p. 133.
144. Waldock, op. cit., note 141, at p. 131.
145. For details, see Chapter 2, section 2.
146. (First) UNCLOS, Official Records, vol. III, p. 25.
147. Press Release No. 3 of the United States Delegation, 11 March 1958.
148. Doc. A/CONF. 13/C.1/L.59. (First) UNCLOS, Official Records, vol. 3, pp. 172ff.
149. Jens Evensen, 'Certain Legal Aspects Concerning the Delimitation of the Territorial Waters of Archipelagos', UN Doc. A/CONF./13/18, in (First) UNCLOS, Official Records, vol. I, pp. 289–302, at p. 302.
150. ibid.
151. Typifying this group were Fiji, Mauritius, Indonesia and the Philippines.
152. Report of the Seabed Committee (Committee on the Peaceful Uses of the Seabed and Ocean Floor Beyond the Limits of National Jurisdiction) to the General Assembly, vol. I, Official Records, 28th Session, Supplement No. 21, Doc. A/9021, p. 55, para. 79.
153. UN Doc. A/AC. 138/SC. II/L.15 of 14 March 1973. The other two principles were: (1) An archipelagic State, whose component islands and other natural features form an intrinsic geographical, economic and political entity, and historically have or may have been regarded as such, may draw straight baselines connecting the outermost points of the outermost islands and drying reefs of the archipelago from which the extent of the territorial sea of the archipelagic State is or may be determined. (2) The waters within the baselines, regardless of their depth or distance from the coast, the seabed and the subsoil thereof, and the superjacent airspace, as well as all their resources, belong to, and are subject to the sovereignty of the archipelagic State.
154. Draft Articles on Archipelagos, UN Doc. A/AC.138/SC.II/L. 48 of 6 August 1973, particularly Article V.
155. UN Doc. A/AC.138/SC.II/SR. 73 of 22 August 1973, p. 12.
156. Rodgers, op. cit., note 137, p. 157.
157. UN Doc. A/CONF.62/C.2/L.52 of 12 August 1974, Third UNCLOS, Official Records, vol. III, p. 228, and vol. II, pp. 261 and 267.

Chapter 2

The right of innocent passage as the classical exception to coastal State sovereignty in coastal waters

1. Introduction

The right of innocent passage is the main universally recognized manifestation of limitations imposed by international law on sovereignty in coastal waters. This has been repeatedly affirmed in various international law fora and by authors.[1] However, to ascertain the complete content of that right exclusively on the basis of customary international law might be hazardous. Thus, prior to the Third United Nations Conference on the Law of the Sea, the Seabed Committee issued a report in which it wrote: 'With respect to the regime of passage through the territorial sea, reference was made to the right of innocent passage and to the need to elaborate that concept further.'[2] The doubt inherent in this statement was due to the diversity of State practice. Hence, for purposes of clarity, the drafting of a written text has been advocated.

Inevitably, the attempt to codify the customary law on innocent passage has led to 'progressive development' of that principle which, in some circumstances, has spawned new rules.

In this chapter, we intend to ascertain whether customary international law is the source of the right of innocent passage. This will be followed by an analysis of the content of that right *via* an appropriate definition of the key terms 'innocence' and 'passage'. Finally, a distinction will be made between the right of innocent passage and similar but different rights of passage in coastal seas. In this way, we hope to identify the 'place' of the right of innocent passage in international law generally and in the Law of the Sea in particular.

2. The right of innocent passage and customary international law

Although it has been asserted that '[a]s a general principle, the right of innocent passage requires no supporting argument or citation of authority; it is firmly established in international law',[3] evidence tends to show that, contrary to prevailing opinion, innocent passage was not generally considered a rule of customary international law, but one in *statu nascendi*.

There are isolated opinions and localized practices which could be quoted to show the customary basis of the exercise of the right of innocent passage prior to the nineteenth century. At the beginning of the twentieth century, a drive for some sort of statutory and jurisprudential enactments set in. This drive to codify the law on the right of innocent passage was at least partly due to the vagueness of the law on that subject and also illustrative of the doubts as to its customary nature.

Before an analysis is made of the views of learned societies and groups of jurists, in an attempt to trace the evolution of international custom on the subject prior to the 1930 Codification Conference, it should be noted that earlier on, only passing references had been made to the right of innocent passage by writers, and that the right was considered by others as a corollary of the right to trade.[4]

This latter views, strongly advocated by Grotius,[5] was echoed by many authors, especially Sir Philip Medows who observed in 1689:

> As it is a way, it is common to the peaceable traders of all nations. And this is so far from being a damage to any, that it is highly beneficial to all, for as there is no man so selfsufficient as not to need the continual help of another, so neither is there any country which does not at some time or other need the growth and productions of another.[6]

Despite the intimate link between the right of innocent passage and the question of the status of coastal waters, demonstrated in the introductory chapter,[7] many treatises prior to the nineteenth century considered innocent passage as a secondary requirement, akin to mere usage, when studying the nature of coastal waters. Typical of this approach was the classical work of Vattel, who, after treating at length the domination over coastal seas by States, concludes: 'The shores of the sea belong unquestionably to the Nation which possesses sovereignty over the territory of which they form a part, and they come under the head of public property.' This assertion led Vattel to the following conclusion:

> A Nation may appropriate such things as would be hurtful or dangerous to it if open to free and common use . . . It is a matter of concern to their security and their welfare that there should not be a general liberty to approach so near their possessions, especially with ships of war, as to hinder the passage of trading vessels and disturb navigation . . . These marginal seas, thus subject to a Nation, are part of its territory and may not be navigated without its permission.

However, Vattel conceded, with reference to the right of innocent passage, that:

> access may not lawfully be refused to vessels when their purpose is innocent and they are not under suspicion, since every owner is bound to grant free passage to strangers, even by land, when no harm or danger results from so doing.

Not only authors doubted the customary nature of the right of innocent passage in the past century; State practice, too, questioned its foundation. Even though some regional treaties[9] could be seen as guaranteeing the right of innocent passage, these instruments were more concerned with jurisdictional matters than with the right of passage *per se*.

British practice is very illuminating in this respect. As a major maritime nation and, as such, a torch-bearer for rules governing the seas, British conduct may best reflect 'customary' practice in this issue.

By an Act of Parliament of 1878, the British Territorial Waters Jurisdiction Act, power was granted to British courts to exercise competence over any events occurring within the territorial waters of Britain.[10] The immediate goal of the Act was to overrule a decision rendered two years earlier in *R.* v. *Keyn*, in which a court had declined jurisdiction, giving 'full' effect to the right of passage, to try the captain of a foreign ship who had run down an English ship in British territorial waters, causing the loss of a British life.[11]

Due to this state of flux characterized by changing attitudes to the right of innocent passage, learned societies and groups of jurists attempted to define that right as a matter of international legal obligation rather than of national political necessity.

The learned societies and bodies of experts which attempted to 'codify' the right of innocent passage prior to the 1930 Hague Codification Conference were: the Institut de droit international, the International Law Association, the League of Nations Committee of Experts for the Progressive Codification of International Law, the American Institute of International Law, Kokusaīko-Gakkawai (the Japanese branch of the International Law Association), and the Harvard Research in International Law.

From the groundwork accomplished by the 'Institut de droit international' in 1894 up to the rules formulated in 1929 by the Harvard Research team, all the above entities drafted proposals to clarify or confirm the right of innocent passage.

Typical of this trend was the proposal presented by the 'Institut de droit international' in the form of Rules on the status of sovereign coastal waters. The 1894 Rules of the Institute confirmed the right of innocent passage in the following way:[12]

> *Article* 5. Tous les navires sans distinction ont le droit de passage inoffensif par la mer territoriale, sauf le droit des belligérants de réglementer et, dans un but de défense, de barrer le passage dans ladite mer pour tout navire, et sauf le droit des neutres de réglementer le passage dans ladite mer pour les navires de guerre de toutes nationalités.
>
> *Article* 6. Les crimes et délits commis à bord de navires étrangers de passage dans la mer territoriale par des personnes qui se trouvent à bord de ces navires, sur des personnes ou des choses à bord de ces mêmes navires, sont, comme tels, en dehors de la juridiction de l'Etat riverain, à moins qu'ils n'impliquent une violation des droits ou des intérêts de l'Etat riverain, ou de ses ressortissants ne faisant partie ni de l'équipage ni des passagers.
>
> *Article* 7. Les navires qui traversent les eaux territoriales se conformeront aux règlements spéciaux édictés par l'Etat riverain dans l'intérêt et pour la sécurité de la navigation et pour la police maritime.
>
> *Article* 8. Les navires de toutes nationalités, par le fait seul qu'ils se trouvent dans les eaux territoriales, à moins qu'ils n'y soient seulement de passage, sont soumis à la juridiction de l'Etat riverain.

In substance, the pertinent provision contained in the proposal of the League of Nations Committee of Experts did not deviate from Article 5 drafted by the Institut. That provision, Article 7, reads as follows:[13] '*Pacific passage*. All vessels without distinction shall have the right of pacific passage [i.e. innocent passage] . . .' However, Article 7 also contained indications on the manner in which this right was to be exercised:

> In case of submarine vessels, this right shall be subject to the condition of passage on the surface. The right of passage includes the right of sojourn in so far as the latter may be necessary for navigation. The right of free passage includes the right of passage for persons and goods independently of the right of access to the foreign mainland.

The 1924 draft of the International Law Association on the subject contained the following articles, confirming the right of innocent passage in very strong language, reminiscent of the Institute's earlier draft:[14]

> *Article* 6. The ships of all countries, public as well as private, have the right to pass freely through [coastal] waters . . .
> *Article* 7. States shall not be entitled, under any circumstances whatever, by permanent or even temporary works, to forbid or interfere with the transit through their [coastal] waters.

The existence of a general principle on the right of innocent passage was also confirmed by the American Institute of International Law which, in 1925, submitted to the Pan American Union a draft containing this text:[15]

> *Article* 9. Merchant vessels of all countries may pass freely through [coastal] seas, subject to the laws and regulations of the Republic to which the said sea belongs.
> Neither warships nor merchant vessels can sojourn in [coastal] seas, or commit any act involving the violation of those laws and regulations, without the authorization of the said Republic.

In the same vein, the draft prepared by the Japanese Branch of the International Law Association (Kokusaīko-Gakkawai) read:

> *Article* 6. All ships without distinction shall enjoy the right of inoffensive passage through littoral waters, conforming themselves to any rules which may be laid down by the adjacent State for the security of navigation, for the police of the seas, or for the defence and security of its own territory.[16]

Finally, in 1929, just prior to the Hague Codification Conference, researchers of the Harvard Law School prepared a draft convention on the subject of territorial waters. Article 14 of the draft dealt with the right of innocent passage and stated: 'A State must permit innocent passage through its marginal seas by the vessels of other States, but it may prescribe reasonable regulations for such passage.'[17]

In sum, without any substantive variations, all the above-mentioned texts unhesitatingly asserted a right of innocent passage. This could be interpreted as an expression of uncertainty on the part of the various scientific bodies of experts over the rule of customary international law on the subject.

But the inclusion of a right of innocent passage in a series of draft conventions of different and unrelated origins may also show that some type of customary international law exists or is in the making. It can be justifiable to have recourse to uniform clauses to show the existence of customary international law.[18] A similar demonstration might be attempted by pointing to uniform draft conventions. Considering the possibility that *travaux préparatoires* can be cited to interpret a treaty[19] and that sometimes draft conventions can play the same role *vis-à-vis* international conventions, a uniform line of draft conventions could be invoked as evidence.

Independently of the various drafts, the following statement of the Preparatory Committee of the 1930 Hague Codification Conference, made in the light of replies to a request for comments addressed to governments, may be illustrative of State practice:

> The principle that merchant ships have a right of innocent passage is not contested. There is also agreement that there are complementary rules applying the principle to persons and goods and permitting the ship to anchor within territorial waters where this is necessary for purposes of navigation.[20]

Accordingly, the Preparatory Committee offered the following provisions as basis of discussion No. 19:

> A coastal State is bound to allow foreign merchant ships a right of innocent passage through its territorial waters; any police or navigation regulations with which such ships may be required to comply must be applied in such a manner as to respect the right of passage and without discrimination.
> The right of innocent passage covers persons and goods.
> The right of passage comprises the right of anchoring so far as is necessary for purposes of navigation.[21]

Encouraged by these developments, the Second Committee of the 1930 Hague Codification Conference reported that 'the freedom of navigation is of such great importance to all States that the right of innocent passage through the territorial sea has been generally recognized . . .'. Thus, the following phrase was inserted in Article 4 of the Draft Text of this Committee: 'A coastal State may put no obstacles in the way of innocent passage of foreign vessels in the territorial sea.'

It was in these terms that the right of innocent passage was conceived until 1949, when the question of its judicial recognition first came up. This was in the *Corfu Channel* case.

The pertinent point of the International Court's judgment read:

> It is the opinion of the Court, generally recognized and in accordance with *international custom*, that States in time of peace have a right to . . . [transit] . . . without the previous authorization of coastal States [through straits], provided that *passage is innocent*. Unless otherwise prescribed in an international convention, there is no right for a coastal State to prohibit such passage . . . in time of peace.[22]

Despite reference in the judgment to international custom and innocent passage, it can still be argued that the International Court of Justice did not confirm the existence of a customary rule of innocent passage generally for all ships in all coastal waters. Indeed, the Court explicitly refused to make any reference to innocent passage in ordinary territorial seas[23] and instead concentrated on international straits and on the passage of warships.

3. Definition of the right of innocent passage

No matter how broad the interpretation of the right of innocent passage could be made, so as to permit the nationals of one State to use the coastal waters of another State for purposes of navigation, it has never been taken to be the equivalent of the freedom of navigation in the high seas. Whereas the latter merely has to be exercised 'with reasonable regard to the interests of other States in their exercise of the freedom of the high seas',[24] 'and also with due regard for the rights under this Convention with respect to activities in the Area',[25] the extent of the right of innocent passage needs more refinement by defining each of the two key words, 'innocent' and 'passage'.

(a) Characteristics of the right of innocent passage

When these two key words are isolated from each other, their significance emerges more clearly. Whereas the requirement of 'innocence' of the passage essentially safeguards the security of the coastal State, the reference to 'passage' could be said to relate more specifically to the foreign vessel exercising the right of passage. The legal meaning of the term 'passage' has not altered greatly from 1930, when it was first considered in an international conference. By contrast, the significance of the term 'innocent' has changed and become more complex. To determine the content of the right of innocent passage, it is necessary for the two key words to be analysed separately, due attention being given to the more controversial one of the two—'innocent'.

The significance of 'innocent'

Probably in an attempt to give more precision to the term 'innocent' within the context of the exercise of the right of innocent pasqage, the most recent treaty on the issue, the 1982 Convention, lists twelve forms of activity incompatible with the exercise of the right of innocent passage. Nonetheless, the term remains elusive, and its evolution since the 1930s attests to the difficulties involved.

In the context of the exercise of the right of passage, the word 'innocent' has always been defined negatively. Draft Article 3(2) of the 1930 Codification Conference defined 'innocence' in this manner:

> Passage is *not innocent* when a vessel makes use of the territorial sea of a coastal State for the purpose of doing any act prejudicial to the security, to the public policy, or to the fiscal interests of that State.[26]

Before the 1958 Geneva Conference on the Law of the Sea, the question of what amounted to 'innocent' passage was debated at length in the International Law Commission and in the General Assembly of the United Nations.[27]

Article 15(3) of the Commission's Draft once again defined 'innocence' negatively:

> Passage is *innocent* so long as a ship *does not* use the territorial water for committing any acts prejudicial to the security of the coastal State or contrary to the present rules or to other rules of international law.[28]

Close scrutiny of these texts permits the assertion that emphasis is placed on the *conduct* of the ship or vessel to decide on the innocent character of passage. By relying on the specific conduct during passage to determine the innocence or non-innocence of passage, these early provisions restricted the right of the coastal State to interfere with vessels whose passage could, on other grounds, be prejudicial to the 'security considerations' of that State.

When the commentary on draft Article 15(3) is examined, however, it appears that the International Law Commission gave high priority to the security and other interests of the coastal State. In its commentary, the Commission stated:

> For the right in question to be claimable, passage must in fact be innocent . . . The Commission considered that 'fiscal interests of the State'—a term [contained in the Articles of the 1930 Codification Conference] that should be interpreted very broadly, including all matters relating to customs and to import, export and transit prohibitions—could be regarded as being included in the more general expression used in Article 15, paragraph 3. *This expression covers*, inter alia, *questions relating to customs and health as well as the interests enumerated in the comment to article 18.*[29]
>
> Article 15(3) contains only general criteria and does not go into details. There was therefore no need to mention the case—to which attention has been specifically drawn—of ships using the territorial sea for the express purpose of defeating import and export controls, contravening the customs regulations of the coastal State (hovering ships). The Commission considers, however, that passage undertaken for this purpose cannot be regarded as innocent.[30]

The question of what constitutes innocent passage came up in the meetings of the General Assembly in 1957 following the Suez crisis of 1956.

Specifically on the issue of 'innocence', several definitions came up, despite the guidelines resulting from the articles and comments formulated by the International Law Commission. Two trends could be distinguished in the course of the debates in the General Assembly concerning the crisis, one of which was championed by India, while the other was represented by Italy.

The Indian delegate considered that the articles of the International Law Commission Draft had to be read together and that, in particular, Article 16 was bound to Article 17, 'because while Article 16 states the general position, Article 17 refers to the rights of protection of the coastal State'. In support of his position, he quoted paragraph 3 of Article 17 of the ILC draft and concluded:

> Therefore, this so-called right of innocent passage actually means that one must prove innocence. Innocence depends upon the *character* of the party claiming the passage; it depends upon the *purpose* of the passage, and also upon the *freight* that is carried.[31] (emphasis added)

For the Italian delegate, this would be setting an extremely high standard at the detriment of the right of innocent passage. Thus, in response to the Indian suggestion, he said:

> I cannot share the liberal interpretation which the representative of India, Mr. Krishna Menon, gave to this principle . . . This interpretation would nullify the rule of innocent passage, since it is obvious that, if it were valid, the littoral States would no longer have the duty of justifying their refusal of passage to a vessel on specific occasions and for specific reasons; rather, it would rest with the vessel to prove that its passage was innocent.[32]

These apparently opposing opinions are illustrative of a fundamental legal question: whether the coastal State may ward off threats to its security by interfering with passage in advance of overt action or whether the coastal State must wait for 'action' to establish that passage is non-innocent? In other words, can the coastal State decide subjectively what is non-innocent, or can non-innocence be objectively perceived?

As far as the International Law Commission's draft articles were concerned, the Indian delegate's interpretation was correct. As the articles stood, they called for subjective determination of innocence. The 'observance of local regulations' as a requirement for innocence means that the 'right to proceed must be accompanied by the respect of regulations concerning the manner of proceeding. Thus the right of innocent passage is negated when there is a contravention of local regulations on how to pass in the coastal waters'.

This definition of 'innocence' was too subjective for some delegations, and it dangerously deprived the 'right' of any value. The opportunity to alter the definition came in the 1958 Geneva Conference on the Law of the Sea. The opinion expressed by the delegate of Italy earlier in the General Assembly was shared by most delegates from the Western world. The delegations of France, New Zealand, Belgium, Canada and Sweden spoke in this vein. The main premise of their argument was based on statements made by the delegation from the United Kingdom at the beginning of the 1958 Conference.

In expressing concern at suggestions that the right of innocent passage was in some way subordinate to the rights of the coastal State over its territorial sea, Sir Reginald Manningham-Buller said:[33]:

> The right of innocent passage was an independent right, in no way subordinate to any other, and was of particular importance in the case of international straits . . . No established and customary right of passage or access could be done away with by the unilateral action of any of the neighbouring coastal States.

Nevertheless, he admitted that:

> It was not easy to define what was meant by 'innocent passage'. Account must be taken of the position of the coastal State, yet it must also be remembered that the right was one necessary to navigation which it was in the interests of the coastal State itself to afford.

At the 1958 Conference, many amendments were proposed to alter the definition of 'innocence' found in the 1956 Draft Articles of the International

Law Commission. A common denominator of most amendment proposals was the recognition that a close link existed between the definition of 'innocence', the rights of the coastal State, and the duties of the passing vessel, as suggested in the General Assembly by the Indian delegate. This link was borne out by Articles 15(3), 18 and 17 of the International Law Commission Draft.

Only the proposal of the United States, which was amended by India[34] and Turkey[35] to become Article 14(4) of the 1958 Convention on the Territorial Sea and Contiguous Zone, is of direct relevance. This proposal, aimed at indicating 'that the sole test of the innocence of a passage was whether or not it was prejudicial to the security of the coastal State',[36] was opposed as 'inconsistent with existing international law', on the ground that it 'would enable a State to claim that the actual passage of a ship was prejudicial to its security', whereas the real test of innocence was 'the manner in which passage was carried out;.[37]

Nevertheless, the American proposal, as amended by India and Turkey, was adopted and became Article 14(4) of the Convention on the Territorial Sea and the Contiguous Zone.[38]

This provision defines 'innocence' as follows:

> Passage is 'innocent' so long as it is not prejudicial to the peace, good order or security of the coastal State. Such passage shall take place in conformity with these Articles and with other rules of international law.[39]

In trying to avoid any subjective determination of 'innocence', Article 14(4) goes to the opposite extreme: while it has the effect of not making the innocence of passage dependent upon compliance with local regulations, its definition of innocence does not relate to what the ship is doing in the territorial sea. The ship may commit no act considered predudicial to the coastal State while it is in the territorial sea, but its passage may be non-innocent on the ground that it is prejudicial by virtue of something else.[40]

But this something else would, in order to avoid any 'subjective judgment' on the definition of 'innocence', be more than the existence of local laws and regulations—something that could be considered as tainting the passage even if there happened to be no specific domestic law or regulation under which passage was locally illegal.[41]

It follows that it was necessary to dissociate the idea of non-innocence of passage from that of infringement of local laws and regulations, such as ignoring a navigational light, or passing a buoy on the wrong side. If a vessel infringes such a law or regulation, it may indeed be liable to a fine or other penalty. But passage does not, merely on that account, cease to be innocent, or become liable to prevention or denial entirely. The ship must pay, or make satisfactory arrangements for paying, but must then be allowed to proceed.[42]

Unlike the ILC Draft Articles, Article 14(4) of the Convention on the Territorial Sea was aimed at eliminating any such uncertainties. It is doubtful whether the desired result was achieved. Although it can be argued, on behalf of those who favour an 'objective' test of innocence, that paragraph 4 makes it clear that the prejudice must be to the coastal State ('Passage is innocent so long as it is not prejudicial to the peace, good order or security of the coastal State'); and that the fact that passage may be prejudicial to some third State does not affect its innocence in relation to the coastal State, the 'objectivity' is weakened in two respects. Firstly, the words 'prejudicial . . . to the coastal State' are not referring to acts committed only *in* the territorial sea. The paragraph permits the coastal State to consider passage as non-innocent on the ground that the coastal State disapproves generally of the voyage because of its object, or its possible consequences which might have repercussions that would be prejudicial to, or might indirectly affect, the coastal State.[43]

Secondly, as compared to the Commission's draft article, Article 14(4) of the 1958 Convention enlarges the concept of what is non-innocent to include not only prejudice to the 'security', but also to the 'peace' and 'good order' of the coastal State. This affords the latter plausible reasons for prohibiting or impeding passage.[44]

Therefore, the definition of what constitutes 'innocence' cannot be construed solely either subjectively or objectively. O'Connell states:

> Its content is complex: if there is intention to harm, then innocence is lacking, but the problem is one of knowledge of intention; supposition may be sufficient, yet a ship by its mere presence can cause prejudice to the coastal State.[45]

Under such circumstances, some differing views can be identified as regards the proper way of appreciating 'innocence'. Those who conceive of innocence as an 'objective' notion consider that innocence must be presumed until passage is shown to be otherwise[46] and think, therefore, that passage is non-innocent if, whatever the intention, acts prejudicial to the coastal State occur during passage. Conversely, passage remains innocent, whatever the intention, as long as no harm has been overtly done. Thus, the burden of proof of non-innocent passage would lie with the coastal State which is required to establish not only the fact but also its actual prejudicial implications.[47]

For those who conceive innocence as a subjective concept, passage is innocent only when no act is done to threaten the coastal State, or when the ship is not carrying persons or goods dangerous to the coastal State, even though no overt act has been committed but is suspected.[48] Under these instances, no overt act need be committed for passage to be non-innocent; thus, the burden of proving innocence shifts to the ship.[49]

The definition of 'innocence' remained elusive until the Third United Nations Conference on the Law of the Sea. At that Conference, the notion was grappled with and in the final analysis was linked explicitly to an apparently exhaustive list of subject-matters falling within coastal State competence.

The right of innocent passage, in particular the meaning of 'innocence', was debated at length in the Second Committee of the Conference. Three draft proposals served as points of departure for discussions, each containing a series of articles dealing with the right of innocent passage. These drafts were that of the United Kingdom[50] (Draft Articles on the Territorial Sea and Straits), of Malaysia, Morocco, Oman and Yemen[51] (Draft Articles on Navigation through the Territorial Sea, Including Straits Used for International Navigation) and of Fiji[52] (Draft Articles Relating to Passage Through the Territorial Sea).

The meaning of 'innocent' was clearly at the heart of the three draft proposals. Article 16 of the United Kingdom Draft, Article 3 of the Four-Nation Draft and Article 3 of the Fiji Draft provided a definition of that term and specified those activities which would render passage non-innocent.

For the purpose of highlighting the unavoidable differences and particularly of identifying apparent similarities, the definitions of 'innocence', as found in the various drafts, will be reproduced in full hereafter:

United Kingdom Draft Articles on the Territorial Sea and Straits

Article 16

1. Passage is innocent so long as it is not prejudicial to the peace, good order or security of the coastal State. Such passage shall take place in conformity with these articles and with other rules of international law.
2. Passage of a foreign ship shall not be considered prejudicial to the peace, good order or security of the coastal State unless, in the territorial sea, it engages in any threat or use of force in violation of the Charter of the United Nations against the territorial integrity or political independence of the coastal State, or without authorization from the coastal State or justification under international law in any of the following activities:

   (a) any exercise or practice with weapons of any kind;
   (b) the launching or taking on board of any aircraft;
   (c) the launching, landing or taking on board of any military device;
   (d) the embarking or disembarking of any person or cargo contrary to the customs, fiscal, immigration or sanitary laws or regulations of the coastal State;
   (e) any act aimed at interfering with any system of communication of the coastal State;
   (f) any act aimed at interfering with any other facilities or installations of the coastal State.

Four-Nation Draft Articles on Navigation Through the Territorial Sea, Including Straits Used for International Navigation

Article 3: Innocence of passage

1. Passage is innocent as long as it is not prejudicial to the peace, good order or security of the coastal State. Such passage shall take place in conformity with these articles and with other rules of international law.
2. Passage of a foreign ship shall not be considered prejudicial to the peace, good order or security of the coastal State unless it engages in the territorial sea in activities such as:

   (a) Any warlike act against the coastal or any other State or any threat or use of force;
   (b) Any exercise or practice with weapons of any kind;
   (c) The launching or taking on board of any device;

(d) The launching, landing or taking on board of any aircraft;
(e) The embarking or disembarking of any person or cargo;
(f) Any act of propaganda affecting the defence or security of the coastal State;
(g) Any act of espionage or collecting of information affecting the defence or security of the coastal State;
(h) Any act of interference with any system of communications of the coastal State;
(i) Any act of interference with any other facilities or installations of the coastal State;
(j) The carrying out of research operations of any kind.

Fiji Draft Articles Relating to Passage Through the Territorial Sea

Article 3

1. Passage is innocent so long as it is not prejudicial to the peace, good order or security of the coastal State, such passage shall take place in conformity with these articles and with other rules of international law.
2. Passage of a foreign ship shall be considered to be prejudicial to the peace, good order or security of the coastal State, if in the territorial sea it engages in any threat or use of force in violation of the Charter of the United Nations against the territorial integrity or political independence of the coastal State or of any other State, or if it engages in any of the following activities:

(a) Any other warlike act against the coastal or any other State;
(b) Any exercise or practice with weapons of any kind;
(c) The launching or taking on board of any aircraft;
(d) The embarking or disembarking of any person or cargo;
(e) Any act of espionage affecting the defence or security of the coastal State;
(f) Any act of propaganda affecting the security of the coastal State;
(g) Any act of interference with any systems of communication of the coastal or any other State;
(h) Any act of interference with any other facility or installation of the coastal State;
(i) Any other activity not having a direct bearing on passage.

Common to all the three Draft Articles is the first paragraph, emanating from Article 14(4) of the 1958 Convention. The second paragraph, aimed at specifying those activities which would render passage non-innocent, differs in at least two respects in all three drafts.

Whereas the Fiji Draft positively states that passage of a foreign ship should be considered prejudicial to the coastal State if such and such acts are committed, the two other drafts use a negative formulation. Furthermore, whereas the United Kingdom Draft enumerates acts which are not innocent, it is silent on acts of espionage and propaganda. These issues are stressed in the other two drafts. Finally, it is interesting to note that the United Kingdom and the Fiji

Draft Articles, in paragraph 2, make reference to '. . . any threat or use of force in violation of the Charter of the United Nations . . .'[53] Obviously this brings in other acts which could render passage non-innocent.

Unlike the two other texts, the Four-Nation Draft Article gives just a few examples of acts that can be considered non-innocent by the use of the phrase '. . . activities such as . . .' and thus is open-ended. All three texts, however, omit mention of the consequences of pollution on coastal waters, or of fishing activities of foreign vessels exercising the right of passage. The draft article finally adopted filled these lacunae.

The 1982 Convention reflects a trade-off among the authors of the three Drafts, with more weight given to the text presented by Fiji. Article 19(1) of the Convention reproduces the first paragraph of the three Drafts, which are themselves taken from Article 14(4) of the 1958 Convention. This provision states: 'Passage is innocent so long as it is not prejudicial to the peace, good order or security of the coastal State. Such passage will take place in conformity with these articles and other rules of international law.'

Following the Fiji Draft, the scope of this paragraph is clarified in paragraph 2 of Article 19 of the 1982 Convention:

> Passage of foreign ships shall be considered to be prejudicial to the peace, good order or security of the coastal State if in the territorial sea it engages in any of the following activities:
>
> (a) any threat or use of force against the sovereignty, territorial integrity or political independence of the coastal State, or in any other manner in violation of the principles of international law embodied in the Charter of the United Nations;
> (b) any exercise or practice with weapons of any kind;
> (c) any act aimed at collecting information to the prejudice of the defence or security of the coastal State;
> (d) any act of propaganda aimed at affecting the defence or security of the coastal State;
> (e) the launching, landing or taking on board of any aircraft;
> (f) the launching, landing or taking on board of any military device;
> (g) the loading or unloading of any commodity, currency or person contrary to the customs, fiscal, immigration or sanitary laws and regulations of the coastal State;
> (h) any act of wilful and serious pollution contrary to this Convention;
> (i) any fishing activities;
> (j) the carrying out of research or survey activities;
> (k) any act aimed at interfering with any systems of communication or any other facilities or installations of the coastal State;
> (l) any other activity not having a direct bearing on passage.

The question that can be asked is whether this enumeration withdraws any discretionary power from the coastal State subjectively to characterize acts as non-innocent, thus permitting prohibition of passage, interference therewith, and arrest of the foreign ship. If the enumeration of specific acts that could constitute non-innocent passage was meant to furnish an 'objective test', then conduct taking the form of 'intention to harm because of flag or mission' cannot be so qualified. However, Article 19(2) (a) of the 1982 Convention also prohibits passage '. . . in any manner in violation of the principles of international law embodied in the Charter of the United Nations'; and the same Article, in paragraph 2(i), prohibits '. . . any other activity not having a direct bearing on passage . . .'. These very vague formulae give the coastal State more subjective elements to justify its personal appreciation of the passage. Can this trend not lead to a situation where the coastal State could also take into account acts committed or occurring beyond its territorial waters, concerning even third States only, as falling within the scope of Article 19(2) of the 1982 Convention?

Somehow anticipating such an interpretation, a distinguished author remarks:

> Concern for the broad, community interests (including the coastal States interest as a flag State in other contexts) justifies establishing limits on coastal State discretion by providing that the innocence or lack thereof, of passage must be determined only by specific acts occurring during the passage *in* the territorial sea itself. [54]

Thus, it could be claimed that the coastal State's subjective appraisal of passage as non-innocent is limited, restricted objectively by the requirement that the violation occur while the foreign ship is *in* passage. Does this mean that if the coastal State's law is breached by a foreign ship from a point outside the territorial sea, and the ship is subsequently found within territorial waters exercising the right of passage, it is by so doing 'innocent' and immune from the local authorities? This, of course, is not the case if those violations involve coastal State laws and regulations in the contiguous zone or in the exclusive economic zone.[55]

Finally, one ought to ask whether conformity or non-conformity of behaviour with the laws and regulations of the coastal State would affect 'innocence' of passage. Another way of looking at this same issue is to try to differentiate between 'non-innocent passage' and the 'non-observation' of laws and regulations enacted by the coastal State in conformity with the Convention. In practice, the distinction is extremely tenuous. In fact, non-compliance with such laws and regulations may or may not make passage non-innocent. The sanction for non-compliance depends on the nature of the infringement and the degree of its seriousness. Non-payment for services rendered in the exercise of the right of innocent passage would normally give rise to claims for fees, but not necessarily affect the 'innocence' of passage; while a massive violation of the laws and regulations of the coastal State with respect to the preservation of the environment or a fishing vessel's lack of proper storage of fishing equipment pursuant to coastal State regulations would. We shall revert to these points in Chapter 6.

In sum, the elusive nature of the word 'innocent' within the right of passage regime in coastal waters necessitates the taking into consideration both the objective and the subjective significance of the term. Under the present law and practice, inevitably, the discretionary power of the coastal State to determine 'subjectively' non-innocent passage is far-reaching. Reisman very pertinently summarizes the situation in this manner:

> As a general jurisprudential matter, an open-textured normative formulation in a decision process appropriately structured . . . gives discretion to the applier, the same formula may be undesirable and invite abuse if the application is unilateral. When norms whose application threatens severe deprivation to others are to be applied unilaterilly, prudence requires that these norms be framed at lower levels of generality, lest the application itself threaten public order.[56]

Was this achieved in the 1982 Convention? On this point, the delegations which participated in the elaboration of that Convention may not be too sure. A definition of innocence by 'enumeration' of non-innocent acts deprived the right of passage of a great part of its value. For, although it reduces the area of controversy, it does not do away with it completely, particularly in view of the residual open-ended clauses.

The components of 'passage'

Unlike the meaning of 'innocence', the legal significance of 'passage', within the context of the right of innocent passage, has not altered significantly since the 1930 Hague Codification Conference, when those terms were first defined in an international forum.

Article 3 of the adopted Draft Text of the Second Committee (Territorial Sea) of the 1930 Codification Conference[57] defined passage as follows:

> Passage means navigation through the territorial sea for the purpose either of traversing that sea without entering inland waters, or of proceeding to inland waters, or of making for the high sea from inland waters. [Passage] includes stopping and anchoring, but in so far only as the same are incidental to ordinary navigation or are rendered necessary by *force majeure* or by distress.

In a commentary on this provision, the Second Committee noted that:

> when a State has undertaken international obligations relating to freedom of transit over its territory, either as a general rule or in favour of particular States, the obligations thus assumed also apply to the passage of the territorial sea. Similarly, as regards access to ports or navigable waterways, any facilities the State may have granted by virtue of international obligations concerning free access to ports or shipping on the said waterways, may not be restricted by measures taken in those portions of the territorial sea which may reasonably be regarded as approaches to the said ports or navigable waterways.[58]

From these provisions and the commentary, which are to be considered as interrelated, 'passage' is more than a word of 'motion'[59] involving a continuous movement from one end of the territorial waters to another end without any contact with the territory of the coastal State.

For purposes of clarification and simplicity, Gidel's categorization of the three types of passage envisaged in the 1930 Draft provisions are quite interesting. These types are:[60]

— 'Passage latéral', involving no direct contact with the inland waters of the coastal State;
— 'Passage d'entrée', involving access to internal waters and harbours; and
— 'Passage de sortie', departure from a harbour or internal waters, heading for the high seas or the exclusive economic zone.

These three forms of passage will be analysed briefly and separately, a fourth consideration being the stopping and anchoring in the course of ordinary navigation or on account of force majeure or distress.

Lateral passage

The first type of passage in Gidel's categorization is the most typical within the context of the right of innocent passage. This is so because it involves entering the territorial waters at one point and leaving them at another point, without calling at a port, navigable river or other shore locality. At the 1930 Conference, some delegates made this point quite clear. For the United States delegate, '. . . the vessel of another State is not in innocent passage when it is approaching the port of a State through its marginal seas or when she is entering or leaving a port of that State'.[61] On the proper definition of innocent passage, the British delegate stated:

> The right of innocent passage is the right of a foreign ship not proceeding either to or from a port of a coastal State to enter and navigate the territorial waters of that State for the purpose only of passing through them.[62]

The mere fact that a vessel traverses the territorial sea, in the sense that it enters at one point and leaves at another, does not make the operation one of passage if passage as such was not the *purpose*.[63] If the vessel passes through for some other purpose, not necessarily illegal, that operation is not one of passage within the meaning of the term envisaged here.[64]

Criticizing those who consider passage to mean exclusively the lateral crossing of coastal waters, and justifying the majority view in the Second Committee of the 1930 Codification Conference, Gidel considers that:

> Le droit de passage appartient aussi bien aux navires qui font route pour entrer dans un port qu'à ceux qui le quittent. Si le port n'est pas ouvert au commerce international, il n'y a pas lieu de considérer le navire comme étant juridiquement en 'passage'; mais si le port est libre, le régime du passage doit s'appliquer au navire qui s'y rend. Cela n'empêche pas que, lorsque le navire est arrivé au port, l'Etat riverain ne puisse lui imposer même à titre rétroactif, l'observation des conditions auxquelles ses règlements subordonnent l'accès des navires.[65]

Passage to or from internal waters

Although it is rightly pointed out that, according to the draft provisions adopted by the 1930 Codification Conference, '. . . le droit de passage existe quelle que soit la navigation dans laquelle s'encadre le trajet à travers cette mer, quelle que soit la provenance et la destination du navire',[66] it is inconceivable that a coastal State would permit entry into or departure from its inland waters and at the same time deny or disrupt access to its territorial sea.[67]

When the commentary to Draft Article 3 of the Hague Codification Conference is considered in the light of this type of 'passage', it appears that the drafters had in mind the necessary connection between the transit for land-locked States and their right of access to the high seas.[68] Be that as it may, the jurisdictional issues for ships entering or leaving internal waters cast doubt on whether this type of 'passage' can substantially be compared to the lateral passage referred to earlier.

This is all the more so since it is stated in Article 5 of the 1930 Draft Articles on the Territorial Sea that '. . . in the case of vessels proceeding to inland waters [the coastal State can take all necessary steps] against any breach of the conditions to which the admission of those vessels to those waters is subject . . .'.[69] In the commentary on this Article, it is acknowledged that the coastal States' powers are 'wider if a vessel's intention to touch at a port is known, and include, *inter alia*, the right to satisfy itself that the conditions of admission to the port are complied with'.[70]

Stoppage and anchorage as components of passage

Stopping and anchoring at a port or roadstead does not *per se* prevent an operation from being considered one of passage, provided it is incidental to ordinary navigation or compelled by emergency. This is how 'passage' is conceived in Article 3 adopted by the 1930 Codification Conference. To put it differently, if stopping and anchoring were the *purpose* of entering into the territorial waters, then the 'right of passage' regime ceases to operate. In practice, determining whether or not the stoppage or anchorage is 'incidential to ordinary navigation' is not easy. Consequently, some still maintain that, despite textual arguments to the contrary, '. . . if a vessel anchors in the marginal sea of another State the passage is broken and the vessel may be regarded as within the marginal sea for purposes other than that of innocent passage'.[71]

Nevertheless, stoppage and anchorage may pertinently and reasonably be considered 'passage', given the exceptional situations ships at sea could face—exceptional situations which could probably necessitate a request for aid and assistance from the coastal State.

If, in the process of passing through the territorial sea, a ship stops and anchors independently of motives connected with *ordinary navigation* and based on circumstances beyond its control, or on distress,[72] its presence cannot be justified on exercise of the right of innocent passage. In this case, the ship may be considered to be contemplating sojourning in the territorial sea, with the consequence that its status in those waters could be assimilated to that of a ship in internal waters, at the jurisdictional mercy of the coastal State.

Be this as it may, the 1930 definition of 'passage' was subsequently reproduced in the Draft Articles of the International Law Commission and adopted as paragraphs 2 and 3 of Article 14 of the 1958 Convention. As in the 1930s, the most significant area of discord concerned the inclusion of access to and from internal waters in the concept of innocent passage. Some at the International Law Commission thought that this inclusion would blur the differences between the territorial sea and internal waters and that, at least in order to exercise its fiscal prerogatives, the coastal State must have additional powers of jurisdiction over a ship entering or leaving its internal waters and found in its territorial sea. Thus,

Jessup made the following comment on the International Law Commission's draft definition of 'passage' taken from the 1930 Hague Draft:

> a vessel passing through territorial waters en route to or from a port of the coastal State is considered to be exercising a right of innocent passage . . . Access to ports should . . . properly be considered a topic separate from innocent passage. The jurisdictional rights of a coastal State are different in the two cases, exercise of jurisdiction over ships entering or leaving ports being in many instances reasonable or even necessary, while such exercise over a vessel in innocent passage could not be justified.[73]

Nevertheless, the definition given to 'passage' in the 1950s has been confirmed in the 1982 Convention, with just two additions made in the light of proposals included in the three Drafts presented by the United Kingdom, the Four Nations, and Fiji.[74] The most important addition contained in the Draft of the Four Nations was as follows: 'Passage shall be continuous and expeditious. Passing ships shall refrain from manoeuvring unnecessarily, hovering or engaging in any activity other than mere passage.'[75] The second sentence of the above proposal is aimed at threats and intimidation; it would be superfluous, were the first sentence to be interpreted in good faith.[76]

Adopting this argument, the other drafts, those of United Kingdom and of Fiji, merely provided that 'such passage shall be continuous and expeditious'. The 1982 Convention also adopts this view and adds the obligation to render assistance. After some minor drafting, Article 18 of the 1982 Convention on the Law of the Sea (which is similar to Article 14(2) and (3) of the 1958 Geneva Convention on the Territorial Sea; to Article 15(2) and (4) of the ILC draft; and Article 3 of the 1930 Hague Codification drafts) took the following form as regards the definition of 'passage' within the context of innocent passage:

1. Passage means navigation through the territorial sea for the purpose of
   a) traversing that without entering internal waters or calling at a roadstead or port facility outside internal waters; or
   b) proceeding to or from internal waters or a call at such roadstead or port facility.
2. Passage shall be continuous and expeditious. However, passage includes stopping and anchoring, but only so far as the same are incidental to ordinary navigation or are rendered necessary by force majeure or distress or for the purpose of rendering assistance to persons, ships or aircraft in danger or distress.

Despite the strong minority reservations referred to earlier, paragraph 1 of Article 18 considers proceeding to or from internal waters as constituting 'passage' within the framework of the right of innocent passage. Nevertheless, other provisions of the 1982 Convention strongly restrict such 'passage'. Among these provisions, one finds Article 25(2), which states:

> In the case of ships proceeding to internal waters or a call at a port facility outside internal waters, the coastal State also has the right to take the necessary steps to prevent any break of the conditions to which admission of those ships to internal waters or such a call is subject.

Article 27(2) gives the coastal State criminal jurisdiction over such ships by prescribing:

> [Nothing] affects the right of the coastal State to take any steps authorized by its laws for the purpose of arrest or investigation on board a foreign ship passing through the territorial sea after leaving internal waters.

There is, finally, Article 28(3) on the limitations to the exercise by the coastal State of civil jurisdiction in relation to foreign ships:

> [this is . . .] without prejudice to the right of the coastal State, in accordance with its laws, to levy execution against or to arrest, for the purpose of any civil proceedings, a foreign ship lying in the territorial sea, or passing through the territorial sea after leaving internal waters.

(b) Meaning of the right of innocent passage

The complex components of the terms 'innocence' and 'passage' show that it is quite difficult to define the combined words in precise terms. The definition of each component term is kept somewhat vague in order to reconcile the legitimate security and other interests of the coastal State with the inclusive right of other States to 'pass' through territorial waters. A simplistic appraisal would be that a zero-sum game is being played, with articles aimed at cancelling the effects of each other.[77] However, as shall be shown later on, the protection of the right of innocent passage and corresponding duties *vis-à-vis* the coastal State have to some extent been balanced. Without going into further details, it can be said that under present standards the right of innocent passage may be defined simply as the right of the ships of all States to 'pass' (in the various forms and manners indicated) innocently (as formulated above) through the territorial sea. Can this definition be distinguished from other rights of passage in other types of coastal waters and in the superjacent air space?

4. Distinction of the right of innocent passage from other rights of passage in the seas

(a) The right of transit passage in straits

In the *Corfu Channel* case[78] and in the 1958 Convention,[79] passage through (international) straits was conceived of as an exercise of the right of innocent passage, subject to the modalities of the exercise of that right. By contrast, the 1982 Convention conceptualizes three separate types of rights of passage applicable in three categories of straits characterized by their geographical and geophysical nature and by their use for international navigation. The first category is that of Article 36 of the 1982 Convention, to which neither the 'innocent passage' regime nor that of 'transit passage' applies, but different versions of the high seas freedom of navigation. This type of straits is characterized by the existence of 'a route through the high seas or through an exclusive economic zone of similar convenience'.

The second type of straits envisaged in the 1982 Convention are those, referred to in Article 45(1) (b), which connect '. . . a part of the high seas or an exclusive economic zone and the territorial sea of a foreign State'. To this type of straits the non-suspendable though comparatively restricted regime of innocent passage applies. These straits referred to Articles 36 and 45 and do not concern us here. A third type of straits, mentioned in Article 37 and elaborated upon in Article 38, includes straits 'used for international navigation between one area of the high seas or an exclusive economic zone and another area of the high seas or an exclusive economic zone'. To these straits, the regime of *transit passage* is applicable.

Transit passage is a neologism. This right lies, as stated in the previous chapter, between that of innocent passage and the high seas freedom of navigation, but leans more towards the former. Without going into its legislative history, suffice it to say that transit passage represents a compromise between the proposals made by the maritime powers[80] and those presented by the so-called 'straits States'.[81] It may also be viewed as an element within the general package deal in the 1982 Convention, used to secure universal recognition of the 12-mile limit of the territorial sea.

Early statements made by the United States and the Soviet Union could substantiate this assertion and make it possible to anticipate this special type of passage regime. The Soviet position could be ascertained from a draft submitted at the beginning of the Third United Nations Conference on the Law of the Sea which stated in its Article 1(1) that: 'In straits used for international navigation between one part of the high seas and another part of the high seas, all ships in transit shall enjoy equally the *freedom of navigation* for the purpose of transit passage through such straits.[82] Speaking earlier in 1972 in the Seabed Committee, the United States delegate made it clear that:

> The United States and others . . . [consider that] . . . their vital interests require that agreement on a twelve mile territorial sea be coupled with agreement on free transit of straits used for international navigation and these remain basic elements of our national policy which we will not sacrifice.[83]

After some striking additions, deletions, and arrangements, we now have the right of transit passage as a right of its own. 'Transit passage' is defined in Article 38(2) of the 1982 Convention to mean

> the exercise . . . of the freedom of navigation and overflight solely for the purpose of continuous and expeditious transit of the strait between one part of the high seas or an exclusive economic zone and another part of the high seas or an exclusive economic zone. However, the requirement of continuous and expeditious transit does not preclude passage through the strait for the purpose of entering, leaving or returning from a State bordering the strait, subject to the conditions of entry to that State.

From the above definition it can be readily perceived that qualitatively and quantitatively the right of transit passage is quite distinct from the right of innocent passage.

Qualitatively, the definition of 'transit passage' does include a reference to the 'freedom of navigation', while 'innocent passage' does not. It does not apparently include a requirement of surface passage for submarines, which is a must in 'innocent passage'. Quantitatively, the right of transit passage includes the right of overflight, unlike any type of innocent passage regime.

However, as far as the substantive aspect of both rights are concerned, they are more related to each other than to the high seas freedom of navigation. Freedom of navigation on the high seas, as defined earlier, is subject to no limitations or conditions other than the duty of reasonableness, inherent in every right in any case. 'Transit passage' is exercised subject to duties which correlatively are rights of the coastal States. Similarly, the right of innocent passage is exercised subject to the rights of the coastal State. Since the right of innocent passage has a longer history, 'transit passage' seems more a species of the former than a 'reduced' version of the high seas freedom of navigation.

Thus, Article 39 of the 1982 Convention states, as far as duties imposed on passing ships and aircraft are concerned, that:

1. Ships and aircraft, while exercising the right of transit passage, shall:

   (a) proceed without delay through or over the strait;
   (b) refrain from any threat or use of force against the sovereignty, territorial integrity or political independence of States bordering the strait, or in any other manner in violation of the principles of international law embodied in the Charter of the United Nations;
   (c) refrain from any activities other than those incident to their normal modes of continuous and expeditious transit unless rendered necessary by force majeure or by distress;
   (d) comply with other relevant provisions of this Part.

2. Ships in transit passage shall:

   (a) comply with generally accepted international regulations, procedures and practices for safety at sea, including the International Regulations for Preventing Collisions at Sea;
   (b) comply with generally accepted international regulations, procedures and practices for the prevention, reduction and control of pollution from ships.

3. Aircraft in transit passage shall:

   (a) observe the Rules of the Air established by the International Civil Aviation Organization as they apply to civil aircraft; State aircraft will normally comply with such safety measures and will at all times operate with due regard for the safety of navigation;
   (b) at all times monitor the radio frequency assigned by the competent internationally designated air traffic control authority or the appropriate international distress radio frequency.

Except for paragraph 3 on aircraft passage, the other duties enumerated in Article 39 fit into some of the activities considered by Article 19 to be prejudicial to the peace, good order or security of the coastal State if a vessel engages in them in exercising the right of innocent passage. For example, in order for passage to be 'transit passage' ('not prejudicial . . . to the coastal State'—innocent passage formulation), it must not be a 'threat or use of force against the sovereignty, territorial integrity or political independence of States bordering straits' (except that this plural usage appears wider in scope, unlike the *coastal State* restriction for innocent passage). Furthermore, the passage must not 'in any other manner [be] in violation of the principles of international law embodied in the charter of the United Nations'. Consequently, in both instances, the coastal State or the strait State, as the case may be, is empowered to assess the lawfulness of the passage.

If any further distinction could be made between the right of innocent passage and the right of transit passage in straits, it would relate to the degree of coastal State appreciation of submerged navigation and overflight.

In the case of innocent passage, submarines and other underwater vehicles are required to navigate on the surface and to show their flag (1982 Convention, Article 20). In the case of transit passage, no article specifically requires surface navigation, nor specifically and unequivocally obliges submarines to traverse international straits submerged. Article 39(1) (c) of the 1982 Convention only warns ships on transit passage to 'refrain from any activities other than those incident to their *normal modes* of continuous and expeditious transit unless rendered necessary by force majeure or by distress' (emphasis added). Considering that this is the only place when the Convention may have alluded to submerged navigation as being a normal mode of locomotion for submarines, does this actually afford more scope than the requirement of surface navigation in case of innocent passage? This doubt is shared by many authorities in the area. Reisman thinks that in order to reach this assimilation between submerged navigation and 'normal mode', the latter

> must be construed as noncontextual, non-normative, and permanently vessel-specific. But in the text and in general, this interpretation is forced and unreal. Mode of transit of different vessels is, in part, a factual question, but it also has normative and contextual components, for what is 'normal' will depend on context, including the legal environment. It is neither implausible nor inconsistent with [the Convention's] provisions to assume that both the coastal and the flag State will participate in determining 'normality for vessels transiting coastal waters'.[84]

As regards the strait State's appreciation of 'normality', this may well mean an obligation to practise surface navigation as in the case of the right of innocent passage, given the fact that in order to obtain safe passage of ships (Article 42(1), that State can enact laws and regulations (Article 42(1) (a)) on safety of navigation and the regulation of maritime traffic. It would be reasonable and logical for the strait State's laws to require surface navigation in a dense, busy and dangerous strait. *A contrario*, nothing prevents a coastal State or a strait State from granting the right of submerged passage through its waters by virtue of instruments other than the Law of the Sea Convention.

As far as overflight is concerned, there is no such activity implicit in the right of innocent passage.[85] Article 19(2) (e) even considers the launching, landing or taking on board of any aircraft as a non-innocent activity. Transit passage, on the contrary, involves the right of overflight. However, even here, aircraft are restricted by the Rules of the Air issued by the International Civil Aviation Organization and other safety measures and precautions (Article 39(3) of the 1982 Convention).

The Chicago Convention on International Civil Aviation (1944) thus circumscribes the right of overflight:

> all aircraft . . . not engaged in scheduled international air services shall have the right . . . to make flights into or in transit non-stop across (a) territory [i.e. straits, territorial sea, archipelagic waters, etc.] . . . without the necessity of obtaining prior permission, and *subject to the right of the State flown over to require landing*. (emphasis added)

Under Article 39 of the 1982 Convention, State aircraft will normally comply with such safety measures as prescribed by the International Civil Aviation Organization. On the other hand, Article 3(c) of the Chicago Convention prescribes:

> No State aircraft . . . shall fly over the territory of another State or land thereon *without authorisation* by special agreement or otherwise, and in accordance with the terms thereof. (emphasis added)

Of course, the requirement for special authorization could be one of the major safety measures to be enacted for State aircraft.

In sum, the right of 'innocent passage' and the right of 'transit passage' are quite similar so far as the attributions of the coastal or strait State are concerned, but quite distinct in at least one respect, namely, suspension of passage. Article 23(3) of the 1982 Convention provides that:

> The coastal State may, without discrimination . . . *suspend* temporarily in specified areas of its territorial sea the innocent passage of foreign ships if such suspension is essential for the protection of its security, including weapons exercise.

Article 44 of the same Convention, however, presribes that, in international straits,

> States bordering straits shall not hamper transit passage and shall give appropriate publicity to any danger to navigation or overflight within or over the strait of which they have knowledge. There shall be *no suspension* of transit passage.

This has been a recurrent theme even when transit passage was considered an aspect of the right of innocent passage. Thus, in the 1958 Convention, it was stated that 'there shall be no suspension of innocent passage of foreign ships through *straits* . . .'.[86] This was reflecting the view expressed by the International Court of Justice in the *Corfu Channel* case, where the Court had said: 'Unless otherwise prescribed in an international convention,[87] there is no right for a coastal State to prohibit such passage through *straits* in time of peace.'[88]

Do all these requirements of non-suspension of passage; circumscribed but explicit, textual, provision for overflights; and the non-textual condition on surface transit of submarines in straits, equally apply to the right of archipelagic sealanes passage and, in that case, would these requirements distinguish it from the right of innocent passage?

(b) Right of archipelagic sealanes passage

The right of archipelagic sealanes passage is comparable in all respects to the right of transit passage in international straits. It is thus different from the right of innocent passage in the same way as the regime of transit passage differs from that of innocent passage.

Article 53 of the 1982 Convention, which covers the right of archipelagic sealanes passage, runs as follows:

1. An archipelagic State may designate sealanes and air routes there above, suitable for the continuous and expeditious passage of foreign ships and aircraft through or over its archipelagic waters and the adjacent territorial sea.
2. All ships and aircraft enjoy the right of archipelagic sealanes passage in such sea lanes and air routes.
3. Archipelagic sea lanes passage means the exercise in accordance with this Convention of the rights of navigation and overflight in the normal mode solely for the purpose of continuous, expeditious and unobstructed transit between one part of the high seas or an exclusive economic zone and another part of the high seas or an exclusive economic zone.
4. Such sealanes and air routes shall traverse the archipelagic waters and the adjacent territorial sea and shall include all normal passage routes used as routes for international navigation or overflight through or over archipelagic waters and, within such routes, so far as ships are concerned, all normal navigational channels, provided that duplication of routes of similar convenience between the same entry and exit points shall not be necessary.
5. Such sealanes and air routes shall be defined by a series of continuous axis lines from the entry points of passage routes to the exit points. Ships and aircraft in archipelagic sealanes passage shall not deviate more than 25 nautical miles to either side of such axis lines during passage, provided that such ships and aircraft shall not navigate closer to the coasts than 10 per cent of the distance between the nearest points on islands bordering the sealane.
6. An archipelagic State which designates sealanes under this article may also prescribe traffic separation schemes for the safe passage of ships through narrow channels in such sealanes.
7. An archipelagic State may, when circumstances require, after giving due publicity thereto, substitute other sealanes or traffic separation schemes for any sealanes or traffic separation schemes previously designated or prescribed by it.

8. Such sealanes and traffic separation schemes shall conform to generally accepted international regulations.
9. In designating or substituting sealanes or prescribing or substituting traffic separation schemes, an archipelagic State shall refer proposals to the competent international organization with a view to their adoption. The organization may adopt only such sealanes and traffic separation schemes as may be agreed with the archipelagic State, after which the archipelagic State may designate, prescribe or substitute them.
10. The archipelagic State shall clearly indicate the axis of the sealanes and the traffic separation schemes designated or prescribed by it on charts to which due publicity shall be given.
11. Ships in archipelagic sealanes passage shall respect applicable sealanes and traffic separation schemes established in accordance with this article.
12. If an archipelagic State does not designate sealanes or air routes, the right of archipelagic sealanes passage may be exercised through the routes normally used for international navigation.

From the above, it can be deduced that, as in the case of transit passage, express provision is made for overflight in various paragraphs. There is no obligation of surface navigation for any submarine but, rather, of 'navigation or overflight in the *normal mode*', which arguably could involve submerged navigation for underwater vessels. Since Article 54 of the 1982 Convention concedes that Articles 39, 40, 42 and particularly 44 (the transit passage provisions) apply *mutatis mutandis* to archipelagic sealanes passage, it can be inferred that the right of archipelagic sealanes passage may never be suspended, not even temporarily, contrary to what is the case for innocent passage.

Nevertheless, the regime of the archipelagic sealanes passage, unlike those of innocent passage and transit passage, depends on the delimitation of its geographical scope, on the delimitation of the sealanes by reference to their axis, unless no sealanes are designated by the archipelagic State. In the latter case, the routes normally used for international navigation will be assimilated to sealanes or air routes.

Last but not least there are provisions in the articles on transit passage and innocent passage where passage is defined as 'entering, leaving or returning from a State bordering the strait' (Article 38(2)), or as calling at a roadstead or port facility (Article 18(1) (b)). No such contact is warranted nor conceivable in the context of archipelagic sealanes passage.

It is quite interesting to note that the rights of archipelagic sealanes passage and of transit passage, basically modern offsprings of the more traditional right of innocent passage, allow one major mode of international transportation—air navigation—while innocent passage has always been limited to the passage of 'all ships'.

(c) The problem of air navigation

The right of innocent passage has never been conceived of as including the right of overflight.[89] Neither has that right featured in cases concerning overflight of land territory, despite efforts to the contrary.[90] Generally, the regime prevailing on the surface of the earth has influenced the status of the superjacent airspace, except for the polar regions which are subject to special agreements. Owing to this influence, the airspace above the high seas is subject to the freedom of the high seas regime, i.e. freedom of overflight without the consent of other States. In the exclusive economic zone, where coastal States enjoy only sovereign economic rights, the high seas freedom of overflight prevails (Article 58 of the 1982 Convention). The same obtains in the contiguous air zone—analogous to the 'contiguous zone'[91] in the Law of the Sea—subject to the controversial 'Air Defence Identification Zones'[92] aimed at identifying and controlling aircraft as they approach the territorial sea.

In the territorial sea, where foreign States enjoy the right of innocent passage, there is no such thing as a right of innocent overflight.[93] For the land territory, as seen earlier, the absence of such a right is understandable, because there is neither an absolute right of innocent land transit nor a right of innocent air transit. The lack of any right of overflight over the territorial sea is thus due to the fact that land territory and territorial sea are subject to the same sovereignty.[94]

For the purpose of this Convention, says Article 2 of the 1944 Convention on International Civil Aviation, 'the territory of a State shall be deemed to be the land areas and territorial waters adjacent thereto under the sovereignty, suzerainty, protection or mandate of such State'. Article 1 of the same Convention emphasizes that: '[T]he Contracting States recognize that every State has complete and exclusive sovereignty over the airspace above its territory.'[95]

In principle, no State can use the airspace of another, including the airspace above the territorial seas, without the prior consent of the concerned State. Article 3 of the Chicago Convention (which governs mainly international civil aviation), distinguishes between 'scheduled' and 'non-scheduled' ('charter') international air services. Scheduled international air services over or into the territory or territorial sea of a Contracting State require the prior consent of the State concerned (Article 6 of the Chicago Convention); as regards non-scheduled 'chartered' flights, aircraft of Contracting States may, according to Article 1, make flights into or across the territory and territorial sea of member States without prior permission but this right, as probably in the case of warships exercising the right of innocent passage, is subject to the right of the State territory or territorial waters overflown to require landing, and for each Contracting State, for reasons of safety of flight, to require aircraft desiring to proceed over regions which are inaccessible, or without adequate air navigation facilities (as is the case in the territorial seas) to follow prescribed routes or to obtain special permission.

For non-civil aircraft, i.e. State aircraft, including aircraft used in military, customs and police services, the Civil Aviation Convention of 1944, expressing the opinion and practice of States, quite categorically subordinates overflight to the consent of the territorial State.

Article 3(c) of the Chicago Convention provides that '[n]o State aircraft of a contracting State shall fly over the territory [territorial sea] of another State or land thereon without authorisation by special agreement or otherwise, and in accordance with the terms thereof'.

In sum, except within the limits of Article 5 of the Convention (for cases of non-scheduled civil aviation), or under some special authorization, foreign aircraft do not enjoy a right of aerial passage over the territorial sea and land area of another State.[96]

Accordingly, in the absence of treaty provisions to the contrary, the right of innocent passage of foreign ships through the territorial sea does not include a 'right of innocent passage of foreign aircraft' through the airspace above the territorial sea unless such a right results from 'Bermuda'[97]-type agreements or from the International Air Services Transit Agreement'.[98] There is, therefore, no independent right of the 'innocent passage' category.

The 1982 Convention entertains no doubts in this respect. Part II, Section 3, of that Convention, dealing with the right of innocent passage, considers only 'all ships' and, where aircraft are mentioned (Article 19(2) (e)), overflight is considered a 'non-innocent' exercise of the right of innocent passage.

Notes

1. Consistent with the codification attempts undertaken since 1894 by the Institut de droit international, an eminent member of that Institute wrote in 1954: 'La règle de droit international la plus importante qui limite le droit de l'Etat riverain sur la mer territoriale est celle qui établit de droit des navires de commerce étrangers au passage dit passage inoffensif'. cf. Castberg Frede, 'Distinction entre les eaux territoriales et les eaux intérieures', IDI, *Annuaire* 1954, vol. I, pp. 113–73, at p. 121.
2. *Report of the Committee on the Peaceful Uses of the Seabed and Ocean Floor Beyond the Limits of National Jurisdiction to the General Assembly*, Official Records, 28th Session, Supplement No. 21 (Doc. A/9021), p. 50, paragraph 42.
3. Jessup, P.C., *The Law of Territorial Waters and Maritime Jurisdiction*, New York, Jennings and Co., 1927, p. 120.
4. This was one of Grotius's foremost propositions: 'the most specific axiom of the law of nations; called a primary rule or first principle, the spirit of which is self-evident and immutable, to wit: every nation is free to travel to every other nation and to trade with it'. cf. *The Freedom of the Seas or the Right which Belongs to the Dutch to Take Part in the East Indian Trade*, Oxford, Oxford University Press, 1916, p. 7. See also Castberg, op. cit., note 1, p. 121.
5. Grotius made a blanket assimilation of passage regimes in all other zones, even where there is private ownership, by asserting: '. . . lands, rivers, and any part of the sea tht has become subject to the ownership of a people ought to be open to those who, for legitimate reasons, have need to cross over them; as for instance, if a people . . . desires to carry on commerce with a distant people . . . ownership was introduced with the reservation of such a use, which is of advantage to the one people and involves no detriment to the other. Consequently, it must be held that the originators of private property had such a reservation in view'. *De jure belli ac pacis*, lib. II, cap. 2 (translation of the 1646 edition by Francis W. Kelsey, *The Classics of International Law*, J.B. Scott (ed.), vol. II, Oxford, The Clarendon Press, 1925, pp. 196–7.
6. Quoted in Colombos, C.J., *International Law of the Sea*, 6th ed, London, Longmans, 1967, p. 63.
7. See Jessup, op. cit., note 3, p. 120, who states: 'The right of innocent passage seems to be the result of an attempt to reconcile the freedom of oceean navigation with the theory of territorial waters'.

8. Vattel, E. de, *The Law of Nations or the Principles of Natural Law applied to the Conduct and to the Affairs of Nations and Sovereigns* (translation of the 1758 edition by Charles G. Fenwick, *The Classics of International Law*, J.B. Scott (ed.), vol. III, Washington, Carnegie Institution, 1916, pp. 106–10.
9. For details on these treaties, see Jessup, op. cit., note 3, pp. 72ff. For the US anti-liquor and anti-smuggling enactments, see Fulton, T.W., *The Sovereignty of the Sea*, Edinburgh and London, W. Blackwood, 1911, pp. 534ff.
10. Quoted in Jessup, op. cit., note 3, p. 130.
11. (1876) Exch. 63, quoted in O'Connell, D.P., *The International Law of the Sea*, vol. I, Oxford, Clarendon Press, 1982, p. 264.
12. IDI, *Annuaire*, vol. XIII, 1894–1895, pp. 329–30.
13. Found in AJIL, vol. 23, 1929, Special Supplement, p. 367. For further comments on this proposal, see Brown, P.M., 'The Law of Territorial Waters', *AJIL*, vol. 21, 1927, p. 101.
14. International Law Association, Report of the Thirty-Third Conference, Stockholm, 1924, p. 263.
15. *AJIL*, vol. 20, 1926, Special Supplement, pp. 318ff.
16. Extract found in *AJIL*, vol. 23, op. cit., note 13, p. 376.
17. The complete draft was published, ibid., pp. 243–5. In a commentary on this Article, at pp. 295/296, it was stated: 'Notwithstanding the fact that the sovereignty of a State extends over its marginal sea, the State may not prevent the innocent passage of vessels of other States through such waters, free of all tolls, rights, dues or other exactions . . . In inland waters the right of innocent passage is not recognised. If a vessel anchors in the marginal sea of another State, the passage is broken and the vessel may be regarded as within the marginal sea for purposes other than that of innocent passage.'
18. Lauterpacht, E., 'Freedom of Transit in International Law', *Grotius Society Transactions*, vol. 44, 1958/1959, pp. 311–56, at p. 323.
19. In fact, this method was used by the International Court of Justice in at least two instances: *Reservations to the Genocide Convention*, ICJ, *Reports* 1951, pp. 22ff., and *Barcelona Traction, Light and Power Co., Ltd.*, ICJ, *Reports* 1964, pp. 31ff. cf. Article 32 of the Vienna Convention on the Law of Treaties.
20. LON Doc. C.74.M.39.1929.V., p. 71.
21. ibid., p. 75. Note, however, the use of the words 'merchant ships'. In the course of the discussions, there was majority opinion that innocent passage, as a matter of right, does not extend to warships. For the details of the discussion, see LON Doc. C.251(b).M.145(b).1930.V, *in* League of Nations, *Conference for the Codification of International Law* (1930), Shabtai Rosenne (ed.), vol. 4, New York, Oceana, 1975, pp. 1260ff.
22. The *Corfu Channel* case (Merits) (United Kingdom v. Albania), judgment of 9 April 1949, ICJ *Reports* 1949, p. 28 (emphasis added).
23. ibid., p. 30.
24. 1958 Convention on the High Seas, Article 2.
25. 1982 Convention, Article 87(2).
26. LON Doc. C.351.M.145.1930.V, which contains most of the resolutions and draft articles of the 1930 Codification Conference, which are quoted in full *in* UNCLOS General Assembly, Doc. 13/21 of 14 February 1958, pp. 1ff. For our purposes, see p. 19.
27. The General Assembly had an opportunity to do so after the 1956 Suez crisis. See UN General Assembly, Official Records, 11th Session, 1956/1957, vol. 11 (Docs. A/PV.665, A/PV.666 and A/PV.667), pp. 1265ff.
28. Report of the International Law Commission Covering the Work of the Eighth

Session, April 23–July 4, 1956. General Assembly, 11th Session, Official Records, Supplement No. 9 A/3159, p. 6 (hereinafter referred to as ILC *Report* 1956).

29. The comment on Article 18 ran thus: 'International law has long recognized the right of the coastal State to enact, in the general interest of navigation, special regulations applicable to ships exercising the right of passage through the territorial sea.

Ships entering the territorial sea of a foreign State remain under the jurisdiction of the flag State. Nevertheless, the fact that they are in waters under the sovereignty of another State imposes some limitation on the exclusive jurisdiction of the flag State. Such ships must comply with the laws and regulations enacted by the coastal State in conformity with the present rules and other rules of international law and in particular, with the laws and regulations relating to transport and navigation. At its seventh session, the Commission thought it useful to give the following examples:

a) The safety of traffic and the protection of channels and buoys;
b) The protection of the waters of the coastal State against pollution of any kind caused by ships;
c) The conservation of the living resources of the sea;
d) The rights of fishing and hunting and analogous rights belonging to the coastal State;
e) Any hydrographical survey.'

Found in ILC *Report* 1956, p. 20.

30. ibid., p. 19. In other words, passage could be considered non-innocent if the vessel carried 'goods' which, within the foreign territorial sea, could be used to violate that coastal State's laws.
31. Doc. A/PV.665, op. cit., note 26, pp. 1271, paragraph 62.
32. Doc. A/PV.667, op. cit., note 26, pp. 1287, paragraph 51.
33. (First) UNCLOS, Official Records, vol. III, p. 9.
34. The Indian representative proposed to insert, after the word 'prejudicial to', the words 'the peace, good order or'. ibid., p. 85, para. 3.
35. The Turkish amendment proposed to add, in the second sentence of the American proposal, the words 'and to the other rules of international law'. ibid., p. 98, para. 40.
36. ibid., p. 83, para 22.
37. ibid., p. 85, para. 4. Speaking on this point, the delegate of the United Kingdom 'considered that any reference to the interests of the coastal State was also unacceptable, since it widened the whole concept to a degree which would make a farce of the right . . .'. ibid., p. 85, para. 7.
38. (First) UNCLOS, Official Records, vol. II, p. 65, para. 3.
39. Doc. A/CONF.13/L.52, p. 6, 28 april 1958, ibid., p. 133.
40. O'Connell, D.P., *The International Law of the Sea*, vol. I, 1982, Oxford, Clarendon Press, p. 273.
41. Sir Gerald Fitzmaurice, 'Some Results of the Geneva Conference on the Law of the Sea', *ICLO*, vol. 8, 1959, pp. 73–121, at p. 95.
42. ibid., p. 94.
43. cf. the *Corfu Channel* case (Merits), op. cit., note 22, pp. 31ff., where more emphasis was placed on the *manner* than on the object of the passage. See also Fitzmaurice, op. cit., note 41, p. 97.
44. Even if these terms are construed restrictively. cf. Fitzmaurice, op. cit., note 41, p. 98.
45. O'Connell, op. cit., note 40, p. 272.
46. Among them are L. Gross, 'The Geneva Conference on the Law of the Sea and the Right of Innocent Passage in the Gulf of Aqaba', *AJIL*, vol. 53, 1959, pp. 564–94, at p. 564, and D. Pharand, 'Innocent Passage in the Arctic' in *Canadian Yearbook of International Law*, 1968, pp. 3–60, at pp. 7ff.

47. cf. Ward, R.E., 'The Mayaguez: The Right of Innocent Passage and the Legality of Reprisal', *San Diego Law Review*, vol. 13, 1976, pp. 765–78, at p. 670.
48. This is borne out by a comparative reading of the relevant articles in the 1958 and 1982 Conventions.
49. This is the conclusion of O'Connell, op. cit., note 40, p. 273.
50. Doc. A/CONF. 62/C.2/L.3, of 3 July 1974.
51. Doc. A/CONF. 62/C.2/L.16, of 22 July 1974 (hereafter the four-nation draft).
52. Doc. A/CONF.62/C.2/L.19, of 23 July 1974.
53. Article 2(4) of the United Nations Charter.
54. Burke, W., 'Contemporary Law of the Sea: Transportation, Communication and Flights', *Occasional Paper No. 28*, Law of the Sea Institute, University of Rhode Island, Kingston, 1985, p. 12.
55. Article 73 of the 1982 Convention.
56. Reisman, M., 'The Regime of Straits and National Security: An Appraisal of International Law-Making', *AJIL*, vol. 73, 1980, pp. 48–76, at p. 65.
57. LON Doc. C.351(b).M.145(b).1930.V, *in* Rosenne, op. cit., note 21, pp. 1404–5.
58. Doc. A/CONF.13/21, p. 20; see also Rosenne, op. cit., note 21, p. 1405.
59. Smith, H.A., *The Law and Custom of the Sea*, 3rd ed, London, Clarendon Press, 1959, p. 46.
60. Gidel, G., *Le droit international public de la mer*, Paris, Sirey, 1932–1934, vol. III, p. 204.
61. op. cit., note 21, p. 1260.
62. LON, Doc. C.351(b).M.145(b).1930.V, in Rosenne, op. cit., note 21, p. 1264.
63. Fitzmaurice suggests an instance where a ship enters the territorial sea out of her normal course because of weather conditions or other emergency circumstances, for the purpose of anchoring and of eventually leaving the territorial sea by the same route, and not of passing through it and leaving at another point. op. cit., note 41, p. 93.
64. ibid. This seems to cater for the case of semi-enclosed seas, such as the Black Sea, or gulfs entirely within one nation, where one can navigate without necessarily transiting to other destinations.
65. Gidel, op. cit., note 60, p. 206.
66. ibid., p. 206.
67. Khoshkish, A., *The Right of Innocent Passage*, Geneva, Edition Internationale, 1954, p. 38.
68. It should be noted, however, that generally navigation exercised between the sea and port situated on an international river falls within the scope of river navigation and, consequently, under the regime of that navigation. Vitanyi, B., *The International Regime of River Navigation*, Alphen a.d.R., Sijthoff and Noordhoff, 1979, at p. 8.
69. op. cit., note 26.
70. ibid.
71. Comment on Article 14 of the Harvard Draft Articles on the Law of the Sea, *AJIL*, vol. 23, 1929, Special Number, p. 296.
72. Instances of this include bad weather, the presence of fog, engine failure, and the shallow nature of the territorial sea. It is difficult to contemplate that the distress of a foreign vessel carrying nuclear materials, hence likely to emit dangerous radiation, could still be considered exercising the right of innocent passage and thus prevent the coastal State from 'interfering' to protect itself. cf. Article 17 of the 1962 Brussels Convention on Liability of Operators of Nuclear Ships, in *AJIL*, vol. 57, 1963, p. 268.
73. Jessup, P.C. 'The International Law Commissions. Report on the Regime of the Territorial Sea', *AJIL*, vol. 49, 1955, p. 226.

74. op. cit., notes 50, 51 and 52, respectively.
75. op. cit., note 51, Article 3.
76. Good faith should not be confused with the new Soviet concept of equating 'Continuously and expeditiously with the ratio of reasonable speed . . . along sea corridors or traffic separation systems (where necessary) established by the coastal State . . . or along the shortest traditional transit routes within the territorial sea'. cf. Butler, W.E. 'Innocent Passage and the 1982 Convention: The Influence of Soviet Law and Policy', *AJIL*, vol. 81, pp. 331–47, at pp. 342–3.
77. Hence Butler's proposition that '. . . the international legal system operates on a presumption in favour of innocent passage . . . subject to the rules of international law and *coastal State legislation*'. In ibid., p. 346.
78. Referring to the mine-sweeping operations conducted by the United Kingdom, the Court stated: 'the Court recognises that the operation . . . could not be justified as the exercise of a right of innocent passage, and . . .' *Corfu Channel* case, op. cit., note 22, pp. 28ff.
79. By prescribing as regards passage in straits that: 'There shall be no suspension of innocent passage of foreign ships through straits which are used for international navigation between one part of the high Seas and another part of the high seas or the territorial sea of a foreign State.' Article 16(4) of the 1958 Convention.
80. cf. United Kingdom, Draft Articles on the Territorial Sea and Straits, Doc..A/Conf. 62/C 2/L.2 (Article 29), in which 'transit passage' is used. See also the Draft Articles on Straits Used for International Navigation submitted by Bulgaria, Czechoslovakia, GDR, Poland, Ukrainian Soviet Socialist Rep. and USSR as draft articles on straits used for international navigation. Doc. A/CONF. 62/C.2/L.11.
81. cf. Draft Articles on Navigation in Straits submitted by Malaysia, Morocco, Oman, Yemen, Doc. A/CONF. 62/C.L.2/6. Article 21 called for the application of the regime of innocent passage.
82. Doc. A/CONF.62/C.2/L.11, op. cit., note 80, Article 1(1).
83. Statement made by John R. Stevenson before Subcommittee II of the Seabed Committee on 28 July 1972, UN Doc. A/AC.138/SC.11/SR.37, at pp. 2ff.
84. Reisman, op. cit., note 56, p. 71.
85. Although overflight may be permitted by treaties such as the Chicago Convention of 1944 on International Civil Aviation.
86. Article 16(4) of the 1958 Convention.
87. This was an oblique reference to the Montreux Convention of 1936 governing passage in the Turkish Straits.
88. The *Corfu Channel* case, op. cit., note 22, p. 30.
89. A Romanian proposal in the 1930 Hague Codification Conference to extend for the first time to foreign aircraft a right of innocent passage was withdrawn when the French delegate persuaded all the other delegations that '. . . air navigation was regulated by the Paris Convention of 1919, and that it was therefore preferable that reference should be made to the provisions of that Convention as regards all matters concerning aircraft'. Rosenne, S. (ed.), League of Nations, *Conference for the Codification of International Law* (1930), vol. IV, Dobbs Ferry, NY, Oceana, 1975, p. 1262.
90. From the beginnings of air law, there were two schools of thought on this point. One considered territorial airspace as open to complete freedom, like the high seas, while the other school favoured subjecting the airspace above State territory to absolute State sovereignty. For further details, see Wagner, W.J., *International Air Transportation as Affected by State Sovereignty*, Bruxelles, Bruylant, 1970, pp. 13ff.
91. According to Article 33 of the 1982 Convention, the coastal State may exercise in the contiguous zone the control necessary to prevent or punish infringement of its

customs, fiscal, immigration or sanitary laws and regulations within its territory or territorial sea.

92. These zones, however, have no international customary or conventional basis and thus constitute unilateral encroachment on the high seas. cf. McDougal, M.S. and Burke, W.T., *The Public Order of the Oceans*, New Haven, Yale University Press, 1962, pp. 626ff; Delupis, I., 'Passage Through Air', in *International Law and the Independent State*, New York, Crane, Russak, 1974, at p. 82; de Vries Lentsch, P., 'The Right of Overflight over Strait States and Archipelagic States: Developments and Prospects', *Netherlands Yearbook of International Law*, vol. 13, 1983, pp. 165–225, at p. 173.

93. 'The airspace above the territorial sea is wholly assimilated to the airspace above the territory, the movements of aircraft (flight, take-off and landing) in both spaces are subject to identical conditions. Aircraft do not enjoy in the airspace above the territorial sea the right of innocent passage enjoyed by ships in the territorial sea itself.' At the 1930 Hague Codification Conference this indication was thought necessary since there was no customary law on innocent passage through the air above a territory. Doc. A/CN.4/SR.172, paragraphs 18, 21 and 22. cf. Doc. A/CONF. 13/4, 'The Law of the Air and the [Draft] Articles Concerning the Law of the Sea Adopted by the International Law Commission', particularly pp. 4–12.

94. The idea of having a right of innocent overflight in the airspace above the territorial sea is untenable, partly because vessels in the territorial sea are subject to gravitations and viscosity which limit their movement and speed, whereas aircraft confront no such limitations and thus can cruise at supersonic speed with heightened security problems (accidents, higher noise levels, and environmental pollution).

95. The idea is that in this way the territorial State would protect itself against risks of falling objects and ballast, violation of national laws on, say, customs duties and contraband; and, of course, avoid exposure to disadvantages of a strategic character such as espionage and the photographing of strategic objects and sites on the territory of the State concerned. cf. Wagner, op. cit., note 90, p. 14. As shown in the introductory chapter, the territorial sea originated also from the thought of protecting the security of the territorial State by a 'belt of marginal sea'.

96. cf. comments by the International Civil Aviation Organization on the Draft Articles concerning the Law of the Sea adopted by the International Law Commission in 1956, in (First) UNCLOS, Doc. A/CONF.13/31 of 24 January 1958, p. 3.

97. The 'Bermuda Agreement' is a bilateral air services agreement signed between the United States and Great Britain on 11 February 1946 and used as a model for other bilateral agreements to authorize overflight by foreign aircraft in sovereign airspace (in both land territory and the territorial sea).

98. The International Air Services Transit Agreement, like the International Air Transport Agreement, both concluded jointly with the Convention on International Civil Aviation in 1944, are examples of multilateral treaties granting '. . . the *privilege* to fly across territories and territorial seas and land for non-traffic purposes' (Article 1(1); Bermuda Agreement, Annex, Article 1).

Chapter 3

The scope of the right of innocent passage in certain coastal zones

1. Introduction

In the previous chapter, it was noted that the right of innocent passage takes different shapes according to the geophysical nature of the area envisaged. Thus there is a suspendable right of innocent passage within the territorial sea proper, a non-suspendable right of innocent passage in the straits mentioned by Article 45 of the 1982 Convention, and a suspendable right of innocent passage through archipelagic waters outside archipelagic sealanes (Article 52 of the 1982 Convention). There is also a suspendable right of innocent passage in parts of the internal waters (Article 8). These various rights of innocent passage will be analysed in greater detail in the pages that follow. The emphasis will be on how these rights came to be applied in the various zones and how they are regulated by the present Law of the Sea regime.

2. The Territorial Sea Proper

What is here termed territorial sea proper is the area seaward of the low-water mark to a distance presently taken to be a maximum of twelve nautical miles.[1] We exclude the special cases of bays, of islands located within a distance of 12 nautical miles, and of areas within groups of islands. These special situations will be dealt with in another section of this chapter.

The right of innocent passage in its original customary law connotation was mainly viewed with the framework of the territorial sea proper. That major thrust has not altered, despite the extension of innocent passage to archipelagic waters beyond the archipelagic sealanes and in the straits described in Article 45 of the 1982 Convention. Consequently, from the Draft Proposals of the 1930 Hague Codification, *via* the International Law Commission's work and the 1958 Convention on the Territorial Sea and the Contiguous Zone, to the Articles of the 1982 Convention, the right of innocent passage has consistently been associated with the legal status of the territorial sea proper. Just considering the 1982 Convention, it is conceivable that all ten articles of Part 1, Section 3, subsection A, dealing with the passage rules, rights and obligations, are either of the variety, '. . . through the territorial sea . . .', or of the variety, '. . . in the territorial sea . . .'. Does it mean that all internal or interior waters are excluded from the innocent passage regime?[2]

3. Internal Waters

The internal waters of a State are defined in Article 8(1) of the 1982 Convention, as waters on the landward side of the baseline used for measuring the breadth of the territorial sea. This definition naturally excludes the waters within archipelagos. This definition would appear to cover inland waters such as rivers, lying wholly within the territory of one State from source to mouth,[3] and lakes within the same territory. However, for our purposes, 'internal waters' refer to maritime waters enclosed by baselines, especially by straight closing lines or straight baselines warranted by geographical or historical circumstances. In other words, but for some delimitation hazards or historical circumstances, these portions of the seas would be high seas, or the territorial seas proper, wherein the regimes of freedom of navigation or of innocent passage would apply.

Although coastal States exercise about equally complete and absolute sovereignty over these internal waters as they exercise over their land territory, the right of innocent passage is considered still operational.[4] This despite the fact that the right of innocent passage was conceived of as characterizing only the legal status of the territorial sea proper, generally excluding internal waters.[5] Prior to its codification in both the 1982 Convention and the 1958 Geneva Convention, this exception to the established rule was first judicially acknowledged in the 1951 *Fisheries* case between the United Kingdom and Norway. A brief analysis of this evolution would help elucidate the *raison d'être*, the judicial scope and the nature of the right of innocent passage in internal waters.

(a) The *Fisheries* case (United Kingdom v. Norway) (1951)

This case concerned, among other issues, fishing rights off the Norwegian coast, the territoriality of some types of bays and the delimitation system applicable to deeply indented coasts. We shall focus on the portions of the judgment dealing with the acceptance of the straight-baselines method of delimitation and with the territoriality of 'historical waters'. Emphasis will be placed on the existence of a right of innocent passage in these portions of the seas despite their new status as internal waters.

The Court was asked to decide on the lawfulness of a Norwegian Royal Decree of 12 July 1935 including in the internal waters of Norway certain maritime areas. According to the United Kingdom, these waters were part of the high seas. The Court had thus to decide whether the Royal Decree was in conflict with the rules of international law. For Norway, the 1935 Decree was an application of a traditional system of delimitation which was in conformity with international law, because the 'rules of international law take into account specific cases and therefore concedes that the drawing of [straight] baselines must be adapted to the special conditions obtaining in different regions'.[6] By the use of this delimitation method incorporated in the 1935 Decree as well as in other Decrees dating back to 1812, 47 straight lines were drawn all along the northern coast of Norway, between the headlands of bays, across fiords and sounds, and where there were islands, islets and reefs off the mainland, between the salient and most extreme of these features.

The United Kingdom for its part conceded only that Norway was entitled to claim as Norwegian internal waters, on historic grounds, all fiords and sounds falling within the conception of a bay as defined in international law, whether the length of the closing line of the indentation was more or less than ten nautical miles.[7] Furthermore, for the United Kingdom international law did not give a State a right to choose baselines which conflicted with accepted customary rule, namely, that baselines should not be straight but should follow the low-water mark along even an indented coast with island fringes or, for cases of bays, the proper closing lines.[8]

In rejecting these two contentions, the Court directly admitted the inclusion in the internal waters of areas of the sea which, under 'earlier' delimitation criteria, would have formed part of the territorial sea, thus subjecting them automatically to the right of innocent passage. On the maximum permissible length of closing lines for bays, the Court noted that:

> Although the ten-mile rule has been adopted by certain States both in their national law and in their treaties and conventions, and although certain arbitral decisions have applied it as between these States, other States have adopted a different limit. Consequently, the ten-mile rule has not acquired the authority of a general rule of international law.[9]

On the question of whether the straight baselines method of delimitation applied by Norway on her coast was in compliance with the rules of international law, the Court expressed the view that the Norwegian method was not contrary to those rules but was the 'application of general international law to a specific case'. The judgment on this point read:

> It has been contended, on behalf of the United Kingdom, that Norway may draw straight lines only across bays. The Court is unable to share this view. If the belt of territorial waters must follow the outer line of the 'skjaergaard', and if the method of straight baselines must be admitted in certain cases, there is no valid reason to draw them only across bays, as in Eastern Finnmark, and not also to draw them between islands, islets and rocks, across the sea areas separating them, even when such areas do not fall within the conception of a bay. It is sufficient that they should be situated between the island formations of the 'skjaergaard', *inter fauces terrarum*.
> Consequently, the court is unable to share the view of the United Kingdom Government, that 'Norway, in the matter of baselines, now claims recognition of an exceptional system'. As will be shown later, all that the Court can see therein is the application of general international law to a specific case.[10]

Another issue, which was treated at length by the Court and which is pertinent to our topic, concerned internal waters claimed for 'historical reasons' over fiords and sounds lying between the island fringes and the mainland of Norway. In tackling this issue, the Court first of all defined 'historic waters' in these terms: 'By "historic waters" are usually meant waters which are treated as internal waters but which would not have that character were it not for the existence of an historic title.'[11]

It then stressed the peculiar character of the Norwegian coast within a historical and economic context: 'In these barren regions the inhabitants of the coastal zone derived their livelihood essentially from fishing.'[12] As regards Norwegian historic rights, the Court went on to state that:

> The Court notes that, in respect of a situation which could only be strengthened with the passage of time, the United Kingdom Government refrained from formulating reservations. The notoriety of the facts, the general toleration of the international community, Great Britain's position in the North Sea, her own interest in the question, and her prolonged abstention would in any case warrant Norway's enforcement of her system against the United Kingdom.[13]

In conclusion, the Court summarized its findings by saying that:

> the method of straight lines, established in the Norwegian system, was imposed by the peculiar geography of the Norwegian coast; . . . even before the dispute arose, this method had been consolidated by a constant and sufficiently long practice, in the face of which the attitude of Governments bears witness to the fact that they did not consider it to be contrary to international law.[14]

Although admitting the drawing of straight baselines instead of following the low-water mark along the coast to set the limit between internal waters and territorial seas, the Court subjected its use to certain considerations. There is, first, the principle that the 'drawings of baselines must not depart to any appreciable extent from the general direction of the coast.'[15] Secondly, there must be a connection between the sea areas involved and the land formations separating or surrounding them. In other words, according to the Court, 'the real question raised in the choice of baselines is . . . whether certain sea areas lying within these lines are sufficiently closely linked to the land domain to be subject to the regime of internal waters.'[16] Third, there is the requirement for the straight baselines to be conceived with moderation and fairness, that is, to be drawn in a 'reasonable manner'.[17]

The juridical regime of the enclosed waters

Central to any question regarding the juridical regime of the waters enclosed by appropriate straight baselines was the right of 'international' passage. This was dependent on the *degree* of connection existing between the sea areas enclosed and the land formations surrounding them. For Norway, this degree could be properly assessed geographically, by considering whether or not the waters intervening between the islands and the mainland operated as a unifying or a separating element.[18] For the United Kingdom, the test was whether or not the position and configuration of the islands tended to close waters to international navigation.[19] To put its case forcefully, the United Kingdom mentioned the waters of the navigational route known as the Indreleia by way of example.

Connecting the North Sea and the Arctic Sea (both of which are open seas), the Indreleia, although forming part of the waters of the 'skjaergaard', should constitute a legal strait where the regime of innocent passage should prevail, as in the territorial sea. This British argument clearly envisioned the possibility of a strip of territorial waters lying within a belt of internal waters.[20] For the Court, however,

> [t]he Indreleia is not a strait at all, but rather a navigational route prepared as such by means of artificial aids to navigation provided by Norway. In these circumstances the Court is unable to accept the view that the Indreleia, for the purposes of the present case, has a status different from that of the other waters included in the 'skjaergaard.[21]

Can the inference therefore be made that the Court was overruling its earlier decision in the *Corfu Channel* case, in which a right of innocent passage was recognized for legal straits?[22] Unless, of course, the Court took the Indreleia not to be a real legal strait in that context. The view expressed by one writer, which we share entirely, is that

> the Court's statement *for the purposes of the present case*. . . it was unable to treat the Indreleia channels as having a different status from the rest of the waters within the 'skjaergaard'. The Court may have intended, by the italicized words, to reserve the question of the right of passage. In the past the principal distinction between inland and territorial waters lay in the existence of a right of passage through the latter but not through the former. . . It is hoped that the Corfu Channel doctrine prevails, even if this means recognising a right of innocent passage through inland waters in certain circumstances.[23]

Fitzmaurice suggested in an article[24] that, although by the application of the doctrines of the *Fisheries* case 'some legal straits' or 'channels' can be converted from territorial into internal waters, the consequences of this conversion can be avoided. By recognizing that the regime of innocent passage ought to apply to all waters normally used by international shipping since these waters are not actually inserted into the true mainland coast, these waters could be given the status of internal or national waters.

In sum, the Court did not pronounce, and did not have to, on navigational rights in internal waters, in view of Norway's assurances that although it regarded such water areas as internal, 'there would be no interference with international navigation'. Probably if the Court had been pressed to take a stand on the issue, it would have reiterated Norway's assurances in the form of an obligation imposed on Norway.

(b) Legal status of internal waters in the sessions of the Institute of International Law (1954)

The judgment in the 1951 *Fisheries* case provided some scholars with the opportunity of examining the juridical nature of 'internal waters'. The Institute of International Law discussed the notion of internal waters in its 1954 session at Aix-en-Provence.

In a report on the distinction between territorial waters and internal waters, F. Castberg, a member of the Institute, with the decision of the *Fisheries* case in mind, pertinently observed that:

> Un Etat peut être autorisé, en se fondant sur des raisons historiques,

> économiques ou sociales, à fixer de longues lignes de base entre les îles et les rochers (. . .) surtout lorsqu'il est question de la limite territoriale du droit acquis exclusif de la population aux pêches côtières (. . .) Il peut estimer équitable ou utile d'étendre le droit de passage des navires d'autres Etats, en temps de paix aussi, à une partie des eaux qui se trouve en deçà des lignes de base.[25]

On the last point, quoting a passage written by Raestad in 1931,[26] Castberg said that:

> En tout cas, il est naturel que les Etats étrangers intéressés s'opposent à ce que toutes les portions d'eaux qui se trouvent à l'intérieur des lignes de base soient déclarées être des eaux intérieures dans toute l'acception de ce terme.

In the conclusion of his lengthy report, Castberg, referring to the possibility of different types and limits of the so-called internal waters, observed that:[27]

> Les limites des eaux intérieures de l'Etat riverain peuvent être tracées de manière différente dans des buts différents, par des dispositions législatives édictées par cet Etat, à condition toutefois qu'il ne soit pas porté atteinte par cette mesure aux droits des autres Etats, surtout à leur droit de libre passage inoffensif dans la mer territoriale.

In the debates following the presentation of this report, the above conclusion was severely criticized by some members of the Institute, with Gidel making the most vocal representations. Sir Gerald Fitzmaurice would have preferred to express the idea differently:

> I would prefer to say that all waters inside the baseline from which territorial waters are measured, are internal waters; but that a further distinction is to be drawn between those internal waters which are genuinely inland waters (e.g. rivers, creeks, island, lakes, canals etc.) and those which are not (e.g. large bays and waters between the mainland and islands off the coast). Generally speaking, there is no right of passage through the former waters, but there is, or should be, through the latter . . . Under no circumstances should the extension of internal waters made possible by the new baseline method operate so as to impede the right of innocent passage through what would be territorial sea if the older coast-line (or tide-mark) rule were still applied.[28]

For Gidel, the partitioning of internal waters for different purposes, at the discretion of the coastal State, as suggested by Castberg,

> serait, je le crains, infiniment dangereux et ne ferait que jeter le trouble là où nous avons la bonne fortune de voir régner l'accord dans la pratique comme parmi les auteurs. Ce morcellement impliquerait que chaque Etat riverain pourrait composer à sa guise pour ses eaux intérieures un statut juridique particulier; il retiendrait dans ce statut individuel des eaux intérieures toutes les compétences qu'il estimerait lui être avantageuses et éliminerait toutes celles auxquelles correspondrait une charge. Or c'est le propre d'un statut dégagé par le droit que de constituer un tout dans lequel s'équilibrent pour celui qui y est astreint les avantages et les inconvénients. Cette notion a une particulière importance dans le droit international où les membres de la

communauté internationale doivent de trouver, en droit, dans des conditions comparables entre elles quant à leurs rapports mutuels.

L'hypothèse où un Etat ne va pas dans telle ou telle partie de ses eaux intérieures jusqu'au bout des compétences que le droit international commun lui donne sur ces eaux n'entraîne ni modification substantielle au statut juridique des eaux intérieures de cet Etat ni changement de délimitation de ces eaux par rapport aux eaux territoriales.[29]

Ending his criticisms of Castberg's conclusions and apparently restating international law regarding 'international' waters Gidel concluded:[30]

Il n'est pas au pouvoir d'un Etat riverain de se créer pour ses eaux intérieures un statut juridique particulier dérogatoire à la catégorie juridique du droit international 'eaux intérieures'. Mais l'Etat riverain demeure libre de renoncer soit conventionnellement soit législativement à l'exercice de telle ou telle des compétences que le droit international commun reconnaît à l'Etat riverain comme tel dans ses eaux intérieures.

(c) Legal status of internal waters under the Draft Articles of the International Law Commission

Following the judgment of the International Court of Justice in the *Fisheries* case (1951), the International Law Commission, at its eighth resumed session in 1956, was faced with the problem of passage in internal waters. The question was prompted by the replies of governments to the Draft Articles prepared by the Commission.[31] Article 5 of the Draft recognized the use of straight baselines as a delimitation criterion in appropriate circumstances but said nothing on the navigational status of the waters enclosed.

The most articulate comment on the issue of navigation through internal waters was made by the British Government. The comments by that Government, the relevant parts of which are reproduced in full, stated *inter alia* that:

Her Majesty's Government regard it as imperative that, in any new code which would render legitimate the use of baselines in proper circumstances, it should be clearly stated that the right of innocent passage should not be prejudiced thereby, even though this may involve that, in certain cases, this right shall become exercisable through internal as well as through territorial waters. Her Majesty's Government consider that the Commission would be performing a most useful function if it were to give mature consideration to the problem how the use of baselines is to be reconciled with existing rights of passage. For their part, Her Majesty's Government can only say at this stage that, in their view, in case of conflict, the right of passage, as a prior right and the right of the international community, must prevail over any alleged claim of individual coastal States to extend the areas subject to their exclusive jurisdiction.[32]

A new Draft Article 5 of the International Law Commission put forward for consideration at the 1958 Law of the Sea Conference contained a paragraph 3 incorporating the above views. It read:

> Where the establishment of a straight baseline has the effect of enclosing as internal waters areas which previously had been considered as part of the territorial sea or of the high seas, a right of innocent passage, . . . through those waters will be recognized by the coastal State in all those cases where the waters have normally been used for international traffic.

By so wording the last lines of the provision (where those waters 'have normally been used for international traffic'), the Commission acknowledged that the right of innocent passage will not be allowed in certain categories of internal waters, i.e. those which have 'not normally been used for international traffic'.

In other words, the status normally enjoyed by internal waters, i.e. exclusive and inclusive sovereign coastal State territorial prerogatives could only be conditional to the right of passage where there was proof of a 'historic' right of 'international' passage in that portion of the 'internal' waters. At least the commentary by the International Law Commission on Article 5(3) bears out this interpretation. The commentary states:

> The question arose whether in waters which become internal waters when the straight baseline system is applied the right of passage should not be granted in the same way as in the territorial sea. Stated in such general terms, this argument was not approved by the majority of the Commission. The Commission was, however, prepared to recognize that if a State wished to make a fresh delimitation of its territorial sea according to the straight baseline principle, thus including in its internal waters part of the high seas or of the territorial sea that had previously been waters through which international traffic passed, other nations could not be deprived of the right of passage in those waters. Paragraph 3 of the article is designed to safeguard that right.[33]

Nevertheless, the idea that there existed a historic right of innocent passage in internal waters created by straight baselines if such waters had been subject to such a right appears to be tautological. It is easily conceivable that in areas or portions of the sea subject to the straight-baseline method of delimitation, but which have not yet been so delimited and are still considered to form part of the territorial sea or the high seas, the right of innocent passage and/or the high seas freedom of navigation apply. In these circumstances, it is absurd to use the phrase 'where the waters have normally been used for international traffic' because, as a portion of territorial sea or high seas, even if not used for international traffic, these waters are subject to innocent passage or freedom of navigation. Consequently, there is an overwhelming presumption that the area is used for international traffic regardless of whether it is effectively so used.

Except what is contemplated is that in certain territorial seas the intensity of international navigation strengthens or weakens the notion that '. . . it is used or not used for international traffic . . .' with the consequence of altering the navigational rights therein.

In the 1953 Geneva Conference on the Law of the Sea, where the Draft Articles of the International Law Commission were further examined for inclusion in an international convention, the phrasing of paragraph 3 above was altered, eliminating any chance whatsoever of any portion of the sea, when mapped by the straight baseline method of delimitation, being named internal waters and '. . . use for international navigation . . .', so as to avoid the notion of a historical right of innocent passage.

Finally, Article 5(2) of the 1958 Geneva Convention on the Territorial Sea and the Contiguous Zone stated:

> Where the establishment of straight baselines . . . has the effect of enclosing as internal waters areas which previously had been considered as part of the territorial sea or of the high seas, a right of innocent passage . . . shall exist in those waters.

Article 8(2) of the 1982 Convention is a verbatim reproduction of this provision. Thus, it is conceivable, under present international Law of the Sea, that in some cases internal waters (mainly waters lying on the landward side of the inner limit or baseline of the territorial sea) can be divided into two navigational portions. The first portion of the internal waters consists of the waters lying between the low-water line along the coast and the new straight baselines joining appropriate points on the coast. In this area of internal waters, there exists a right of innocent passage. In the other portion of internal waters, consisting of parts of the sea lying between the low-water mark and the land territory *stricto sensu*, there is no such right.[34] Both portions of the internal waters stand on precisely the same footing in all other respects. As internal waters, both are national waters and thus form part of the national territory.

In sum, a coastal State with an indented coast, islands, and bays could exercise the discretion to draw the limits of its internal waters differently for different purposes. But where it chooses the method of straight baselines, the internal waters so created, to the limit of the low-water mark, do not prejudice the right of innocent passage of other States.

4. Straits

Generally, a strait is a narrow passage of the sea separating or connecting two parts of the high seas or of exclusive economic zone.[35] Straits are found either between an island and the mainland or at the narrow 'meeting points' of two continents.

As was shown by the arguments in the *Fisheries* case, the Indreleia passage, as a water route between the coastal islands and the Norwegian mainland connecting the North Sea and the Arctic Sea, was, according to the United Kingdom's main premise, a legal strait. For the International Court of Justice, on the other hand, the use of the straight-baselines method of delimitation resulted in making the waters of the Indreleia internal waters, although other States retained the right of innocent passage, those waters having always been used for that purpose. Where the use of straight baselines is excluded between an island and the mainland[36] (which would make the channel waters internal), that channel is a strait.[37] Although it is called a strait as far as international navigation is concerned, the very liberal regime of transit passage (overflights and submerged navigation) is not applicable in those waters. This is particularly so if there exists, seaward of the island (as is generally the case), a route through the high seas or through an exclusive economic zone of similar convenience with respect to navigational and hydrographical characteristics.[38]

There are other types of straits which, instead of connecting one part of the high seas or one exclusive economic zone and another part of the high seas or another exclusive economic zone, link the high seas or an exclusive economic zone to the territorial waters of a foreign State.[39] In these straits, the regime of transit passage is inapplicable as well.

In these two types of straits, the 'island-mainland straits', and 'the high seas/economic zone—territorial sea straits', there exists, according to Article 45 of the 1982 Convention, 'a non-suspendable right of innocent passage, provided these are *straits used for international navigation*'. Although the category of straits *not* used for international navigation may be limited or insignificant, the overall qualification 'straits used for international navigation' reflects customary international law as evidenced by the *Corfu Channel* judgment and adopted wholesale by Article 16(4) of the 1958 Convention. It is our intention to analyse the uncertainty of the meaning of 'straits used for international navigation' by a thorough survey of the *Corfu Channel* case, where the phrase was used for the first time in an international adjudication, before being included in the Law of the Sea Conventions of 1958 and 1982. It should be remembered that this judgment also confirmed the right of innocent passage in international straits.[40]

(a) The *Corfu Channel* case (United Kingdom v. Albania) (1949) and the exercise of 'innocent passage' in straits

Brief summary of facts with emphasis on navigation

On 15 May 1946, two British cruisers proceeding south through the North Corfu Channel were fired on by Albanian shore batteries. In the inconclusive exchange of notes which followed, the whole question of the right of passage in the Corfu Channel was argued by both parties at length. Considering the Corfu Channel as falling within its territorial waters, Albania emphasized the fact that 'the passage of foreign . . . vessels in Albanian territorial waters was subject to previous notification to, and authorisation by, the Albanian Government'.[41] This view was expressed in a communication of the Albanian Chief of Staff dated 17 May 1946. The United Kingdom Government objected to this and, in a final note dated 2 August 1946, restated its position with regard to the right of innocent passage. The United Kingdom considered innocent passage through straits forming routes for international maritime traffic between two parts of the high seas to be a right recognized by international law. The note ended with the warning that if Albanian coastal batteries in the future opened fire on any British warship passing through the Corfu Channel, the fire would be returned.[42]

Barely six months after the first incident, on 22 October 1946, two British warships, proceeding northward through the North Corfu Channel, struck mines which caused damage to these vessels and some loss of life. The ships were not proceeding in battle formation but in single line with their guns apparently trained fore and aft and not loaded. After some preliminary debate on the whole affair at the United Nations Security Council, as required by Articles 35 and 36 of the Charter, the dispute was brought before the International Court of Justice.[43]

Contentions of the parties

As expected the position of the Albanian Government regarding the Corfu Channel incident of 22 October 1946 was based on two contentions: firstly, that the British vessels had no right to pass through the Channel, which constituted Albanian waters, and secondly that the passage was not innocent. These two contentions embody two different features. The second contention opens up the whole question of the rules of innocent passage and of the character of the passage of 22 October, that is essentially an issue of fact and law. The first contention addresses issues of direct relevance to our consideration, namely, the right of passage of foreign vessels through territorial waters and the regime of passage in international straits in this respect. By a vote of 14 to 2, the Court rejected the two Albanian contentions.

Without going into the judgment of the Court, it is interesting to note the following statements made in the pleadings to counter Albania's contentions.

The United Kingdom agent first stated:

> This is a court of law, and you will draw the proper inferences from the evidence which is put before you. But you are also a tribunal of fact, and, if I may say so with great respect, you are not obliged to leave your common sense behind with your hats and coats in the robing room.

Then, on a point of law, the agent asserted:

> Now, Mr. President, I am going to deal with passage through straits. . . . Our main submission [is] that in an international strait [vessels] have a right of innocent passage unqualified by any right whatever in the coastal State to interrupt the passage and that the Corfu Channel is such a strait.[44]

And, on a point of fact, he emphasized that:

> Although the Corfu Channel may be used principally (but not exclusively) by coastal traffic, this does not deprive it of its status as an international highway and it does not appear very profitable to discuss the question whether such a highway is of major or minor importance . . . Albania is not . . . the only State with an interest in the waters of the Channel or the traffic passing through it. One half of the Channel at its narrowest portion is Greek territorial waters and the Channel is principally used as an approach to Corfu and other Greek ports. Albania is, in fact, trying to claim control of the traffic in an international strait, which is of more importance to Greece than to Albania.[45]

On the question of whether or not there exists an alternative route without passing through the Channel, the agent of the United Kingdom went on: 'To have taken a course west of Corfu, instead of through the Strait, would have involved for these ships an additional distance of 100 miles.'[46]

Countering the United Kingdom agent on these points, the Albanian agent said:

> Le canal de Corfou est un détroit latéral naturel reliant deux libres espaces maritimes de la Mer Ionienne . . . [Il] n'est qu'une voie latérale d'importance fort secondaire . . . éloignée des grands courants de communication méditerranéens. La caractère latéral et secondaire de cette voie ressort en outre par le fait que les mêmes espaces maritimes qui communiquent par le canal nord à l'est de l'île de Corfou, peuvent non seulement être reliés aussi par les eaux à l'ouest de l'île, mais leur communication par cette dernière route est en effet plus courte et se fait dans des mers libres et larges . . . à travers le canal de Corfou . . . [ce] principalement des bateaux de cabotage (voiliers et voiliers à moteur) et de petite navigation . . . Il résulte clairement de ces données que le canal de Corfou n'est point une artère maritime internationale de première importance, 'an international highway', comme l'affirme le Gouvernement britannique.[47]

From the above statements made by the agents of the United Kingdom and Albania, the question of an autonomous regime of international straits could be perceived. The United Kingdom, basing itself on a purely geographical criterion, argued that the strait connects two parts of the high seas and that such straits should be open for free passage of all foreign vessels. The Albanian agent, on the other hand, relied on the argument that there was no common regime of international straits, but he insisted even more on the fact that the Corfu Channel was not a useful strait for the international community.

Observations of the Court on these issues

Both views were weighed by the Court in three sequences. First, the Court affirmed the concept of an international strait with freedom of navigation as rule. Second, it examined whether or not the Corfu Channel qualified as an international strait. Third, on the basis of those premises, it ruled in favour of the United Kingdom. The relevant portion of the judgment read:

> It is, in the opinion of the Court, generally recognized and in accordance with international custom that States in time of peace have a right to send their [vessels] through straits used for international navigation between two parts of the high seas without the previous authorization of a coastal State, provided that passage is innocent. Unless otherwise prescribed in an international convention, there is no right for a coastal State to prohibit such passage through straits in time of peace.[48]

By this statement, the International Court of Justice acknowledged the right of innocent passage in international straits, regardless of whether the strait lies in territorial waters or is a corridor to the high seas; provided, once again, that the strait could 'historically' be established to have been 'used for international navigation before'. However, as we saw in Chapter 2, under present Law of the Sea provisions, the more liberal 'right of transit' in international straits would now be applicable to the Corfu Channel if the Court's findings on the international importance of that strait were confirmed. Transit passage, not innocent passage, would be justified for two reasons. First, the Corfu Channel is not formed by an island and a mainland belonging to the same State; consequently, the regime of the 'right of non-suspendable innocent passage' established in Article 38 of the 1982 Convention is not applicable. Second, the channel does not lead to the territorial sea of a foreign State, which would have justified the non-suspendable right of innocent passage provided for in Article 45(1) (b) of the 1982 Convention.

Be that as it may, for some members of the Court there was no general right of innocent passage or transit passage in international law. The dissenting opinion of one of the judges involved in the Corfu Channel case illustrates this philosophy. Judge Krylov said:

> There is no common regulation of the legal regime of straits. Every strait is regulated individually . . . by convention. The regime of the Corfu strait has not been juridically regulated. If the regime of the strait is not defined by a multilateral convention, it appertains to the coastal State or States to regulate it . . . The political tension between Albania and Greece made it impossible to regulate the regime of the North Corfu strait by an agreement between them. Therefore, Albania had the right to regulate the passage of [vessels] through her own territorial waters provided that she conformed to the rules of international law.[49]

Nevertheless, the law laid down by the Court, establishing a general regime of international straits, is sound. To sum up the judgment, not every strait but only those 'used for international navigation' must yield innocent passage to vessels in time of peace. The judgment is unambiguous in its outright denial of the right of the coastal State to prohibit such passage in time of peace. There is no disagreement among writers in so far as these points are concerned.[50] What is important in our context is the test qualifying a strait to be such an international highway.

(b) Characteristics of straits governed by the regime of innocent passage

We are more concerned here with straits falling within the category defined in Article 45 of the 1982 Convention, i.e. straits allowing for the exercise of a non-suspendable right of innocent passage. In this regard, it should be noted that all straits not used for international navigation, regardless of their geographical situation, lying within territorial seas, are subject to the provisions on suspendable right of innocent passage of Part II of the 1982 Convention.[51] Thus, whereas the objective geographical criterion—a body of water connecting high seas or exclusive economic zones, and/or the latter with the territorial sea of a foreign State—cannot be controversial, the subjective test of an international strait, in the sense of its being used for international navigation, is still uncertain.

Part III of the 1982 Convention, which covers Article 45 dealing with innocent passage regime in straits, is conspicuously entitled 'Straits Used for International Navigation'. However, nowhere is a definition given of the meaning of 'straits used for international navigation'. Nevertheless, in the *Corfu Channel* case and in the debates of the International Law Commission, indications may be found regarding the content of a definition. But prior to the notion being considered in these fora, a well-known writer on international straits had already expatiated on the subject.

Erik Brüel and the definition of straits used for international navigation

Writing in 1947, Erik Brüel, in his treatise on *International Straits*,[52] considered that it was safer to view all waters covered by the geographical conception of straits as being included in the legal regime of straits. He nevertheless clarified his views when he added:

> It being, however, universally recognised that not all waters covered by the geographical conception of straits shall enjoy this peculiar legal position, the question is next, what test should be applied to reach a conclusion in this respect.

In responding to this question, he squarely[53] addressed the question of what could be called a 'strait used for international navigation' by saying:

> As to this, it would seem that the degree of importance of the particular strait to the international sea commerce, taken in its broadest sense, covering the passage of both mercantile ships and warships, must be the decisive factor. How extensive and how deeply rooted this interest should be, cannot be determined by any hard and fast rule, but is a question of fact, depending upon such facts as f.e. the number of ships passing through the strait, their total tonnage, the aggregate value of their cargoes, the average size of the ships, and especially, whether they are distributed among a greater or smaller number of nations—all of which seem to give good guidance, no single factor, however, being decisive: altogether it does not seem possible to reach any comprehensive formula beyond saying that only those straits that are of some, not quite inconsiderable importance to the international sea-commerce, enjoy the peculiar legal position accorded to straits. This is the one quality of the strait, which this treatise attempts to characterize by the word 'international', whereby is simply meant that the interest attached to the use of these straits is worldwide, while no opinion is expressed either as to the territorial status or at all as to the legal status of these straits.[54]

In a search for a definitive criterion, Brüel further attempted a comparative linguistic analysis:

> emphasis has been laid soon on one or another of the factors that may come under consideration: expressions like 'routes maritimes indispensables' and 'routes maritimes nécessaires à la navigation' lay stress on the absolute indispensability of the passage, while the term 'grandes routes maritimes' permits of an interpretation that has regard also to the actual importance of the straits, besides emphasizing that this is in relation to the 'big' i.e. the international shipping. The latter element is likewise prevalent in the English terms 'international highways' or 'highways for international traffic', while an expression as 'passage habituel' stresses the importance of what is accustomed. Fitting to a degree is likewise the expression 'natural traffic routes' used in various Danish regulations, as f.e. the Danish Rules of Neutrality of 1938.[55]

Brüel finally concludes his attempt at a definition of 'straits used for international navigation' by a non-exhaustive enumeration of such straits existing in the world at his time.[56] Curiously, he made no mention whatsoever of the Corfu Channel.

The Corfu Channel case and the notion of straits used for international navigation

While considering the position of the Corfu Channel and the idea of a strait used for international navigation, the International Court of Justice examined the Albanian contention

> that [the channel did not belong to the class of international highways], being of secondary importance and not even a necessary route between two parts of the high seas, and that it is used almost exclusively for the local traffic to and from the ports of Corfu and Saranda.[57]

For the Court, on the other hand, the real test of a strait used for international navigation, necessarily implying that it was an international highway, had more to it than the apparently subjective criterion of 'importance' formulated by the Albanian agent.

On this point the Court made it quite clear that:

> It may be asked whether the test is to be found in the volume of traffic passing through the strait or in its greater or lesser importance for international navigation. But in the opinion of the Court, the decisive criterion is rather its geographical situation as connecting two parts of the high seas and the fact of its being used for international navigation. Nor can it be decisive that this strait is not a necessary route between the Aegean and the Adriatic seas. It has nevertheless been a useful route for international maritime traffic.[58]

The Court then quoted the figures given by the United Kingdom agent on the traffic through the Channel relating to the period from 1 April 1936 to 31 December 1937 as regards the number of ships, their nationality, the regularity of the traffic, etc.[59] The Court went on to affirm that:

> There were also regular sailings through the Strait by Greek vessels three times weekly, by a British ship fortnightly, and by two Yugoslavian vessels weekly and by two others fortnightly. The Court is further informed that the British Navy has regularly used this Channel for eighty years or more, and that it has also been used by the navies of other States. One fact of particular importance is that the North Corfu Channel constitutes a frontier between Albania and Greece, that a part of it is wholly within the territorial waters of these States, and that the Strait is of special importance to Greece by reason of the traffic to and from the port of Corfu.[60]

Then the Court concluded its findings by saying:

> Having regard to these various considerations, the Court has arrived at the conclusion that the North Corfu Channel should be considered as belonging to the class of international highways through which passage cannot be prohibited by a coastal State in time of peace.[61]

Some criticism has been levelled against the conclusion of the Court on this particular point.[62]

Our interest remains how to determine the meaning of the phrase 'straits used for international navigation'. Brüel considered that this could be done on the basis of the 'importance of the particular strait to international sea commerce', an 'interest' which is non-quantifiable and thus cannot be derived from any hard and fast rule but only from the 'factual situation' of each strait. The majority of the International Court of Justice, on the other hand, thought that the 'importance of a particular strait' and the 'facts of each' were contributory rather than determining factors because of their essentially subjective qualities. The Court then tried to outline, tautologically to some extent, objective criteria to determine the nature of 'straits used for international navigation'. From the paragraph quoted in the judgment these are objective geographical factors—a strait constituting a connection between two parts of the high sea and serving as an international frontier. As regards the tautological 'objective' pre-condition that the strait serve as a useful route for international maritime traffic, it was 'immaterial' that the strait was not a necessary but only an alternative route between the two parts of the high seas concerned.[63]

In an article written in 1953, Brüel systematically and, in our opinion, convincingly refuted the criteria applied by the International Court for defining 'straits used for international navigation', i.e. international straits to which, under present Law of the Sea Conventions, the non-suspendable regime of innocent passage applies.

As to the geographical criterion—the fact of connecting two parts of the high seas—Brüel stated:

> If all straits connecting two parts of the high seas were to be considered international straits, a very great number of straits without any importance whatsoever for international navigation would fall within this category of straits . . . the legal reason for giving straits a legal position of their own is not their geographical position but their function as passages for international traffic . . .[64]

On the fact that it should constitute an 'international frontier', he went on to say:

> that a strait constitutes a frontier between two countries, in this case Albania and Greece, is completely irrelevant as to the qualification of the strait as international. The expression 'international' has no reference whatsoever as to the territorial status of the strait. It does not mean that the shares of the strait are divided between other States or that it constitutes a frontier between them, but is only a short expression of the fact that the interest attached to the use of the strait is worldwide.[65]

Finally, on the contention that the strait must be a 'useful' route for international maritime traffic, Brüel asserted that:

> is not sufficient to qualify it as international. If such were the case, States interested in sending warships through a strait needed only to claim that it was

useful to them. The individual State could in this way be able, only by saying that a strait was 'useful' to it, to make a strait international and restrict the rights of the coastal State.[66]

Brüel concludes his criticism of the Court's criteria by quoting the dissenting Judge Azevedo and affirming that:

> [there exist] two groups of rights, the conflict of which is to be solved by the regulation of the legal position of international straits, namely the interests of international navigation, and the interests of the coastal State. Both groups of rights are vital, and the conflict, therefore, must be solved very cautiously.[67]

All said and done, it would be difficult and illusory to assert that a 'strait used for international navigation' could not connect two seas, or not be an international frontier, or not be useful for international navigation. However, it would be an over-simplification to stress only one of those criteria independently or to the detriment of the others. But one thing is certain, 'the degree of importance of the particular strait to the international sea-commerce, taken in its broadest sense, covering the passage of both mercantile ships and warships, [is] . . . the decisive factor'. Consequently, it is essential for an appropriate appreciation of the 'use for international navigation' of any strait that an examination be made of the circumstances in order to appreciate the *intrinsic importance* of each individual route.[68]

Judge Azevedo, emphasizing this view in his dissenting opinion in the *Corfu Channel* case, further brought out the relativity of 'use for international navigation'. He asserted that:

> every strait offers a passage that shipping may make use of; but conversely, it might be argued that no strait [is] indispensable for shipping; for it is always possible to find some other route connecting two seas, as happened, for example, before the Suez and Panama Canals were opened.

With a view to the security and other interests of the coastal States around such straits, Judge Azevedo adds that it would be wrong to

> approve unreservedly a restriction of the rights of the coastal State in order to satisfy . . . third States . . . No other view could be admitted unless the closing of the strait rendered navigation impossible or very difficult—conditions which have led to the regulation of the more important straits and have justified certain other exceptions. The notion of an international strait is always connected with a minimum of special utility, sufficient to justify the restriction of the rights of coastal State—which must be assumed to be complete and equal to those of other States.[69]

Reappraisal of the definition of 'straits used for international navigation' since the Corfu Channel case

Neither the 1958 Geneva Convention on the Territorial Sea and the Contiguous Zone, nor the 1982 Convention, nor the draft proposals made in various conferences have attempted to determine 'objective' criteria to characterize 'straits used for international navigation'. It should be recalled that in the *Corfu Channel* case, the Court presented statistics as to the amount of traffic in the Corfu Strait, cited the 'geographical situation [of the Strait] as connecting two parts of the high seas', mentioned the Strait's 'special importance to Greece . . .', and concluded that it 'has nevertheless been a useful route for international maritime traffic.'[70]

This 'somewhat artificial wording . . ., regarded as a sign of an uncertainty amongst the judges as to the international character of the strait',[71] has nevertheless been adopted and incorporated with few changes into later conventions. This was, in particular, the approach chosen by the International Law Commission.

During two meetings in 1955 and 1956, and with the idea that the *Corfu Channel* case considered 'straits used for international navigation' as dependent upon their 'importance' as a sea route, members of the Commission proposed alternative expressions such as 'straits indispensable to international navigation' and 'straits essential to international navigation'. However, the final draft of the Commission's provision, as presented to the (First) Conference of the Law of the Sea of 1958, contained only the expression 'straits normally used for international navigation'.[72] Whether such phrasing covered cases of commercial shipping only, and straits leading to the territorial sea of one State, was answered by one delegate with the words: '. . . the question sounded far more like a case for the International Court of Justice [once more] than a matter on which the Commission would enunciate a general rule.'[73]

During the (First) Conference of the Law of the Sea of 1958, the word 'normally' contained in the Commission's wording was deleted,[74] probably in order to avoid arguments as to the amount of traffic using the strait in each particular case. Although the new expression, 'straits which are used for international navigation', was more liberal than that used by the Court and the Commission, the basic question remained unanswered.

In Article 16(4), its only provision dealing with passage in straits, the 1958 Geneva Convention on the Territorial Sea and the Contiguous Zone prescribes:

> There shall be no suspension of the innocent passage of foreign ships through straits which are used for international navigation between one part of the high seas and another part of the high seas or the territorial sea of a foreign State.

What constitutes a 'strait used for international navigation' is and will remain a moot question, since the 1982 Convention on the Law of the Sea does not attempt either to define or to indicate factors which could edify potential users on whether they are entitled to a non-suspendable right of innocent passage because the strait prima facie can be considered as being 'used for international navigation'.

In sum, such a determination would consist in a classification by charts of existing 'straits used for international navigation'.[75] However, for those charts to be accurate and not to be biased in favour of any particular interest, an international panel[76] would have to set up such charts with the possibility of periodic adaptation. For a strait which could not have been considered a 'strait used for international navigation' at one time could eventually become one, whereas another which was so classified before could be demoted to the category of straits *not* used for international navigation. Be that as it may, the non-suspendable right of innocent passage would only be applicable in cases where such straits are 'used for international navigation', at least under present Law of the Sea conventions.[77]

5. Archipelagic waters

Like archipelagic sealanes passage, the right of innocent passage is exercisable in archipelagic waters,[78] although the different types of passage take place in principle in different areas of these waters. However, beyond archipelagic waters, in areas seaward of the archipelagic baselines which are considered territorial sea,[79] the right of innocent passage also applies. These are the results of the 1982 Convention which recognizes the sovereignty of an archipelagic State over archipelagic waters.[80]

An appraisal of the exercise of the right of innocent passage in archipelagic waters requires a brief historical analysis of the concept 'archipelagic waters'.

The earliest treaty law dealing with islands and island groups—i.e. the Geneva Convention on the Territorial Sea and the Contiguous Zone—concerns itself exclusively with single islands or groups of islands situated in the immediate vicinity of the coast. As far as islands are concerned, the Convention acknowledges that every island has its own territorial sea.[81] As regards groups of islands, in keeping with the findings of the judgment in the 1951 *Fisheries* case, a provision of the Convention prescribes:

> In localities where the coastline is deeply indented and cut into, or if there is a fringe of islands along the coast in its immediate vicinity, the method of straight baselines joining appropriate points may be employed in drawing the baseline from which the breadth of the territorial sea is measured.[82]

This provision refers to coastal archipelagos situated 'in the immediate vicinity of a main coast'. It therefore excludes mid-ocean archipelagos. In the *Fisheries* case just referred to, there was indeed a trend towards separating the problem of coastal archipelagos from that of other archipelagos. It should be recalled that the judgment referred to 'groups of islands or coastal archipelagos' in very broad terms, ruling out any limitation of the length of straight baselines to ten miles. However, a further geographical criterion for resorting to straight baselines, i.e. that the baseline 'must not depart to any appreciable extent from the general direction of the coast',[83] could not conceivably apply to mid-ocean archipelagos far off the 'main coast'.

Of course, one of the main considerations always invoked against application of the straight baseline method of delimitation prior to the adoption of Article 5(2) of the 1958 Convention[84] was the question of the legal status of the waters enclosed by such baselines.

The 1958 Convention and other proposals on the issue had always assumed that the areas of the sea which were enclosed by such straight baselines should have the status of internal waters. In an authoritative document submitted by the Secretariat of the United Nations, its author, Jens Evensen,[85] asserted that waters enclosed by baselines should be considered internal waters but open to innocent passage of foreign ships where they formed a strait.

However, in the case of mid-ocean archipelagos, where some of the waters between islands have the status of high seas, the conversion into internal waters makes a considerable difference. For example, where the geography of the islands permits the assimilation of passages as 'straits connecting two parts of the high seas' (old formulation), a non-suspendable innocent passage regime for foreign vessels could be allowed (cf. Article 16(4) of the Geneva Convention) in those passages, too.

As regards specifically mid-ocean archipelagos, the use of straight baselines would create large 'internal seas'. From these waters, once part of the high seas, a number of freedoms pertaining to the high seas (like freedom of overflight) would be eliminated. The maintenance of a mere right of innocent passage in these internal seas rather than of the freedom of navigation shows the importance of the security and other interests of the archipelagic States.

It was apparently in this light that Indonesia, considering itself an archipelagic State, promulgated in 1957 the 'archipelago principle' which read *inter alia*:

> all waters surrounding, between and connecting the islands constituting the Indonesian State, regardless of their extension or breadth, are integral parts of the internal or national waters which are under the exclusive sovereignty of the Indonesian State. Innocent passage of foreign ships in these internal waters is granted as long as it is not prejudicial to or violates the sovereignty and security of Indonesia . . .[86]

As expected, some major maritime nations, such as the United States, Great Britain, Australia and Japan, lodged protests[87] against the 'Indonesian archipelagic principle', which was deemed to violate the established principle of the freedom of the high seas and to hamper passage through the important searoutes connecting South East Asia with Australia. However, the Indonesian Government rejected these protests and, in an Explanatory Memorandum on the disadvantages of the pre-1957 situation, explained that:

> Pockets of high seas in the islands of or in between the land-territories [islands] of Indonesia were putting functionaries in a difficult situation as they had to observe all the time whether they were finding themselves in national waters or on the high seas, because their rights of taking any step depend on their position. In case of war between two parties, with their battle-fields moving to and fro on the high seas between Indonesian islands, our unity would be threatened.[88]

Nevertheless, the Indonesian claims did not gain general recognition. More so since the 1958 Geneva Convention on the Territorial Sea and the Contiguous Zone completely ignored the issue of ocean archipelagos and merely contained provisions on individual islands. However, in the Third United Nations Conference on the Law of the Sea positions were to alter dramatically.[89]

At the start of that Conference, in a document presented by Fiji, Indonesia, Mauritius and the Philippines and entitled 'The Archipelagic Principles',[90] these States spelled out three principles to be incorporated into any future Convention on the Law of the Sea. The first principle advocated the drawing of straight baselines connecting the outermost points of the outermost islands and drying reefs in order to measure the breadth of the territorial sea. The second principle subjected the waters within the baselines to the sovereignty of the archipelagic State. The third principle, which is of direct importance here, was formulated as follows:

> Innocent passage of foreign vessels through the waters of the archipelagic State shall be allowed in accordance with its national legislation, having regard to the existing rules of international law. Such passage shall be through sealanes as may be designated for that purpose by the archipelagic State.

In order to concretize this principle, the four States submitted five Draft Articles relating to archipelagic States[91] to the Second Committee of the Third United Nations Conference on the Law of the Sea in 1974. In this Draft, it was asserted, for the first time, that the waters enclosed by the baselines would be called archipelagic waters (Article 3); that ships of all States would enjoy the right of innocent passage through the archipelagic waters (Article 4); and that the archipelagic State would be entitled to designate sealanes suitable for the safe and expeditious passage of foreign ships through its archipelagic waters, and to restrict the passage of such ships, or of any types or classes or such ships, to such sealanes (Article 5).

Fierce negotiations followed between, on the one hand, the group of major seafaring nations and, on the other, the major archipelagic States. The first group advocated freedom of passage through the archipelagic waters, or at least a right of passage corresponding as much as possible to the traditional right of innocent passage, while the other group was prepared to permit only a very restricted right of passage.[92]

Articulating the latter position was the Government of Indonesia, which, in a statement issued in March 1976, acknowledged the right of passage for normal commercial vessels in its archipelagic waters without any restriction, but stated that 'an archipelagic State may require prior notification for the passage through its archipelagic waters exercised outside the sealanes by foreign warships and by foreign vessels with special characteristics.[93]

Notwithstanding the above, the final compromise arrived at and contained in the 1982 Convention on the Law of the Sea caters to both the interests of the archipelagic States and of the major seafaring States, and particularly to their rights of navigation and overflight.

Part IV of the 1982 Convention spells out the main innovations in this regard. Included are the following: whereas waters enclosed by the use of straight baselines are called generally 'internal waters', Article 49 of the 1982 Convention maintains that the waters between the islands of an archipelagic State enclosed by (straight) 'archipelagic' baselines have a new status called 'archipelagic waters'. Had they been turned into internal waters, only a right of innocent passage in those areas could have been envisaged, and the right of overflight would have been excluded given the complete and exclusive nature of sovereignty over the airspace above internal waters. However, Article 52 of the 1982 Convention merely provides that the ships of all States enjoy a right of innocent passage through archipelagic waters; this does not convert the latter into internal waters, for in these archipelagic waters, according to Article 53(1) of the Convention, an archipelagic State is asked to designate sealanes and air routes suitable for the continuous and expeditious passage of foreign ships and aircraft. Furthermore, all ships and aircraft enjoy, within these lanes and routes, a new right of archipelagic sealanes passage (paragraph 2), which was described in Chapter 2.

In sum, the right of innocent passage under Part II, Section 3 of the 1982 Convention may be exercised in two areas of an archipelagic State's waters: in the territorial sea of the archipelagic State, as determined by Article 48 of the 1982 Convention, and in the archipelagic waters outside of archipelagic sealanes.

Whether the right of innocent passage in these waters fully benefits all ships, i.e. normal commercial vessels, foreign warships, submarines and vessels with other characteristics such as nuclear propelled ships, and ships carrying nuclear weapons and other dangerous substances, will be examined in the chapters that follow.

Notes

1. 1982 Convention, Article 3.
2. '[T]he rights possessed by a State over its territorial waters are rights of sovereignty . . . but no one has yet seriously suggested that the well-established distinction in international law between territorial and interior waters has disappeared . . . Territorial waters have long been regarded as not only different in status from interior waters but as possessing in some degree the quality of being part of the high seas, at any rate for purposes of navigation'. Per Eric Beckett, in ICJ, *The Corfu Channel* case, Pleadings, Oral Arguments, Documents, vol. III, 1950, p. 272.
3. If they pass through two or more States, they are called international rivers subject to certain conventional laws.
4. 1982 Convention, Article 8.
5. cf. ibid., Articles 2(1), 7(3), 8(1) and 17.
6. *Fisheries* case (United Kingdom v. Norway), ICJ *Reports* 1951, p. 131.
7. Ibid., p. 121.
8. Ibid., p. 123.
9. Ibid., p. 131.
10. Ibid., pp. 130–1.
11. For a thorough analysis of the concept of 'historic waters', see the 'Memorandum Concerning Historic Bays', UNCLOS, United Nations General Assembly, Doc. A/CONF.13/1 of 20 September 1957, pp. 3–110.
12. Ibid., p. 128.
13. Ibid., pp. 138–9.
14. Ibid., p. 139.
15. Ibid., p. 133.
16. Ibid.
17. Ibid., pp. 140–1, 142.
18. ICJ, *Fisheries* case (United Kingdom v. Norway), Pleadings, Oral Arguments and Documents, 1951, vol. 1, pp. 465–8, particularly paragraph 422 which contains the following passage: '[i]l n'y a pas que l'élément physique à prendre en considération. L'élément social n'a pas moins d'importance. Si les eaux qui se glissent entre l'archipel et le continent apparaissent socialement comme une barrière, comme un agent de désunion, l'interdependance ne sera pas la même que si elles jouent, au

contraire, le rôle d'un agent de fusion. La réalité sociale, la tradition, l'usage effectif sont, en pareille matière, des données essentielles.'

19. Ibid.
20. Rodgers, P.E.J., *Midocean Archipelagos in International Law*, New York, Vintage Press, p. 63.
21. *Fisheries* case, op. cit., note 6, p. 132.
22. The *Corfu Channel* case, ICJ *Reports* 1949, p. 3, at pp. 28–9.
23. Waldock, C.H.M., 'The Anglo-Norwegian Fisheries Case', *BYBIL*, vol. 28, 1951, pp. 114–71, at p. 158. Waldock also criticized the idea that 'artificial aids' provided by a coastal State would influence the status of the waterway by mentioning the fact that navigational aids are supplied by coastal States in many comparatively wide straits the waters of which are not internal waters. He thus drew the inference that what the Court meant was that the Indreleia was more akin to an inland river or canal.
24. Fitzmaurice, G., 'The Law and Procedure of the International Court of Justice, 1951-54: Points of Substantive Law—1', *BYBIL*, vol. 31, 1954, pp. 341–429, at pp. 419–20.
25. IDI *Annuaire* 1954, vol. 1, pp. 113–73, at pp. 126–7.
26. Raestad, A., 'Le problême des eaux territoriales à la Conférence pour la codification du droit international', *Revue de droit international*, vol. 7, 1931, pp. 107–46, at p. 134. On the same page Raestad nevertheless affirmed: '. . . Il est difficile d'appliquer ici les règles relatives au passage inoffensif . . . le cas échéant, les navires étrangers seraient forcément soumis à d'autres conditions et revêtiraient forcément un tout autre caractère que dans le cas de la mer territoriale ordinaire.'
27. Op. cit., note 25, p. 172.
28. Ibid., p. 206.
29. Ibid., pp. 219–21.
30. Ibid., p. 223.
31. For details, see the Report of the I.L.C. Covering the Work of its Seventh Session, General Assembly, Official Records, 10th session, Supplement No. 9, Doc. A/2934, New York, 1955, pp. 25–49.
32. Ibid., pp. 43–4.
33. ILC *Yearbook* 1956, vol. II, p. 268.
34. It is possible that by artificial means (dredging, for example) this part of internal waters becomes navigable at least in certain seasons.
35. Brüel, Erik, *International Straits*, London, Sweet and Maxwell, 1947, vol. I, pp. 15ff.
36. cf. Article 7 of the 1982 Convention.
37. Typical examples of such straits are the Pemba strait (between Pemba Island and the Tanzanian mainland) and the strait of Messina (between the Italian mainland and Sicily).
38. cf. Article 38(1) of the 1982 Convention.
39. Examples include the Strait of Georgia, the Gulf of Honduras, Head Harbour Passage and the Strait of Tiran.
40. cf. *Corfu Channel* case, op. cit., note 22, dissenting opinion of Judge Krylov, at p. 74: 'Contrary to the opinion of the majority of the judges, I consider that there is no such thing as a common regulation of the legal regime of straits. Every strait is regulated individually. That applies to the Bosphorus and the Dardanelles, to the Sound and the Belts, to the Straits of Magellan, etc. The legal regime of all those straits is defined by the respective international convention. The regime of the Corfu Strait has not been juridically regulated. Owing to its insignificance, the regime of that Strait has not been found worthy of special attention.'
41. Ibid., p. 27.

42. Ibid.
43. For details, see the Report of the Security Council to the General Assembly, United Nations, General Assembly, Doc. A/366 of 21 August 1947, pp. 89–108.
44. *Corfu Channel* case, Pleadings Oral Arguments and Documents, 1950, vol. III, p. 277.
45. Ibid., vol. II, pp. 242–3.
46. Ibid.
47. Ibid., pp. 34–5.
48. The *Corfu Channel* case, op. cit. note 22, p. 28.
49. Ibid., pp. 74–5.
50. Chung, I., *Legal Problems Involved in the Corfu Channel Incident*, Geneva, Droz, 1959, p. 205.
51. cf. The *Corfu Channel* case, op. cit., note 22, p. 28. 'The Court expressly declines to pronounce one way or the other on the question of passage through territorial waters not forming part of international straits, this not being necessary to their decision in the Corfu case.'
52. Erik Brüel, op. cit., note 35.
53. Ibid., p. 42.
54. Ibid., pp. 42–3.
55. Ibid., p. 43.
56. Ibid., p. 44. For a complete list of international straits, see Larson, D.L., 'Security Disarmament and the Law of the Sea', *Marine Policy*, January 1979, pp. 40–58, at pp. 56–8.
57. The *Corfu Channel* case, op. cit., note 22, p. 28.
58. Ibid.
59. Ibid., p. 29. A British note attested that during the period of one year and nine months, the total number of ships putting in at the Port of Corfu after passing through or just before passing through the Channel was 2,884, the flags of the ships being Greek, Italian, Roumanian, Yugoslavian, French, Albanian and British. Small vessels were included, with the proviso that one vessel could have made several journeys. It was also alleged that a large number of vessels went through the Strait without calling at the Port of Corfu.
60. Ibid., p. 29.
61. Ibid.
62. Brüel, E., 'Some Observations on Two Statements Concerning the Legal Position of International Straits (Made by the I.C.J. in its Judgment of April 9th 1949, in the *Corfu Channel* case), in Constantopoulos, D.S.and Wehberg, H. (eds), *Gegenwartsprobleme des internationalen Rechtes und der Rechtsphilosophie*; Hamburg, Girardet, 1953, pp. 259–78, particularly, pp. 272ff. See further Khoshkish, A., *The Right of Innocent Passage*, Geneva, Editions générales, 1954, pp. 126ff.; Chung, I.Y., op. cit., note 50, p. 208; dissenting opinion of Judge Azevedo in the *Corfu Channel* case, op. cit., note 22, at pp. 105ff. and dissenting opinion of Judge Krylov, ibid., pp. 74ff.
63. Fitzmaurice remarks that the pronouncements of the Court as to the meaning of 'straits used for international navigation' 'have practical importance, because the tests . . . of the importance of the waterway, the nature and quantity of the traffic utilising it, whether it is the only, or the principal or a secondary route [argument advanced by Albania in the *Corfu Channel* case and, to some degree, by Brüel] are all open to the objection that in many cases it would be impossible to know in advance . . . whether a given waterway had the character of an international strait or not, since it would depend on matters of *opinion* . . .'. Fitzmaurice, G., 'The Law and Procedure of the International Court of Justice: General Principles and Substantive Law', *BYBIL*, vol. 27, 1950, pp. 1–41, at p. 28.

64. Brüel, op. cit., note 62, p. 276.
65. Ibid., p. 227.
66. Ibid., pp. 266–7.
67. Ibid., p. 227.
68. The *Corfu Channel* case, op. cit., note 22, p. 105 (dissenting opinion of Judge Azevedo).
69. Ibid., pp. 105–6.
70. Ibid., pp. 28–9.
71. Brüel, op. cit., note 61, p. 277.
72. Report of the ILC to the General Assembly, United Nations, General Assembly, 11th Session, Official Records, Supplement No. 9 (Doc. A/3159), p. 6, Article 17(4).
73. ILC, *Yearbook* 1956, vol. 1, (Doc. A/CN.4/Ser.A/1956), p. 203.
74. Two delegates at the Conference made statements on this point. For the British delegate, '[normally] was vague, and might well become a source of argument, friction and dispute between nations as to what was or was not the "normal" use of a particular strait'. For the delegate of Saudi Arabia, 'it should be recalled that the term "normally" had been used in several international instruments, and had been specifically included in the Convention and Statute on the International Regime of Maritime Ports, adopted at Geneva in 1923, to remove any doubts and ambiguity'. (First) UNCLOS, Official Records, vol. III, 1958, p. 95, paragraph 36, and p. 96, paragraph 5.
75. For attempted charts, see Cdr. Kennedy, 'A Brief Geographical and Hydrographical Study of Straits Which Constitute Routes for International Traffic' (First) UNCLOS, Official Records, vol. I, 1958, pp. 114–64; Lay, H., Churchill, R., Nordquist, M. (eds), *New Directions in the Law of the Sea*, New York, Oceana, 1973, vol. II, pp. 885–91.
76. For O'Connell, as regards most of those charts, '. . . [t]he statistics are a little misleading, because many of these straits are dubiously "international" in the sense of being habitually used by shipping as required by the principles laid down by the International Court of Justice in the *Corfu Channel* case and indeed find themselves in the list only because of assiduous cartographical scrutiny on the part of those who seek to produce arresting figures'. O'Connell, *The Influence of Law on Sea Power*, Manchester, Manchester University Press, 1975, p. 97.
77. Caminos, H., 'Legal Regime of Straits in the 1982 United Nations Convention on the Law of the Sea' *(Recueil des Cours) Collected Courses of the Hague Academy of International Law*, 1987, vol. 5, pp. 13–245.
78. 1982 Convention, Article 52. For an exhaustive analysis of this concept, see Rodgers, op. cit. note 20; O'Connell, D.P., 'Midocean Archipelagos in International Law', *BYBIL*, vol. 45, 1971, pp. 1–77; and Dubner, B.H., *The Law of Territorial Waters of Midocean Archipelagos and Archipelagic States*, The Hague, Nijhoff, 1976.
79. 1982 Convention, Article 48.
80. Ibid., Articles 2(1) and 49(1) and (2).
81. 1958 Convention on the Territorial Sea and the Contiguous Zone, Article 10(2).
82. Ibid., Article 4(1).
83. *Fisheries* case, op. cit., note 6, p. 131.
84. Acknowledging the right of innocent passage in enclosed waters, whatever their denomination.
85. Evensen, Jens, 'Certain Legal Aspects Concerning the Delimitation of the Territorial Waters of Archipelagos' (First) UNCLOS, Official Records, vol. 1, 1958, pp. 289–305.
86. Rodgers, op. cit., note 20, p. 85.
87. *Keesing's Contemporary Archives*, 1–8 March 1958, p. 16043.

88. Syatauw, J.J.G., *Some Newly-Established Asian States and the Development of International Law*, The Hague, Nijhoff, 1961, p. 184.
89. For a complete analysis of the negotiations of the Third UNCLOS on this matter, see Rodgers, op. cit., note 20.
90. *International Legal Materials*, vol. XII, 1973, pp. 581; also UN Doc. A/AC.138/SC.III/L.15 of 14 March 1973.
91. Third UNCLOS, Official Records, vol. III, p. 226, Doc. A/CONF.62/C.2/L.49.
92. Lentsch, P. de Vries, 'The Right of Overflight over Strait States and Archipelagic States', *Netherlands Yearbook of International Law*, vol. 14, 1983, pp. 165–225, at p. 183.
93. Leifer, M., *International Straits of the World, Malacca Singapore and Indonesia*, Alphen a.d.R., Sijthoff, 1978, p. 144. Such vessels include, according to Leifer, nuclear-powered ships, ships carrying nuclear substances or dangerous materials, fishing vessels, research and hydrographic ships, and tankers.

Chapter 4

Ocean vessels and their exercise of the right of innocent passage: private vessels

1. Introduction

As may be concluded from the previous chapter, the right of innocent passage could in principle be exercised in the territorial sea proper, in some internal waters, in some straits and in certain portions of the archipelagic waters. However, whether all ships, including those 'with special characteristics', can exercise this right to a similar degree is another question. Although it can be argued that customary international law, and both the 1958 and 1982 Conventions, grant the right of innocent passage to 'all types' of sea vessels, the contrary can equally be maintained. The practice of many key coastal States, including their legislation, clouds the apparently 'clear' treaty provisions.

It is therefore our intention, in the present and the next chapter, systematically to identify the legal status and autonomy of private and public vessels in the exercise of the right of innocent passage, in terms of criminal, civil and administrative and other law enforcement measures of the coastal State, given the constraints of both treaty law and coastal State legislation. Private ships, unlike public vessels (particularly warships), have customarily, and without encountering objections, enjoyed the right of innocent passage. Public vessels *stricto sensu* cannot be subject to seizure, attachment or detention by legal process, nor to judicial proceedings *in rem*, while private ships exercising the right of innocent passage may be submitted to such proceedings at the discretion of the coastal State.[1]

Given the historical designation 'merchant ship' to cover private vessels, be they private yachts or private hospital ships, we have decided to use similar terminology for purposes of convenience.

The terms 'merchant ships' and 'private vessels' are used interchangeably because the legal status of each is the same while exercising the right of innocent passage. The expression 'merchant ships' nonetheless offers the advantage of clarity and in no way undermines the principal points developed in this work.

Merchant ships are large sea-going vessels used primarily for purposes of international trade. One of the major reasons for the existence of the right of innocent passage was—and still is—to encourage, facilitate and promote such trade. It will thus be easily understood why, in both municipal and treaty law, pride of place is given to merchant ships as first beneficiaries of the right of innocent passage. Although contemporary international law envisions innocent passage as a right relating to international communication and navigation generally,[2] and not only to trade-related navigation, historical evidence shows the contrary.[3]

Technically speaking, a foreign merchant ship cruising in the territorial sea by way of a general exercise of the right of innocent passage is considered to be on the high seas. On no account is the merchant ship's passage to be impeded, nor is the said passage subject to conditions, be they notification, authorization or other restrictions, except in furtherance of established criteria determining 'passage' to be prejudicial to the peace, good order or security of the coastal State, or to coastal State laws and regulations relating thereto.[4]

However, whereas in the high seas, administrative, criminal and civil jurisdiction belong to the flag State,[5] except in cases of *erga omnes* obligations,[6] in the territorial sea that State does not necessarily have these powers, since the right of innocent passage must be exercised with due respect to the sovereignty of the coastal State. The first major presumption in matters of jurisdiction is that the latter is territorial.[7] It is therefore obvious that merchant ships exercising the right of innocent passage are subject to the jurisdiction of the State whose territorial sea is being used. However, innocent passage is an independent right which in principle, if properly exercised, excludes jurisdiction of the coastal State over the merchant ship.

This being the case, there must be limitations placed on the coastal State's jurisdiction over foreign vessels in innocent passage. Logically, a coastal State should exercise jurisdiction over such vessels if an act committed on board has consequences which tend to disturb the peace and tranquility of the territorial sea. However, if the act itself and its consequences remain confined to the vessel, wisdom and logic should lead the coastal State to refrain from exercising jurisdiction.

Two subsidiary questions can be asked regarding the exercise of criminal and civil jurisdiction by the coastal State over foreign vessels exercising the right of innocent passage.

Firstly, in criminal matters, is it enough for such an act to have consequences reaching beyond the vessel, or must the act at the same time be of a nature to disturb the peace and tranquillity of the territorial sea?

Secondly, on civil matters, should coastal State jurisdiction only cover acts committed by the vessel or by persons on board during the exercise of the right of innocent passage, or should it include acts committed before the vessel entered the territorial sea? Furthermore, can process be served on persons on board a merchant ship for any action arising before the vessel entered the territorial sea to engage in innocent passage?

Focusing mainly on the 1982 United Nations Convention on the Law of the Sea, an attempt will be made to analyse how the jurisdictional conflicts regarding merchant ships exercising the right of innocent passage in territorial seas have been resolved in criminal, civil and administrative matters. However, a brief comment on how customary international law views the issue and how the latter has been handled in previous cases could be enlightening. An examination of some national laws would be very interesting, too, to identify present State practice.

2. Criminal jurisdiction

Since a merchant ship is not a floating portion of the flag State's territory, acts committed on board such ships in the territorial sea are reputed to be accomplished within the territory of the coastal State.[8] This being the case, criminal acts occurring on board merchant ships exercising the right of innocent passage are in principle subject to the courts of the coastal State. This could be an acknowledgement of the so-called objective territorial principle, according to which jurisdiction exists when any essential constituent element of a crime is localized on State territory.[9]

The Permanent Court of International Justice, in a series of *obita dicta* in the '*Lotus*' case,[10] made these propositions adequately clear. In this case, a French steamer and a Turkish collier collided. The Turkish vessel sank, and Turkish lives were lost. Although the collision did not take place in the territorial sea, criminal jurisdiction was exercised over an officer of the French steamer when it came to port in Turkey.

No matter how unrelated the case may be to the principles of criminal jurisdiction viewed in our context, two passages in the Court's judgment *prima facie* justify the refusal of flag State jurisdiction in certain circumstances, when the ship is exercising the right of innocent passage in the territorial sea.

Justifying the refusal of flag State criminal jurisdiction within the territory of another State, the Permanent Court stated in one passage:

> International law governs relations between independent States. The rules of law binding upon States therefore emanate from their own free will as expressed in conventions or by usages generally accepted as expressing principles of law and established in order to regulate the relations between these co-existing ïndependent communities or with a view to the achievement of common aims. Restrictions upon the independence of States cannot therefore be presumed.
>
> . . . The first and foremost restriction imposed by international law upon a State is that—failing the existence of a permissive rule to the contrary—it may not exercise its power in any form in the territory of another State.
>
> In this sense, jurisdiction is certainly territorial; it cannot be exercised by a State outside its territory except by virtue of a permissive rule derived from international custom or from a convention.[11]

On the priority of coastal State criminal jurisdiction when the effects of the act are felt on that State's territory, or in its territorial sea, the Court held:

> It is certain that the courts of many countries, even of countries which have given their criminal legislation a strictly territorial character, interpret criminal law in the sense that offences, the authors of which at the moment of commission are in the territory of another State, are nevertheless to be regarded as having been committed in the national territory if one of the constituent elements of the offence, and more especially its effects, have taken place there.[12]

However, as stated earlier, the right of innocent passage is an independent right that derogates from the territorial sovereignty exercised by the coastal State in its territorial sea. Accordingly, that right could be considered as entailing a permissive rule depriving the coastal State of its complete power to exercise jurisdiction, as it does on land territory, to the advantage of the flag State.

To avoid unnecessary meddling with navigation in the territorial sea, not all acts on board merchant ships exercising the right of innocent passage are subject to coastal State jurisdiction. Although this could naturally be the 'correct' solution, customary international law as reflected in draft proposals of the 1920s is unclear. Whereas at one extreme there was a proposal to give exclusive criminal jurisdiction to the coastal State, at the other, jurisdiction was to depend on certain conditions.

Draft No. 12 on 'Jurisdiction', submitted to the Inter-American Commission of Jurists at Rio de Janeiro in April 1927 by the American Institute of International Law, stated in one of its provisions[13]: 'Merchant vessels within the territorial waters of a Nation shall be subject to the administrative and criminal laws and procedures of the said Nation.'

A 1928 draft of the 'Institut de droit international', on the other hand, provided that:

> Les crimes et délits commis à bord des navires de commerce de passage dans la mer territoriale ne tombent pas comme tels sous la juridiction de l'Etat riverain. Par exception, les crimes et délits dont l'effet dépasse les bords du navire sont soumis à la juridiction pénale de l'Etat riverain en tant qu'ils sont de nature à troubler la tranquillité publique de ce pays et qu'ils constituent des faits punissables selon ses lois et que ses tribunaux sont compétents pour en connaître.[14]

Stating the same view, but very vaguely and imprecisely, particularly regarding the nature of the act and the question of whether it was in violation of the criminal law of the coastal State, the International Law Association, at its 34th Conference in 1926, adopted a Draft Convention on the Law of Maritime Jurisdiction in Time of Peace where it was stated that:

> When a vessel is passing through the territorial waters of another State, the vessel, its master, officers, crew, passengers and cargo are only subject to the jurisdiction of such State for acts which take effect outside the vessel or for those which involve the public order or the peace of the coastal State. All other acts relating to such persons or property shall be governed by the law of the State whose flag the vessel is entitled to fly.[15]

The trend portrayed by the above individual proposals has been to grant the flag State jurisdiction over crimes committed on board its merchant ships exercising the right of innocent passage, except where the crime is of a 'serious nature' that goes beyond the ship and is punishable under the laws of the coastal State. Then the coastal State is entitled to exercise primary criminal jurisdiction.

Subsequent developments, particularly those within international fora, have gone further to confirm this view.

(a) Criminal jurisdiction on merchant ships in innocent passage as viewed by international conferences

The 1930 Hague Codification Conference

On the basis of point XII, which dealt with the limitations placed upon the exercise of sovereignty by the coastal State and which had been drawn up by the

League of Nations Preparatory Committee,[16] and of the replies obtained from governments, a draft Article 8 on criminal jurisdiction was included in the 1930 Hague Draft Articles on the Territorial Sea.[17]

Article 8 ran as follows:

> A coastal State may not take any steps on board a foreign vessel passing through the territorial sea to arrest any person or to conduct any investigation by reason of any crime committed on board the vessel during its passage, save only in the following cases:
>
> (1) If the consequences of the crime extend beyond the vessel; or
> (2) If the crime is of a kind to disturb the peace of the country or the good order of the territorial sea; or
> (3) If the assistance of the local authorities has been requested by the captain of the vessel or by the consul of the country whose flag the vessel flies.
>
> The above provisions do not affect the right of the coastal State to take any steps authorized by its laws for the purpose of an arrest or investigation on board a foreign vessel in the inland waters of that State or lying in its territorial sea, or passing through the territorial sea after leaving the inland waters.
>
> The local authorities shall, in all cases, pay due regard to the interests of navigation when making an arrest on board a vessel.

In a series of observations made by the Second Committee of the Hague Conference, it was noted that although navigation ought to be interfered with as little as possible, Article 8 was aimed at making the criminal laws of coastal States *effective* throughout its territory. This notwithstanding, the observations went on to say that:

> The coastal State cannot stop a foreign vessel passing through the territorial sea without entering the inland waters of the State simply because there happened to be on board a person wanted by the judicial authorities of the State for some punishable act committed elsewhere than on board the vessel. It would be still less possible for a request for extradition addressed to the coastal State in respect of an offence committed abroad to be regarded as a valid ground for interrupting the vessel's voyage.

The observations finally contained the following passage:

> The inconvenience caused to navigation by the stopping of a large liner outward bound in order to arrest a person alleged to have committed some minor offence on land can scarcely be regarded as of less importance than the interest which the State may have in securing the arrest of the offender. Similarly, the judicial authorities of the coastal State should, as far as possible, refrain from arresting any of the officers or crew of the vessel if their absence would make it impossible for the voyage to continue.[18]

Commenting on Article 8, some writers seem to think that the provision was not exhaustive and that criminal jurisdiction over passing merchant ships is a matter of expediency or politics rather than of law.

In his analysis, Gidel correctly suggests that:

> L'article 8 ne tend pas à faire le départ entre les compétences respectives de l'Etat des pavillons et de l'Etat riverain en matière répressive à l'égard de navires en passage dans la mer territoriale. Ce qu'il a en vue, c'est de limiter les mesures par lesquelles l'Etat riverain—dans le cas où il est compétent—pourra exercer cette compétence sans porter atteinte aux intérêts légitimes de la navigation du navire en passage.[19]

Article 8 is not exhaustive. Among the matters which are beyond the purview of that article, Gidel cites the

> mesures d'instruction ou des arrestations à raison d'actes commis à une époque où le navire supposé être en passage dans la mer territoriale n'était—lors de la commission des actes—ni en passage dans la mer territoriale, ni en sejour dans ta merterritoriale, ni en navigation ou séjour dans les eaux intérieures de l'Etat riverain.[20]

The categories of criminal acts which touch on the 'rights' of the coastal State are called by Gidel 'actes qui donnent lieu à ce que l'on appelle généralement, dans le langage de l'Ecole, la compétence quasi-territoriale de l'Etat'. These acts he defines as

> des actes qui, même s'ils ont été commis à l'étranger par des étrangers et, à plus forte raison, par des nationaux, sont assimilés par l'Etat qui les prévoit dans sa législation à des actes commis sur son propre territoire, c'est-à-dire peuvent faire l'objet de poursuites pénales malgré l'absence des éléments de territorialité qui fondent normalement la compétence: actes contre la sûreté de l'Etat, complots contre la famille régnante, contrefaçon du sceau de l'Etat, fabrication de fausses monnaies de l'Etat, etc.[21]

Georges Scelle, on the other hand, reduces the whole perspective to a political question. He makes a distinction between crimes which are in violation of the right of innocent passage or are related to the latter, where the coastal State has complete competence and ordinary crimes, which are unrelated to the right of innocent passage.

As regards the latter, he holds:

> pour les délits de droit commun commis à bord et *sans liaison avec le passage* (notamment les délits antérieurs), la règle nous paraît devoir être celle de l'incompétence des autorités locales (et sans aucune distinction entre la nationalité des délinquants, c'est-à-dire même s'il s'agit d'un national).[22]

In conclusion, Scelle notes:

> En réalité, il s'agit, comme dans les eaux intérieures, mais plus nettement encore, d'une question de 'politique', davantage que d'une question de compétence. La légitimité de l'intervention soulève ou ne soulève pas de difficultés, selon les circonstances de l'affaire et l'état des rapports diplomatiques entre les Etats intéressés. C'est dire qu'il s'agit plutôt d'un modus vivendi que d'un état de Droit positif.[23]

Be that as it may, the provisions of Article 8 were subsequently adopted with minor alterations in other international fora.

The International Law Commission

The Initial Draft and the Final Draft submitted by the International Law Commission in 1956 in preparation of the 1958 Geneva Conference on the Law of the Sea contained a provision similar to Article 8 on criminal jurisdiction of foreign ships in innocent passage. Although subscribing to most observations made earlier in connexion with Article 8, the Commission, in its commentary on that provision (which was to become Article 20 of its Final Draft on the Regime of Territorial Sea), added two other remarks.

The first observation related to collisions in the territorial sea. The Commission thought it wise to abstain from laying down specific rules on criminal jurisdiction owing to the wide scope of the subject and to the existence of the International Convention for the Unification of Certain Rules Relating to Penal Jurisdiction in Matters of Collisions or Other Incidents of Navigation, signed at Brussels on 10 May 1952.

Second, the Commission raised the issue of jurisdiction over crimes which extend beyond the merchant ship but whose consequences remain limited to the territory of the flag State. On this point, the Commission observed that:

> It is obvious that, particularly in such cases, the coastal State must act very warily, but it may well be that sometimes in these cases the arrest would also be in the interest of the flag State; hence, it would not be justifiable to forbid the coastal State to intervene.[24]

However, as is shown by the 1958 Geneva Convention on the Territorial Sea and the Contiguous Zone, the majority of States felt that such a view would lead to an over-extensive interpretation of coastal State criminal jurisdiction. Thus, the wording of the phrase was altered. Instead of allowing for coastal State jurisdiction 'if the consequences of the crime extend beyond the vessel', as had been done in the 1930 Draft and in the Final Draft of the International Law Commission of 1956, the 1958 Geneva Convention limits such jurisdiction to cases where '. . . the consequences of the crime extend to the coastal State'.

The (First) United Nations Conference on the Law of the Sea (1958)

At the (First) Geneva Conference on the Law of the Sea of 1958, the provision on criminal jurisdiction contained in the Draft of the International Law Commission was altered in light of proposals presented by delegations and aimed at reconciling national criminal procedure with the needs of navigation in the territorial sea.

Without going into the details of the debate on this issue, we shall consider the rephrasing of the International Law Commission's Draft article in conjunction with the explanations offered by delegates to the Conference.

While Article 21(1) of the International Law Commission's Draft had said '. . . A coastal State may not take . . .', the United States delegation suggested substitution of the phrase: 'The criminal jurisdiction of the coastal State *should* generally not be exercised on board a foreign ship. . . .'[25] This alteration was explained in the following way: '. . . the declaration that a coastal State "may not" make arrests or conduct investigations except in such cases is a departure from the strict theory of international law. Such theory holds that the criminal jurisdiction of the coastal State in its territorial sea is unlimited.'[26] For some delegations, the use of the word 'should' greatly weakened the force of the paragraph as a statement of legal principle and made it nothing but a polite request to coastal States to be reasonable in the exercise of their jurisdiction. Nevertheless, by a vote of 33 to 21, with 20 abstentions, out of 74 States participating in the Conference, the United States' proposal was adopted.[27]

Other changes concerned the first of three exceptions permitting the coastal State to exercise criminal jurisdiction on merchant ships, namely, the situation where the ship is in innocent passage in the territorial sea but where 'the consequences of the crime extend *beyond the vessel*'. Whether these consequences did have to affect the coastal State was made clear by the British delegation which introduced an amendment to substitute the words '*to the coastal State*' for 'beyond the ship'. This proposal was adopted by a majority of 56 votes to 4 with 13 abstentions.[28] In addition, the British delegation proposed a paragraph which read: 'A coastal State may not take any steps . . . to arrest any person or to conduct any investigation in connection with any crime committed elsewhere than on board the ship during its passage through the territorial sea.'[29]

In explaining the reasons for these amendments, Fitzmaurice said that his delegation was introducing 'greater clarity' to the whole text. Since

> under those provisions the coastal State did not take cognisance of offences committed on board a ship during its passage through the territorial sea, in cases where the offences were confined to the ship itself and did not directly affect the coastal State . . ., [and] in the case of an offence committed outside the territorial sea and before the ship's arrival in the territorial sea, the authorities of the coastal State would not be in a position to conduct an investigation or to arrest any person in respect of a vessel which was merely passing through the territorial sea of that State.[30]

The Pakistani delegation further suggested an exception which would allow coastal States to exercise criminal jurisdiction wherever 'it is necessary for the suppression of illicit traffic in narcotic drugs.'[31] This proposal was adopted unanimously.

Finally, Greece suggested a paragraph requesting the coastal State which is about to exercise criminal jurisdiction to inform the consular authorities of the flag State and to facilitate contacts between the latter and the ship's crew.[32] This proposal was carried as well.

The new provision on criminal jurisdiction which was adopted by the Conference became Article 19 of the 1958 Geneva Convention on the Territorial Sea and the Contiguous Zone. This Article reads as follows:

> 1. The criminal jurisdiction of the coastal state should not be exercised on board a foreign ship passing through the territorial sea to arrest any person or to conduct any investigation in connexion with any crime committed on board the ship during its passage, save only in the following case:
>   a) If the consequences of the crime extend to the coastal State; or

b) If the crime is of a kind to disturb the peace of the country of the good order of the territorial sea; or
c) If the assistance of the local authorities has been requested by the captain of the ship or by the consul of the country whose flag the ship flies; or
d) If it is necessary for the suppression of illicit traffic in narcotic drugs.

2. The above provisions do not affect the right of the coastal State to take any steps authorized by its laws for the purpose of an arrest or investigation on board a foreign ship passing through the territorial sea after leaving internal waters.
3. In the cases provided for in paragraphs 1 and 2 of this Article, the coastal State shall, if the captain so requests, advise the consular authority of the flag State before taking any steps, and shall facilitate contact between such authority and the ship's crew. In cases of emergency, this notification may be communicated while the measures are being taken.
4. In considering whether or how an arrest should be made, the local authorities shall pay due regard to the interests of navigation.
5. The coastal State may not take any steps on board a foreign ship passing through the territorial sea to arrest any person or to conduct any investigation in connexion with any crime committed before the ship entered the territorial sea, if the ship, proceeding from a foreign port, is only passing through the territorial sea without entering internal waters.

Criminal jurisdiction over merchant ships in the Third United Nations Conference on the Law of the Sea

In the Third United Nations Conference on the Law of the Sea, attempts were made to alter the use of the word 'should' in the first paragraph of Article 19 so as to exclude coastal State criminal jurisdiction in coastal waters.

Attempts in this sense may be found in the Draft Articles presented by Fiji,[33] on the one hand, and in the Draft Articles submitted by Bulgaria, the German Democratic Republic, Poland and the Soviet Union.[34] These proposals rephrased Article 19(1) of the 1958 Geneva Convention to read: 'The criminal jurisdiction of the coastal State shall not be exercised on board a foreign ship passing through the territorial sea . . .'

The proposed change was to make it mandatory for the coastal State to refrain from exercising criminal jurisdiction, save in the four cases mentioned in Article 19 of the 1958 Convention. However, the word 'should' was finally retained, and all the other provisions of Article 19 were maintained without any alterations or additions, except for the fact that in the new Convention on the Law of the Sea that provision became Article 27 and had to be harmonized with the new notions and principles embodied in that Convention.

Article 27(1) of the 1982 Convention runs as follows:

> The criminal jurisdiction of the coastal State should not be exercised on board a foreign ship passing through territorial sea to arrest any person or to conduct any investigation in connection with any crime committed on board the ship during its passage, save only in the following cases:

(a) If the consequences of the crime extend to the coastal State;
(b) If the crime is of a kind to disturb the peace of the country or the good order of the territorial sea;
(c) If the assistance of the local authorities has been requested by the master of the ship or by a diplomatic agent or consular officer of the flag State; or
(d) If such measures are necessary for the suppression of illicit traffic in narcotic drugs or psychotropic substances.

The above-quoted text shows that there is no obligation for the coastal State to refrain from exercising criminal jurisdiction. Article 27(1) expresses a wish which, however, does not extend to the four situations outlined in sub-paragraphs (a) to (d).

In other words, the question of whether the coastal State should exercise criminal jurisdiction is not just one of basic competence but should be considered in connection with the rights of the State of the foreign ship or flag State.[35] This was in direct recognition of the principle admitted in the *Franconia* case,[36] where a British ship was struck by a foreign ship in British territorial waters. It was decided that the English courts had no jurisdiction, the actual place of the collision being immaterial. Although this position was subsequently altered by statute[37] and could be considered as being limited to the English context, the fact is that in exercising its criminal jurisdiction over foreign merchant ships in innocent passage, a careful use of discretion is required on the part of the coastal State.

Otherwise, as was affirmed by Gidel many years ago and as is still valid today, '[l']Etat riverain qui exercerait mal à propos ou abusivement son droit engagerait sa responsabilité . . . à l'égard de l'Etat du pavillon du navire en passage, objet de mesures inutilement dommageables à sa navigation'.[38]

Another conclusion that can be drawn from the above provisions on coastal State criminal jurisdiction over merchant ships relates to sub-paragraphs (a) and (b) of Article 27(1), i.e. to the cases where the consequences of a crime on board ship extend to the coastal State or disturb either the peace of that State or the good order in its territorial sea. These exceptions have to some degree filled the lacunae mentioned by Gidel in relation to the 1930 Draft Article.

The two exceptions mentioned in sub-paragraphs (a) and (b) substantiate instances of the exercise of quasi-territorial competence, such as counterfeiting.[39] In this case, the coastal State can exercise criminal jurisdiction, more so if the counterfeit bills are in the merchant ship.

As far as sub-paragraphs (c) and (d) are concerned, namely, cases where local assistance is requested by officials of the flag State and cases of universal jurisdiction, such as those relating to illicit traffic in narcotic drugs, the exercise of criminal jurisdiction by the coastal State is, under normal circumstances, also in the interest of the flag State. There are situations, however, where the interests to be protected are essentially those of the coastal State. The subsequent paragraphs of Article 27 bear this out.

In cases of conspiracy, violation of emigration laws, etc., Article 27(2) provides: '. . . the right of the coastal State to take any steps authorized by its laws for the purpose of an arrest or investigation on board a foreign ship passing through the territorial sea after leaving internal waters.'[40]

In all instances of exercise of criminal jurisdiction, there is, under Article 27(3), an obligation to inform and consult with officials of the flag State before completion of any criminal procedure. Where an arrest is contemplated, warns Article 27(4), the local authorities shall have due regard to the interests of navigation.

On the other hand, contrary to what is the case for merchant ships leaving internal waters, the coastal State may not take any steps, on board a foreign merchant ship passing through the territorial sea, to arrest any person or to conduct any investigation in connection with any crime committed *before* the ship entered the territorial sea, provided that the ship, proceeding from a foreign port, is only passing through the territorial sea *without entering internal waters*.[41] However, the coastal State is not prevented from enforcing in its territorial sea regulations on the exclusive economic zone and the contiguous zone.

In sum, the coastal State has a broad range of discretionary powers to exercise criminal jurisdiction over merchant ships in innocent passage. Thus, a contextual interpretation of the 1982 Convention leads to the conclusion, in cases of collisions of merchant ships, or of requests for extradition of persons on board, or of other crimes involving a ship exercising the right of innocent passage, that the coastal State has a primary right to exercise criminal jurisdiction. However, this does not prevent the flag State, in view of the silence of the text, from exercising concurrent jurisdiction, particularly when the act under consideration violates the laws of both the coastal State and the flag State.

By and large, and according to their nature, it could be said that criminal acts performed on merchant ships in innocent passage are not committed in the jurisdictional domain of the flag State. This, undoubtedly, is a restriction of the right of innocent passage. Nevertheless, considerations of international comity require coastal States to refrain from the exercise of criminal jurisdiction over merchant ships in innocent passage. Yet, the hortatory rather than prohibitory language of Article 27 of the 1982 Convention increases the temptation for coastal States to claim such jurisdiction over merchant ships in innocent passage at the slightest 'provocation'. This is borne out by some laws and by the practice of some States.

(b) State practice and municipal law provisions

United States of America

United States legislation[42] stipulates that the territory 'subject to the laws includes land, ports, harbours, bays and the three-mile belt'.[43] Foreign merchant ships entering territorial waters submit themselves to coastal State jurisdiction.

This means that United States jurisdiction over merchant ships and other objects in the territorial sea is assumed by virtue of mere *presence*. Nevertheless, the United States Supreme Court, in several cases to which we shall refer, also acknowledges that a sovereign may renounce the exercise of its jurisdiction, but that this is a matter in its own discretion.

The above principles, still valid today, were enunciated by the United States Supreme Court in *Cunard* v. *Mellon*[44] and in *Schooner Exchange* v. *M'Faddon*.[45] It was held in the former case that:

> It is now settled in the United States and recognized elsewhere that the territory subject to its jurisdiction includes land areas under its dominion and control, the ports, harbours, bays and other enclosed areas of the sea along its coast and a marginal belt of the sea extending from the coast line outward a maritime league or three geographical miles.[46]

In the *Schooner Exchange* case, Chief Justice Marshall stated that:

> The jurisdiction of a nation within its own territory is necessary, exclusive and absolute. It is susceptible of no limitation not imposed by itself. Any restriction upon it deriving validity from an external source would imply a diminution of its sovereignty to the extent of the restriction, and an investment of that sovereignty to the same extent in that power which could impose such restriction. All exceptions, therefore, to the full and complete power of a nation, within its own territories, must be traced up to the consent of the nation itself. They can flow from no other legitimate source.[47]

This position has been endorsed in the 1982 United Nations Convention on the Law of the Sea; it will be recalled that the 1958 equivalent of Article 27(1)—Article 19(1)—had been proposed by the United States delegation. Although this position was traditionally aimed at reconciling a long practice against the smuggling of liquor into the United States, it now included other activities even beyond the territorial sea.

By claiming a right of approach or visitation on the high seas,[48] which would obviously be legitimate were it exercised in its territorial sea, the United States establishes criminal jurisdiction over merchant ships even beyond that belt.[49] The latest manifestation of this trend is found in *United States* v. *Postal et al.*[50] In this case, a United States Court of Appeals upheld the jurisdiction of the courts of the United States over persons arrested by the Coast Guard aboard a merchant ship of foreign registry, seized beyond the 12-mile limit, even though the seizure apparently violated Article 6 of the 1958 Convention on the High Seas (now Article 92(1) of the 1982 Convention) which declares the exclusivity of a nation's jurisdiction over the vessels entitled to fly its flag in areas beyond the territorial sea.

The Soviet Union

Soviet criminal legislation covers the full range of Soviet territory and extends to 'all persons who commit crimes on the territory of the U.S.S.R.'.[51]

Inasmuch as Soviet territorial waters are placed under the full sovereignty of the Soviet Union, the above provision applies to all crimes committed on board foreign merchant vessels while in these waters.

As part of the sweeping revisions undertaken in 1960 in several areas of Soviet legislation, and in response to the 1958 Geneva Convention on the Territorial Sea and the Contiguous Zone, the Soviet Union adopted a new Statute on the Protection of the State Boundary of the U.S.S.R.[52]

This Statute provides that, in cases of merchant ships (foreign non-military vessels) moving in Soviet waters, the Soviet border guard has the right to take from the vessel and to detain persons who have committed crimes and who are subject to criminal responsibility under USSR legislation, and to transfer them to appropriate agencies. But, the legislation continues,

> these measures may not be applied to a person on board a foreign vessel traversing U.S.S.R. territorial waters who has committed a crime prior to the entrance of the vessel in the territorial waters if the vessel is proceeding from a foreign port, restricts its passage to territorial waters, and does not enter internal waters.[53]

Another pertinent piece of legislation, which is still considered operative despite the 1960 Statute, is a Decree of 24 May 1927 which governs the procedure of arrests on foreign merchant vessels. The Decree prescribes that:

> Appropriate authorities of the R.S.F.S.R. [U.S.S.R.] shall have the right to make arrests of criminals on foreign merchant vessels only in those instances when the crime was committed by them wholly or partly on the shore or when the consequences of these crimes may bring forth serious complications on shore.[54]

However, the Soviet Union is said customarily to refrain from interfering with merchant ships, in accordance with international practice, if the crime does not threaten the security or public order of the Soviet Union or the humane principles of Soviet socialist laws.

The United Kingdom

The practice of the United Kingdom regarding the exercise of criminal jurisdiction over merchant ships in innocent passage has been influenced by the decision of the House of Lords in 1876 in the case of *Reg.* v. *Keyn.*[55]

As stated earlier, in this case an indictable offence of manslaughter was committed within the territorial waters of England by a foreigner on a foreign ship; and the question raised was whether the British Admiral's Criminal Court had jurisdiction to try him. By a majority, the House of Lords held that the court lacked jurisdiction.

Subsequently, the British Parliament passed the Territorial Waters Jurisdiction Act of 1878, which is still valid today.[56]

The Act provides that offences committed on the open seas within the boundaries of the territorial waters are within the jurisdiction of the Admiralty and are punishable accordingly. However, a proviso refers to the offences as limited to such as would, if committed within England, be punishable on indictment. In other words, summary offences committed by foreigners on foreign ships within British territorial waters are excluded from the jurisdiction of the coastal State.

A fairly recent application of this principle by the House of Lords may be found in the case of *Bernard Pianka and Another* v. *The Queen.*[57]

The pertinent facts of the case were that on 10 August 1974 the defendants, Pianka and Another, United States citizens on board a ship registered in the

United States, were intercepted by the coast guard within the territorial waters of Jamaica. The ship contained 3,277 lbs of ganja (narcotics). Pianka and his associate were charged on information before a resident magistrate with possessing ganja and with using a conveyance for carrying it contrary to the Dangerous Drugs Law. Both offences were special statutory summary offences triable by a resident magistrate. The offenders were convicted. They then appealed to the Court of Appeal against their convictions on the ground that the resident magistrate had no jurisdiction to try them for the offence charged. The Court of Appeal dismissed the appeal. Finally, the defendants appealed to the British House of Lords *via* the Judicial Committee of the Privy Council.

On the question raised in the defendants appeal whether the jurisdiction to try criminal offences committed on a foreign ship within territorial waters was limited by the 1878 Act to indictable offences and whether the trial was contrary to Article 19 of the 1958 Geneva Convention on the Territorial Sea and the Contiguous Zone (now Article 27 of the 1982 Convention),[58] it was held that:

> a resident magistrate was given power to try offences committed within the parish and that part of the parish which was deemed to extend over the territorial waters; that since the power of the State to pass legislation affecting its territorial waters was unlimited, there was no general immunity to foreign ships from the legislation of either England or Jamaica and there was no principle of construction that would imply that a general legislative provision did not apply to foreign ships.[59]

Per curiam, it was held that the exceptions contained in sub-paragraphs (a) and (b) of Article 19(1) (now Article 27(1) should be liberally construed.

It is interesting to highlight some cardinal passages to get a clear view of British practice as portrayed in the *Pianka* case. A member of the House of Lords thus stated the majority view on the exclusive application of British law in the territorial sea:

> I wish, however, to guard myself from being supposed to adopt any words or expressions which may seem to imply doubt as to the competency of Parliament to legislate as it may think fit for these waters. I think that usage and the common consent of nations, which constitute international law, have appropriated these waters to the adjacent State to deal with them as the State may deem expedient for its own interest.[60]

On the question of whether the right of innocent passage impinges on this rule, it is stated in another passage that:

> the legislative power of the coastal State over its territorial waters is as absolute as its authority over its land territory, and that foreign merchant ships, as foreign individuals, entering that territory, of land or sea, submit themselves to its laws unless exempted therefrom.[61]

Whether such an extremely liberal interpretation could run counter to the provisions of sub-paragraphs (a) and (b) of Article 19(1) (or of Article 27(1)) was said to depend to a large extent upon the facts related to the nature of the passage and the nature of the crime.

Two members of the House of Lords voiced their dissent regarding the question of indictable and summary offences committed on merchant ships under the 1878 Act:

> The proper construction . . . [is that] the British Parliament in 1878 did not entirely abrogate the rule in *Reg.* v. *Keyn*, but modified it only as regards indictable offences. Of this there can be no doubt. However desirable it might be that a British Court should have jurisdiction over foreigners committing serious offences against British law in foreign ships in passage on the seas which constitute British territorial waters, it was obviously considered undesirable that British Courts should assume jurisdiction to try in such circumstances every petty act which infringed any part of the vast code of summary offences under British Law. Hence, too, presumably the requirements (section 3) that prosecutions under the 1878 Act should be sanctioned by the Secretary of State (or, in overseas dominions, the Governor). This limitation to indictable offences must have been a solemn act of legislative policy; and we venture again to emphasise that this limitation on the modification of the common law as declared in *Reg.* v. *Keyn* extended to Jamaica.[62]

In sum, the British position can be stated as follows. Whether an offence is indictable or not, its occurrence on board a merchant ship in British territorial waters makes it subject to Her Majesty's criminal jurisdiction regardless of the Law of the Sea Conventions, whose provisions on this issue have to be liberally construed in any case. The exercise of jurisdiction in this respect is thus decided upon, despite the right of innocent passage, by relying on the interest of the coastal State.

France

Until relatively recently, French criminal jurisdiction over foreign merchant ships in territorial waters was defined by the 'Avis' of the Conseil d'Etat of 1806. Although this Opinion was concerned with merchant ships in French ports, it was applied to ships in the territorial sea as well. The cardinal part of the 'Avis' ran as follows:

> Considérant qu'un vaisseau neutre ne peut être indéfiniment considéré comme lieu neutre, et que la protection, qui lui est accordée dans les ports français, ne saurait dessaisir la juridiction territoriale pour tout ce qui touche aux intérêts de l'Etat;
>
> Qu'ainsi le vaisseau neutre, admis dans un port de l'Etat, est, de plein droit, soumis aux lois de police qui régissent le lieu où il est reçu;
>
> Que les gens de son équipage sont également justiciables des tribunaux du pays pour les délits qu'ils y commettraient, même à bord, envers des personnes étrangères à l'équipage, ainsi que pour les conventions civiles qu'ils pourraient faire avec elles;
>
> Mais que si, jusque-là, la juridiction territoriale est hors de doute, il n'en est pas ainsi à l'égard des délits qui se commettent à bord du vaisseau neutre, de la part d'un homme de l'équipage neutre envers un autre homme du même équipage;

> Qu'en ce cas, les droits de la puissance neutre doivent être respectés, comme s'agissant de la discipline intérieure du vaisseau, dans laquelle l'autorité locale ne doit pas s'ingérer, toutes les fois que son secours n'est pas réclamé ou que la tranquillité du port n'est pas compromise.[63]

In 1935, the Conseil d'Etat went even further by holding that roadsteads independent of any port did not form part of the public maritime domain of France. However, the French position changed in 1978. From then onward, France has subjected merchant ships to the exclusive and compulsory civil and criminal jurisdiction of the coastal State.

Following the disaster of the 'Amoco Cadiz' off the French coast, on 17 March 1978, France issued a Decree[64] implying the 'notification' of the coastal State by any merchant ship, especially oil tankers, exercising the right of innocent passage.[65]

Article 1 of the Decree reads:

> Le capitaine de tout navire transportant des hydrocarbures est tenu, dès l'entrée dans les eaux territoriales françaises, d'adresser au préfet maritime par voie radio-électrique, un message indiquant:
> — La date et l'heure d'entrée dans les eaux territoriales;
> — La position, la route et la vitesse du navire;
> — La nature du chargement.

In a Circular relating to the above incident, the French Government directed local maritime authorities to take measures strictly to regulate the passage of tankers in French territorial waters, prohibiting them from approaching the coasts more closely than seven nautical miles, except within international systems of traffic regulation and in access channels to certain ports and roadsteads.[66] The above rule and regulation is taken to apply mainly to oil tankers.

Other States

Regardless of whether the requirements of the Law of the Sea Convention are fulfilled, the tendency of coastal States is to see to it that they are not deprived of primary jurisdiction.

Thus the Canadian Criminal Code of 26 June 1954, as amended,[67] states in its Section 420(1):

> Where an offence is committed by a person, whether or not he is a Canadian citizen, on the territorial sea of Canada, . . . whether or not it was committed on board or by means of a Canadian ship, the offence is within the competence of . . . the territorial division nearest to the place where the offence was committed, and shall be tried in the same manner as if the offence had been committed within that territorial division.

The Nigerian Territorial Waters Decree No. 5 of 8 March 1967[68] states *inter alia*, in its Section 2 (Jurisdiction in Respect of Offences Committed in Territorial Waters):

> (1) Any act or omission which

(a) is committed within the territorial waters of Nigeria, whether by a citizen of Nigeria or a foreigner; and
(b) would, if committed in any part of Nigeria, constitute an offence under the law in force in that part,

shall be an offence under that law, and the person who committed it may . . . be arrested, tried and punished for it as if he had committed it in that part of Nigeria.

(2) . . . The foregoing subsection
(b) in the case of an act or omission committed by a foreigner on board or by means of a foreign ship, shall apply notwithstanding that the ship is a foreign one.

However, in Section 3 (Restriction of Trial of Persons Other than Nigerian Citizens for Offences Committed in Territorial Waters), the Decree further prescribes:

(1) A Nigerian court shall not try a person who is not a citizen of Nigeria for any offence committed on the open sea within the territorial waters of Nigeria unless before the trial the Attorney-General of the Federation has issued a certificate signifying his consent to the trial of that person for that offence.

This provision is similar to a proviso in the United Kingdom Territorial Waters Jurisdiction Act of 1878, which seems to limit coastal State jurisdiction to indictable offences. The British Act had made it clear that foreigners may not be prosecuted unless the Secretary of State certified that it was expedient to do so. The fundamental policy objective of both texts is that it is a waste of time to entertain cases which do not affect national interests. The Nigerian Territorial Waters Act, nevertheless, stipulates that this does not affect the power of arrest, search, entry, seizure or custody exercisable with respect to an offence which has been, or is believed to have been committed, on board a foreign merchant ship.[69]

Conclusion

The State practice so far examined shows that as far as criminal jurisdiction over merchant ships exercising the right of innocent passage is concerned, most domestic laws give unqualified jurisdiction to municipal courts to punish offences committed within the territorial waters. This unqualified jurisdiction, sometimes dictated by 'national interest', is obviously not in conformity with the provisions of Article 27 of the 1982 United Nations Convention on the Law of the Sea. It is, consequently, a restriction on the exercise of the right of innocent passage by merchant ships.

States which become parties to the 1982 Convention are thus under an obligation (for the sake of innocent passage) to harmonize their national legislations with the prescriptions of that convention when it comes into force; unless this is done automatically through a constitutional rule providing for 'the supremacy of International Law, including that established by treaty, over conflicting municipal law.[70] However, it is also recognized that, despite this, most coastal States do not hesitate to pursue a course which violates treaty obligations. As one author rightly puts it:

> because a State is very ambivalent about its attitude towards international law, its courts, when faced with a conflict between municipal law and international law, may prefer to give effect to the provisions of the municipal law even if they are contrary to 'generally acknowledged principles of international law'.[71]

3. Civil jurisdiction

Unlike what they do in the field of criminal jurisdiction, coastal States prefer not to assume civil jurisdiction over merchant ships exercising the right of innocent passage. Except where their direct pecuniary interests are at stake, coastal States find it cumbersome, absurd and inconvenient to be a 'revenue collector' for the flag State. Since jurisdiction in the territorial sea is personal or national (*in rem*), on civil matters merchant ships in innocent passage are usually subject to the rules of private international law to determine the appropriate forum in view of the foreign element inherent in the ship.

It is not our intention to deal with the legal effects of acts such as registrations of births or the validity of marriages taking place on a merchant ship exercising the right of innocent passage, or of acts which might lead to the attribution of nationality.[72] These issues are adequately covered by the principles and rules of private international law and municipal legislation. We shall be concerned with the exercise of civil jurisdiction over merchant ships by the coastal State which could impinge on the right of innocent passage.

The exercise of civil jurisdiction over merchant ships in innocent passage has always been strictly qualified. Proposals by learned societies before the 1930 Hague Codification Conference are illustrative in this regard.

The 'Institut de droit international', at its 1928 Stockholm Session, adopted the following provision as part of its Draft on the Territorial Sea:

> Article 8: Les actes juridiques accomplis à bord d'un navire de commerce de passage dans la mer territoriale ne sont pas, tant au point de vue civil qu'au point de vue commercial, soumis par-là même à la compétence judiciaire et législative de l'Etat riverain.
> L'enfant né sur un navire de commerce de passage dans la mer territoriale doit être considéré comme né sur ce même navire en haute mer.[73]

Less categoric and more on the side of future development was the Draft produced by the Harvard Research in International Law:

> Article 16: A State may not exercise civil jurisdiction over a vessel of another State while it is in course of innocent passage through the marginal sea, except in respect of an act committed by the vessel during the course of that innocent passage and not relating solely to the internal economy of the vessel.[74]

Unfortunately, these individual draft proposals rarely envisaged both personal and *in rem* jurisdiction, nor did they deal with cases of liability incurred in the course of passage.

All these points were covered in Article 9 of the Final Act of the 1930 Codification Conference, which fairly reflected the practice of States at the time:

> A coastal State may not divert a foreign vessel passing through the territorial sea for the purpose of exercising civil jurisdiction in relation to a person on board the vessel. A coastal State may not levy execution against or arrest the vessel for the purpose of any civil proceeding save only in respect of obligations or liabilities incurred by the vessel itself in the course of or for the purpose of its voyage through the waters of the coastal State.
> The provisions are without prejudice to the right of the coastal State in accordance with its laws to levy execution against, or to arrest, a foreign vessel in the inland waters of the State or lying in the territorial sea, or passing through the territorial sea after leaving the inland waters of the State, for the purpose of any civil proceedings.[75]

In an 'observation' attached to this Article, it was stated that the rules on criminal jurisdiction had been closely followed and that in no circumstances should a merchant ship in innocent passage be stopped for the purpose of exercising civil jurisdiction, except when contact was envisaged with internal waters or when events such as collisions or salvage operations had occurred in the territorial waters during the voyage. Jurisdiction also exists for obligations incurred for the purpose of the voyage.[76]

This very strict and restrictive conception of the exercise of civil jurisdiction, which differs from that of criminal jurisdiction over merchant ships in innocent passage, is dictated by several considerations.

Although civil jurisdiction is ultimately accompanied by procedures of enforcement involving criminal sanctions, and though there is thus no great difference between the problems created by the assertion of civil and criminal jurisdictions,[77] Gidel rightly thought that in civil matters, 'l'ordre public de l'Etat riverain est loin d'être intéressé dans la même mesure' and that 'quelques considérations que soient les intérêts pour la défense desquels peuvent agir les autorités de l'Etat riverain, ce sont des intérêts privés en conflit avec d'autres intérêts privés'.[78]

That being the case, he continued, 'lorsqu'il s'agit de différends d'ordre civil, le passage continue très généralement, quels que soient les griefs dirigés contre le navire, à conserver son caractère "inoffensif" '.[79] In conclusion, Gidel, however, moderates his earlier assertions by admitting:

> Cependant il s'agit d'un navire étranger dans la mer territoriale de l'Etat riverain; il est soumis par conséquent en droit et en fait à la souveraineté de cet Etat à même de faire exécuter à l'égard de ce navire ou des personnes se trouvant à son bord les décisions émanant de ses autorités judiciaires, à la suite de procédures légales auxquelles la 'formule exécutoire' vient prêter l'appui éventuel de la force publique.[80]

The text elaborated in 1930 was reproduced in the debates of the International Law Commission and subsequently adopted by the (First) Geneva Conference on the Law of the Sea. At that Conference, there was at one point, a call for the complete deletion of the provision,[81] the reason being that the exercise of civil jurisdiction over merchant ships in innocent passage was taken care of by the

1952 Brussels Convention for the Unification of Certain Rules Relating to the Arrest of Sea-Going Ships. In the end, the original text was, however, amended to reflect the idea that the coastal State is entitled to exercise civil jurisdiction as it thinks fit, as is the case for the exercise of criminal jurisdiction over merchant ships.

Introducing an amendment in this sense at the 1958 Conference, the United States delegation pointed out that no limitation on coastal State exercise of civil jurisdiction existed in international law. That being the case, the delegation proposed and obtained the insertion of the less binding words 'should not' in the first paragraph of Article 20. In this way, the opening phrase would read: 'The coastal State should not stop or divert a foreign ship passing through the territorial sea . . .'.

According to a commentary on this provision,

> no limitation on civil jurisdiction of the coastal State . . . is established in international law. . . . The coastal State's civil jurisdiction extends to the limits of its territorial sea, although recognition is given in the balance of the rule to the existing practice of not exercising such jurisdiction in the case of ships that are traversing the territorial sea without contacting inland waters.[82]

But for this very important alteration, the principles of the 1930 Hague Final Act on the exercise of civil jurisdiction over merchant ships by coastal States were reproduced in the 1958 Geneva Convention on the Territorial Sea and the Contiguous Zone. This same provision has also been reproduced *verbatim* in the 1982 United Nations Convention, except for some minor drafting adjustments.

Article 28 of the 1982 Convention provides:

1. The coastal State should not stop or divert a foreign ship passing through the territorial sea for the purpose of exercising civil jurisdiction in relation to a person on board the ship.
2. The coastal State may not levy execution against or arrest the ship for the purpose of any civil proceedings, save only in respect of obligations or liabilities assumed or incurred by the ship itself in the course or for the purpose of its voyage through the waters of the coastal State.
3. Paragraph 2 is without prejudice to the right of the coastal State, in accordance with its laws, to levy execution against or to arrest, for the purpose of any civil proceedings, a foreign ship lying in the territorial sea, or passing through the territorial sea after leaving internal waters.

In view of the option granted to the coastal State to exercise or not its civil jurisdiction, the enumeration of the circumstances allowing such exercise contained in paragraphs 2 and 3 are indicative rather than exhaustive. Exercising civil jurisdiction when the ship has incurred obligations is necessary and obvious; exercising such jurisdiction when the ship is lying in the territorial sea or passing through the territorial sea after leaving internal waters is justifiable because the obligations in question are connected with the ship's sojourn in these waters rather than with the right of innocent passage. Except for these situations, the exercise of civil jurisdiction over merchant vessels can be cumbersome and wasteful for the coastal State.

4. Administrative jurisdiction over merchant ships in innocent passage

Even if in certain circumstances it could be argued that criminal and civil jurisdiction ought not to be exercised by the coastal State on merchant vessels in innocent passage, administrative jurisdiction is acknowledged as exclusively within the sphere of the coastal State for *all* ships. Without reviewing in detail the administrative prerogatives of a coastal State on all foreign ships in its territorial waters, an issue reserved for a future section, two provisions of the 1982 Convention are worth citing at this stage, namely, Article 21 on the laws and regulations of the coastal State relating to innocent passage, and Article 22 on sealanes and traffic separation schemes in the territorial sea. These provisions purport to give the coastal State a wide range of administrative competences over foreign ships in the territorial sea, not the least being the right to levy charges for services rendered to the ship (Article 26).

5. Conclusion

In sum, merchant vessels exercising the right of innocent passage are not completely free from 'control' by the coastal State. The discretion which coastal States enjoy to exercise criminal, civil and administrative jurisdiction in their territorial sea over foreign merchant vessels limits the exercise of that right. Accordingly, it would not be an exaggeration to say that the exercise of the right of innocent passage by merchant ships is, to some extent, subordinate to the exercise by the coastal State of its full territorial sovereignty over territorial waters.

However, as far as the jurisdictional prerogatives examined above are concerned, the coastal State nevertheless must show circumspection, for although it might in most cases have primary jurisdiction, nothing prevents the flag State from exercising concurrent jurisdiction on the same issue. Whether public or State vessels, which are in principle entitled to sovereign immunity, are faced with the same fate will be our next concern.

Notes

1. Excluded from this consideration is the question of implied or constructive flag State consent to coastal State jurisdiction, as a prerequisite to or result of entry by the foreign vessel into the territorial sea.
2. Under Section III of the 1958 Convention on the Territorial Sea and the Contiguous Zone and under Section 3 of Part II of the 1982 Convention, *all* ships (irrespective of their primary purpose) are entitled to innocent passage in foreign coastal waters.
3. '[C]ommercial passage is justified . . . The interests of the whole world are concerned in the possession of the utmost liberty of navigation for the purposes of *trade* by the vessels of all States.' Per Hall, W.E., *A Treatise on International Law*, 8th edn., Oxford, Clarendon Press, 1924, p. 198.
4. cf. 1982 Convention, Articles 19, 21 and 25.
5. Ibid., Articles 94, 95, 96 and 97(3), read together.

6. According to the 1982 Convention, these include piracy (Article 99), illicit traffic in narcotic drugs or psychotropic substances (Article 108), unauthorized broadcasting (Article 109), and slave trade (Articles 99 and 110(1) (b).
7. Grounds for jurisdiction apart from territoriality are: nationality, passive personality, security and universality. cf. Brownlie, Ian, *Principles of Public International Law*, 3rd edn., Oxford, Clarendon Press, 1979, pp. 300–4.
8. Jessup, P.C., *The Law of Territorial Waters and Maritime Jurisdiction*, New York, Jennings and Co., 1927, p. 122; cf. '*Lotus*' case, PCIJ, Series A, No. 10 (1927).
9. Brownlie, op. cit., note 7, p. 300.
10. loc. cit., note 8.
11. Ibid., pp. 18–19.
12. Ibid., p. 23.
13. Article 8.
14. Article 7.
15. Article 11.
16. Schedule of Points Drawn up by the League of Nations Preparatory Committee, 15 February 1928, LON, Doc. C.44.M.21.1928.V.
17. LON Doc. C.230.M.117.1930.V.
18. Ibid.
19. Gidel, G. *Le Droit international public de la mer*, vol. 3, Paris, Sirey, 1932–34, p. 251.
20. Ibid., p. 261.
21. Ibid., p. 261.
22. Scelle, G., *Manuel de droit international public*, Paris, Domat-Montchrestien, 1948, p. 435.
23. Ibid., pp. 435–6.
24. ILC, *Yearbook* 1956, vol. II, p. 275.
25. (First) UNCLOS, Official Records, vol. III, Doc. A/CONF.13/C.I/L.41, p. 221.
26. Ibid., p. 221.
27. Ibid., p. 117.
28. Ibid., p. 117.
29. Ibid., p. 219 (Doc. A/CONF.13/C.I./L.37).
30. Ibid., pp. 81–2.
31. Ibid., p. 226 (Doc. A/CONF.13/C.I./L.53).
32. Ibid., P. 217 (Doc. A/CONF.13/C.I./L.33).
33. Third UNCLOS, Official Records, vol. III, p. 196, Doc. A/CONF.62/C.2./L.19 (Fiji: Draft Articles Relating to Passage Through the Territorial Sea, Article 8).
34. Ibid., p. 203, Doc. A/CONF.62/C.2/L.26 (Bulgaria, GDR, Poland, USSR: Draft Articles on the Territorial Sea, Article 23).
35. Brownlie, op. cit., note 7, p. 298.
36. *Reg.* v. *Keyn* (1876) 2 Exch. Div. 63.
37. In Territorial Waters Jurisdiction Act (1878), whose Preamble emphasized that an offence committed by a person, whether or not a British subject, within the territorial waters of Her Majesty's dominions was an offence within the jurisdiction of the Lord High Admiral, even though committed on board, or by means of a foreign vessel.
38. Gidel, op. cit., note 19, p. 262.
39. Ibid., p. 261.
40. 1982 Convention, Article 27(2).
41. Ibid., Article 27(5).
42. See United Nations Legislative Series ST/LEG/SER.B/6, pp. 306 and 358 (United States Criminal Code of 1948).
43. By extending the boundaries to the limit of the three-mile belt of territorial sea as part of territory, the implication is that the criminal law extends over the territorial sea.

44. 1923, 43 Supreme Court 504; also see *All England Law Reports*, vol. 27, 1923, pp. 1306ff.
45. 7 Cranch 116, 136 (3 L. Ed. 287).
46. Quoted from Deak, F. and Ruddy F.S. (eds), *American International Law Cases 1783–1968*, New York, Oceana, vol. 5, 1973, p. 400.
47. Ibid.
48. The right of approach, as codified in Article 110 of the 1982 Convention, means that the boarding of a foreign merchant ship is not justified unless there is reasonable *suspicion* that the ship is engaged in piracy, slave trade or unauthorized broadcasting, or is of the same nationality as the warship exercising the right.
49. See, op. cit., note 42, p. 306 (on law enforcement, section 89, Coast Guard).
50. 589 F. 2d 862 (5th Cir. 1979), quoted in Nash, M.L., *Digest of United States Practice in International Law*, Washington, Department of State Publications, 1983, p. 838.
51. Butler, W.E., 'The Legal Regime of Russian Territorial Waters', *AJIL*, vol. 62, 1968, p. 70. cf. United Nations Legislative Series, ST/LEG/SER.B/6, p. 353.
52. Statute on the Protection of the State Boundary of the U.S.S.R., of 5 August 1960 (Gazette of the Supreme Soviet of the U.S.S.R. 1960, No. 34, item 324).
53. Article 36 of the Statute, quoted by Butler, op. cit., note 51, pp. 63–4.
54. Quoted from ibid. at p. 70.
55. *Reg.* v. *Keyn*, (1876) 2 Exch. Div. 63.
56. Found in United Nations Legislative Series, ST/LEG/SER.B/6, p. 355.
57. *Pianka* v. *The Queen* (P.C.), *Weekly Law Reports* 1977, No. 3, p. 859.
58. Although exception (d) in both Articles entitles the coastal State to exercise criminal jurisdiction for the suppression of ganja trade, Jamaican law considered such infringements as summary petty offences.
59. Op. cit., note 51, at p. 860.
60. Ibid., p. 865.
61. Ibid., p. 869.
62. Ibid., p. 875.
63. Found in United Nations Legislative Series, ST/LEG/SER.B/6, p. 336.
64. Décret No. 78–421 du 24 mars 1978, *Journal Officiel de la République Française*, Lois et Décrets 1979, No. 73, p. 1338. In a recent Decree on the subject, it is provided in Article 6 that: 'Les autorités . . . peuvent . . . imposer aux navires étrangers qui exercent le droit de passage inoffensif dans les eaux territoriales françaises, d'emprunter les voies de circulation qu'elles désigneront, et de respecter les dispositifs de séparation du trafic prescrits, notamment s'il s'agit de navires-citernes, de navires à propulsion nucléaires, de navires transportant des substances ou matières radioactives ou autres substances intrinsèquement dangereuses ou nocives.' Décret No. 85–185 du 6 février 1985, *Journal Officiel de la République Française*, Lois et Décrets 1985, No. 34, p. 1734.
65. The United States was among the first countries to protest 'such unilaterally imposed requirement that impinged upon the rights under international law . . . and innocent passage in the territorial seas' (see Nash, op. cit., note 50, p. 999).
66. Op. cit., note 64, at p. 1339.
67. United Nations Legislative Series, ST/LEG/SER.B/15, at p. 245.
68. Ibid., p. 250.
69. Ibid., at p. 251 (Section 3(2) (a) of the Decree).
70. Oppenheim, L., *International Law. A Treatise*, vol. 1: *Peace* (ed. by H. Lauterpacht), London, Longmans, 1962, p. 44.
71. Akinsaya, A., 'The Nigerian Territorial Waters Decrees of 1967 and 1971 in International Law', *Revue égyptienne de droit international*, vol. 32, 1976, p. 154.
72. For further details see Brownlie, I, *Principles of Public International Law*, Oxford,

Clarendon Press, 1979, particularly pp. 388ff.

73. 'Projet de règlement relatif à la mer territoriale en temps de paix', IDI, *Annuaire* 1928, p. 210; see also *AJIL*, vol. 23, 1929, Special Supplement, p. 369.
74. Harvard University, 'Law of Territorial Waters', *AJIL*, vol. 23, 1929, Special Supplement, p. 243.
75. LON Doc. C.230.M.117.1930.V., p. 9.
76. Ibid.
77. Brownlie, op. cit., note 7, p. 299.
78. Gidel, op. cit., note 19, p. 264.
79. Ibid.
80. Ibid.
81. (First) UNCLOS, Official Records, vol. III, p. 218, Doc. A/CONF.13/C.I/L.37.
82. Ibid., p. 243 (United States proposal), Doc. A/CONF.13/C.I/L.42.

Chapter 5

Public vessels and their exercise of the right of innocent passage

1. Public vessels other than warships and submarines

There is a general principle in international law, particularly in the Law of the Sea, which recognizes that public vessels, including warships and other 'State-owned seagoing structures', enjoy sovereign immunity when exercising the right of innocent passage.[1] However, due to the special characteristics of warships, since the Hague Codification Conference in 1930, all the Law of the Sea Conventions have made a distinction between public or State vessels other than warships and warships. A further distinction has been made between State vessels engaging in commerce, on the one hand, and vessels exclusively used for public purposes, on the other. Whereas the coastal State may not for any reason exercise its criminal, civil or administrative jurisdiction over the latter, it has been suggested by some that State vessels engaging in trade ought to be put on the same footing as ordinary merchant ships, without any immunities.

This suggestion was first formally adopted in the 1926 Brussels Convention on the Unification of Certain Rules Relating to the Immunity of State-Owned Vessels[2] which, unfortunately, was ratified by very few States.

However, at the 1930 Hague Codification Conference, the Second Committee, which dealt with the legal status of the territorial sea, adopted an Article 10 which followed the lines of the 1926 Brussels Convention.[3]

Article 10 acknowledged that the exercise of criminal and civil jurisdiction by coastal States over merchant ships was without prejudice to the question of the treatment of vessels exclusively employed in a governmental non-commercial service and of persons on board such vessels. In a commentary, it was noted that, as provided for in the 1926 Brussels Convention, vessels belonging to a government and operated by the latter for commercial purposes were not entitled to privileges and immunity from coastal State jurisdiction.[4]

The aim of subjecting this type of vessels to coastal State jurisdiction was of course to facilitate the presentation of maritime claims. Although the above rule did not reflect the trend in some other States, it was implicitly reaffirmed in the 1952 Brussels Convention Relating to the Arrest of Sea-Going Ships in connection with the propriety of arresting state-owned vessels used for commercial purposes.[5]

In the International Law Commission, opinions were split on the question of the immunity of State vessels operated for commercial purposes and on the merits of the 1926 Brussels Convention. The Special Rapporteur thought that State-owned vessels were to be treated in the same manner as private vessels if they were operated for commercial purposes, the Brussels Convention of 1926 having indicated that 'progressive' line of thought.[6] For other members of the Commission, 'the rule of international law was that State-owned vessels were immune from the jurisdiction of the ordinary courts. Conventions such as the Brussels Convention of 1926 were instruments whereby States voluntarily waived that privilege'.[7] While it was true that the Brussels Convention of 1926 had included for the first time a provision to the effect that State-owned vessels operated for commercial purposes should be treated as merchant ships, this fact proved that, under general international law, government vessels enjoyed immunity.[8]

In its final Draft Report to the General Assembly, the International Law Commission made the following comments on draft Article 22 dealing with government ships operated for commercial purposes:

(1) The Commission followed the rules of the Brussels Convention of 1926 concerning the immunity of government ships. It considered that these rules followed the preponderant practice of States and it therefore formulated Article 22 accordingly.
(2) Certain members felt unable to accept the rules of the Brussels Convention and opposed this Article.[9]

At the (First) Geneva Conference on the Law of the Sea of 1958, similar acrimony characterized the debates on the proposal to follow the rules embodied in the Brussels Conventions. Nevertheless, the resulting Geneva Convention on the Territorial Sea and the Contiguous Zone, in its Article 21, expressly considered subjecting government ships operated for commercial purposes to the same general rules as those applicable to merchant ships exercising the right of innocent passage, i.e. Articles 18 to 20 of that Convention. Thus on civil matters, for example, Article 20 prescribes that the qualified prohibition of execution or arrest of a foreign ship engaged in innocent passage is 'without prejudice to the right of the coastal State, in accordance with its laws, to levy execution against or to arrest, for the purpose of any civil proceedings a foreign ship lying in the territorial sea, or passing through the territorial sea after leaving internal waters'.

As could be expected, several States, while joining the 1958 Convention, have not hesitated to make reservations with respect to this assimilation, on the ground that immunity extends to all government ships irrespective of use or purpose. Several other States have, in turn, objected to these reservations.[10] A typical instance of the former is the reservation made by the German Democratic Republic in 1973 according to which that State 'considers that government ships in foreign territorial waters have immunity and that the measures set forth [for merchant ships] may therefore apply to such ships only with the consent of the flag State'.[11]

The 1982 United Nations Convention on the Law of the Sea virtually repeats the provisions of the 1958 Convention on the Territorial Sea and the Contiguous Zone. This being the case, similar reservations might be made by the same actors as regards the provisions included in the 1982 Convention.

One thing is quite certain, however: foreign government vessels operated for non-commercial purposes are immune from coastal State jurisdiction in the territorial sea. As regards government vessels operated for commercial purposes, many factors, some of which are independent of the provisions of the Convention, would determine their immunity or otherwise from coastal State jurisdiction in the territorial sea.[12] Whether this is the case with the exercise of the right of innocent passage by warships, a special category of government vessels operated for ostensibly non-commercial purposes, will be our next concern.

2. Warships and their exercise of the right of innocent passage

The question of whether or not warships[13] are entitled to the exercise of the right of innocent passage is still a matter of controversy.[14] Customary international law on the topic is not consistent, and State practice and national legislation are contradictory. The two main international instruments that are relevant—the 1958 Convention on the Territorial Sea and the Contiguous Zone, and the 1982 Convention—are not categorical on the issue. This is especially evident when the preparatory work of these instruments is analysed in detail. An extremely liberal interpretation would seem to suggest that the provisions of the two main international conventions acknowledge the 'right' for warships to exercise the right of innocent passage.

For a thorough appraisal of the situation, we should like to trace the evolution from the late nineteenth century, through the draft proposals of academic bodies and the 1930 Hague Codification Conference, until the first international judicial pronouncement on the topic. Then we shall systematically scrutinize the debates in the International Law Commission and in the (First) and Third United Nations Conferences on the Law of the Sea, where some prominence was given to this topic.

The question of the distinction between warships and other sea-going vessels became significant, with respect to the right of innocent passage, only late in the nineteenth century.[15] This was not because prior to that period both types of vessels enjoyed the right of innocent passage, but because, due to the prevalence of the 'property theory' on the territorial sea, a right to exclude *all* foreign shipping was generally conceded to the coastal State, which might tolerate foreign shipping as a matter of practice but was not required to do so.[16] However, although the potential threat represented by warships for the security of the coastal State was not overlooked, and was used in the nineteenth century as an argument against the passage of *all* ships[17] in territorial waters, since the turn of the century the question of the right of passage of warships has assumed increasing importance.[18] Some coastal States consider the exercise of the right of innocent passage by warships as a mere comity which could be withdrawn, the only consequence being that the withdrawal would be regarded as an unfriendly act. They therefore insist upon previous notification and/or authorization before the warship can exercise the right of innocent passage. Other States consider that warships have an unrestricted right of innocent passage which in practice no State has ever objected to in time of peace.

These divergent opinions persisted throughout the 1930 Hague Codification Conference and beyond.

In the course of the *North Atlantic Coast Fisheries* arbitration of 1910,[19] Mr Elihu Root (United States) made an observation that apparently influenced many governments and academic institutions which were preoccupied with draft projects on the territorial sea. The statement denied the existence of a right of innocent passage for warships. The reason given, which is still upheld in some quarters today, was that the simple appellation 'warships' taints the 'innocence' required for passage. Mr Root said: 'Warships may not pass without consent into this zone because they threaten. Merchant ships may pass because they do not threaten.'[20] A survey of the provisions contained in codification projects of the 1920s shows that this view found wide acceptance.

Thus, Article 12 of the 1926 Draft Convention communicated to various governments by the League of Nations Committee of Experts for the Progressive Codification of International Law provided that: 'The exercise by warships of the right of free passage may be subjected by the riparian State to special regulations.'[21]

Article 11 of the Resolution adopted by the Institut de droit international at its 1928 Stockholm session stated the following: 'Le libre passage des navires de guerre peut être assujetti a des règles spéciales par l'Etat riverain.'[22]

Somewhat ambiguously, but still echoing the same denial of warships' right of innocent passage, the Japanese International Law Association, acting in conjunction with the Japanese branch of the International Law Association, adopted in 1926 a draft text providing that: 'A man-of-war may enter the ports, harbours, roadsteads and littoral waters of every foreign State, in so far as her access thereto is in no way prohibited or restricted by the littoral State.'[23]

In the same vein, the text adopted at the 34th Conference of the International Law Association (ILA) in 1926 provided that:

> The ships of all countries, public as well as private, have the right to pass freely through territorial waters, *but are subject to the regulations* enacted by the State through whose territorial waters they pass, provided that such regulations do not infringe any of the provisions contained in this Convention.[24]

Much more ambiguous was Article 6 of Project No. 12 of the American Institute of International Law. This provision, adopted at the Rio de Janeiro session in 1927, began as follows: 'The entry of warships shall depend entirely upon the consent of the Republic sovereign of the port. In time of peace, such consent shall be *presumed*.'[25]

However, the existing ambiguity was dispelled by the commentary accompanying an article which dealt with jurisdiction over warships in foreign territorial waters and which was included in a Harvard Research draft of 1929. That commentary stated:

> The regulation of entrance and sojourn of foreign vessels of war has tended to become uniform and reciprocal in character. A State may properly object to the entrance of such a number of foreign vessels of war as might constitute a threat . . . The minimum of authority consistent with safety is therefore exercised over foreign vessels of war.[26]

That being the case, Jessup, who undoubtedly had some influence on the official American view of the subject at the time, though he was of the opinion that normally the passage of warships in territorial waters was not prohibited, thought that 'legally, it may be forbidden at any time'. He formulated a metaphor which has been seized on by governments and jurists interested in denying the existence of a right of passage for warships. Writing in 1927 and considering the prevailing opinions and State practice, Jessup stated that: 'As to warships, the sound rule seems to be that [warships] should not enjoy an absolute legal right to pass through a State's territorial waters any more than an army may cross the land territory.'[27]

(a) Perspectives in international fora and international judicial precedent

The Hague Codification Conference of 1930

True interaction between the views of academics, as represented by the various draft proposals, and perceptions of governments on the right of innocent passage of warships first occurred at the Hague Codification Conference of 1930. Apparently, the opinions expressed by academics were well received by governments.

Judging from the replies of governments to the Questionnaire addressed to them by the Preparatory Committee of the 1930 Conference, there appeared to be unanimity that the *regulation* of the passage and anchoring of warships by the coastal State was permissible.[28] The main divergence related to the meaning of the word 'regulation'. While some replies interpreted that term to imply previous notification, others took it to mean previous permission.[29] The most lengthy reply, made by Sweden, considered that 'regulation' meant none of the above but referred to the subjection of warships to similar navigational requirements as merchant ships.[30] Accordingly, the Preparatory Committee drafted as Bases of Discussion No. 20 and 21 a tentative article which read:

> A coastal State should recognise the right of innocent passage through its territorial waters of foreign warships, including submarines navigating on the surface.
> A coastal State is entitled to make rules regulating the conditions of such passage without, however, having the right to require a previous authorisation.
> A coastal State is entitled to make rules governing the anchoring of foreign warships in its territorial waters, but may not forbid anchoring in case of damage to the ship, or of distress.
> In foreign territorial waters, warships must respect the local laws and regulations. Any case of infringement will be brought to the attention of the captain: if he fails to comply with the notice so given, the ship may be required to depart.[31]

At the 1930 Conference, the discussion revealed little support for the above Bases of Discussion,[32] as is shown by the attitude of the American and Romanian delegations. The United States representative made the following remarks:

> In my view, the right of innocent passage as a matter of right does not extend to warships. It is ordinarily granted that the right of innocent passage is primarily in favour of commerce, and it seems to me that, so far as warships are concerned, the question is wholly one of usage and the comity of nations.

> A coastal State is, therefore, quite within its competence, at any rate as regards . . . its territorial sea . . . if it says that the right of innocent passage for warships does not exist there . . . If the question of innocent passage of warships through the territorial sea is purely a matter of comity, the coastal State, if it so desires, clearly has the right to require a previous authorisation.

The above view was supported by the Romanian delegate,[33] who justified the requirement of authorization and/or notification in the following way:

> The passage of a foreign warship through the territorial waters of a State, if not notified to it, may constitute a source of danger, especially . . . when the ship flies the flag of a power with which the State concerned has not established diplomatic relations.
> If [the warship] passes through the territorial waters of a State, some ulterior motive may be suspected. The warship may carry out unfriendly acts, such as taking soundings and charting.
> I think, therefore, that we ought to stipulate either that previous authorisation is necessary or that notification must be given, to enable the State concerned to take any precaution it considers advisable.[34]

In the debate, no delegation opposed the above views. The British delegate, who was concerned over the general tendency favouring previous authorization or at least previous notification, preferred to state his mild annoyance thus:

> I would leave matters exactly as they are at the present without attempting to define more precisely what the respective rights and obligations are . . . I . . . support the proposal of the delegate of the United States in so far as he suggests that this [innocent passage of warships] should be treated as a matter of international comity and courtesy . . .[35]

Articles 12 and 13 of the Final Act of the 1930 Conference on the Territorial Sea reflect the compromise finally reached during the discussions.

Article 12 stated that:

> *As a general rule*, a coastal State will not forbid the passage of foreign warships in its territorial sea and will not require a previous authorisation or notification, [although] the coastal State has the right to regulate the conditions of such passage.

And Article 13 provided that:

> If a foreign warship passing through the territorial sea does not comply with the regulations of the coastal State and disregards any request for compliance which may be brought to its notice, the coastal State may require the warship to leave the territorial sea.[36]

The commentary attached to these Articles, which could be used for ascertaining the meaning of the two texts, ran as follows:

> To state that a coastal State will not forbid the innocent passage of foreign warships through its territorial sea is but to recognize existing practice. That practice also, without laying down any strict and absolute rule, leaves to the

> State the power, in exceptional cases, to prohibit the passage of foreign warships in its territorial sea. The coastal State may regulate the conditions of passage, particularly as regards the number of foreign units passing simultaneously through its territorial sea—or through any particular portion of that sea—though as a general rule no previous authorisation or even notification will be required.
>
> Under no pretext, however, may there be any interference with the passage of warships through straits constituting a route for international maritime traffic between two parts of the high sea.
>
> A special stipulation to the effect that warships must, in the territorial sea, respect the local laws and regulations has been thought unnecessary. Nevertheless, it seemed advisable to indicate that on non-observance of these regulations the right of free passage ceases and that consequently the warship may be required to leave the territorial sea.[37]

From the above it could be inferred that, for the first time, an international instrument of such magnitude acknowledged that warships enjoyed extraterritoriality and perhaps, consequently, a 'limited' right of innocent passage through foreign territorial waters.

Extraterritoriality because if the warship violates coastal State laws or regulations, only the flag State could exercise jurisdiction. If the violation caused an injury to the coastal State, the latter would have to appeal directly to the flag State, without involving the ship itself. The only action the coastal State could take would be to ask the warship to leave the territorial sea. But what happens if the ship refuses to leave?

A 'limited' right (of innocent passage for warships) because, while Article 12(1) does recognize a right, albeit *as a general rule*, without requiring previous authorization or notification, Article 12(2) confers on the coastal State the power to regulate such passage. Some eminent authors have construed this as empowering the coastal State to require previous notification and/or authorization.[38]

Among these authors were Bustamante and Gidel. In analysing draft Articles 12 and 13 adopted by the 1930 Hague Conference, Gidel concluded that the formula contained in those provisions

> donne satisfaction à la tendance manifestée par les délégations américaine et britannique. Le passage des bâtiments des marines de guerre étrangères dans la mer territoriale n'est pas un droit mais une *tolérance*. C'est l'opinion qui semble préférable. Elle est mieux de nature à protéger certains Etats contre les abus auxquels ils pourraient être exposés du fait de voisins turbulents ou indiscrets.[39]

Turning to the question of whether the tolerance of the passage of warships provided for in Article 12 would leave room for forbidding such passage, Gidel asserted:

> La formule adoptée par la Commission et par la Conférence s'en tient à une formule empirique qui, tout en s'efforçant d'assurer dans la pratique et en dehors de circonstances exceptionnelles ('en règle générale') le passage des navires de guerre étrangers à travers la mer territoriale, donnerait cependant à

présumer le 'droit' au profit de l'Etat riverain de prendre les mesures qu'il lui est recommandé de laisser, en fait, de côté ('L'Etat riverain n'empêchera pas, etc. L'Etat riverain n'exigera pas, etc.').[40]

Bustamante, for his part, voiced a more qualified view, including practical considerations which might create a need for notification and/or authorization before a warship exercises the right of innocent passage. In a book published in English in 1930, almost simultaneously with the end of the 1930 Hague Codification Conference, he stated that:

> [warships] in principle should not pass through a foreign territorial sea unless the country to which they belong maintains diplomatic relations with the State possessing sovereignty over this sea, they must likewise obey all the special requirements laid down for them, among others perhaps the permission of the competent authority, the prohibition of visits to certain zones, the limitation of the numbers passing at the same time along the coast, the forbidding of the return of the same vessel except at certain intervals, and any other measures that may be imposed or demanded by national security.[41]

The question of innocent passage of warships in the Corfu Channel case

In the *Corfu Channel* case, judicial recognition was undoubtedly given to the existence of a *right* of passage of warships in international straits.[42] By contrast, the International Court of Justice avoided expressing an opinion on the right of warships in the 'ordinary' territorial sea.[43]

The parties in that case, the United Kingdom and Albania, however, referred to the scope of that right in their pleadings, as did some dissenting and individual opinions, despite the majority ruling that '. . . it is unnecessary to consider the more general question, much debated by the parties, whether States under international law have a right to send warships in time of peace through territorial waters not included in a strait.'[44]

In both the pleadings of the parties and the dissenting opinions where the right of passage of warships in 'ordinary' territorial waters was considered, strong reliance was placed on the 1930 Hague Conference and on the writings of various authors to substantiate the grant or the refusal of this right to warships.

In its Memorial, the British Government made the following remarks:

> The published regulations of the large majority of States and their practice previous to the Hague Conference of 1930 acknowledged a right of passage through territorial waters in the ordinary course of navigation for foreign shipping, whether merchant ships or warships . . . In time of peace—and, indeed, in time of war—warships habitually pass through the territorial waters of other States without notice or authorisation when using them as a mere channel of passage.[45]

In its Counter-Memorial, the Albanian Government reminded the Court that the British delegate at the 1930 Hague Conference had agreed with his American counterpart that the passage of warships through territorial waters depended on comity since '[l]e droit de passage inoffensif, en tant que droit, ne s'étend pas aux bâtiments de guerre . . . L'Etat riverain a bien le droit d'exiger une autorisation préalable, si bon lui semble'. The Counter-Memorial then cited the notion of 'tolerance' advocated by Gidel and the statement made by Elihu Root in the *North Atlantic Fisheries* arbitration, to the effect that 'warships may not pass without consent because they threaten'. Article 12 of the Hague Final Act of 1930, with its reference to a 'general rule', was invoked *a contrario* to justify, in exceptional circumstances of which the coastal State was the sole judge, the requirement of previous notification or authorization for passage of warships.[46]

In its Reply, the British Government pointed out that Albania did not refer to the practice of States on the issue, 'which in questions of customary law is of decisive importance as evidence of the existing law'. Consequently, Article 12 cited by Albania in support of the view that the passage of warships was subject to notification or authorization, could not be regarded 'as necessarily stating existing law'. The Reply did admit that the British Government had accepted the United States position at the 1930 Codification Conference, to the effect that the passage of warships through territorial waters was a matter of courtesy rather than of right. But, it explained, this acceptance was a concession to the United States' point of view 'for the sole purpose of promoting an agreement on the draft Convention as a whole and in particular to smooth the way for the settlement of the controversial issue of the extent of territorial seas'. The Reply went on to maintain that that statement, being a mere concession made in the course of a negotiation, had been withdrawn and was of no effect when no agreement was reached as a result of the breakdown of the Conference.[47]

During the oral proceedings, the two sides reiterated and clarified their respective positions. Mr Cot, for Albania, re-emphasized the reasons for the refusal to consider passage of warships as a genuine right and said:

> Ces raisons sont simples et fortes, elles résultent de la nature des choses, du bon sens, de la différence qui existe du point de vue des relations internationales entre la navigation des navires de commerce et celle des navires de guerre . . . En temps de paix, en effet, les navires marchands sont les instruments nécessaires de la vie économique. En temps de paix, au contraire, les navires de guerre sont dans une situation un peu différente: ou bien ils sont des instruments de prestige ou bien ils sont des instruments politiques—on peut même, à cause de leur beauté, les considérer comme des sortes de jouets magnifiques, mais un peu dangereux . . . le passage du navire de guerre doit être toujours considéré en fonction des circonstances et notamment en fonction de la sécurité de l'Etat riverain, ce qui prouve à l'évidence que l'on n'est pas en présence d'un véritable droit—car le droit n'est pas arbitraire—et que l'on se trouve en présence d'une question qu'on laisse régler souverainement, comme il convient, par l'Etat riverain.[48]

Mr Cot then affirmed:

> Il est normal qu'on laisse passer dans ses eaux territoriales les navires de guerre d'un pays allié, d'un pays ami ou d'un pays qui ne peut avoir aucun différend avec vous. Mais il est anormal qu'en période de troubles on accorde les mêmes faveurs, sans aucune discrimination, à tous les navires de guerre étrangers.

To substantiate further and illustrate his points, he went on to quote Root's dictum that 'Warships threaten'; Hall's treatise, where it is written that warships do not have the same right to navigate in territorial seas as merchant ships, which serve the economic objectives of the international community; and Oppenheim's treatise, which limits right of passage of warships to major routes of international navigation. Finally, Mr Cot referred to the negotiations at the 1930 Hague Conference and to draft Article 12 which featured in the Final Act of that Conference. He concluded that the wording of the commentary on that Article invested the coastal State with the power, in exceptional circumstances, to prohibit the passage of foreign warships.[49]

For the counsel of the British Government, Sir Eric Beckett, it was the practice of States that mattered, rather than the opinions of writers on which the Albanian Government had relied. Referring to the 1930 Conference, Beckett pointed out that the Hague draft or Final Act was not an agreed instrument, Article 12 being a 'palpably compromise draft *de lege ferenda*' and not a statement of international law. He further maintained that it was the statements or replies made in the framework of the Conference that represented the views of governments as to the existing law, rather than opinions expressed in the subsequent negotiations. Commenting on the remarks by Hall quoted by Mr Cot, that the right of passage possessed of merchant ships derived from their special importance to the economic life of the international community, Sir Eric quoted Westlake who had stated that '. . . a ship of war as well as a merchantman may have a lawful errand beyond the littoral sea . . .'. He went on to cite authors such as Fauchille[50] and Spiropoulos.[51] As a specific reply to Mr Cot's characterization of warships as instruments of prestige and policy, he contended that:

> even in time of peace, warships may often have other proper services to discharge. Yet, apart from the repression of piracy . . . they police fisheries under international agreement and perform many other useful and humanitarian services. Further, a visit to foreign ports of a fleet or a warship is often as productive of goodwill as the mission of a special ambassador, and to get to the port of the State which is their host, the warships may well wish to pass through the territorial waters of another State.

Nevertheless, stressing what he termed '. . . the international rule . . . which constitutes the compromise formed by practice and the necessities of life', Sir Eric affirmed:

> We say that warships have a right of passage, but a qualified one—qualified by the right of the coastal State to exclude, if in fact it has reasonable and *bona fide* grounds for doing so based on the needs of defence. This surely is a most reasonable compromise. To make the warships' passage a matter of comity merely is not a compromise at all . . . We should agree that if one State alone gives solid grounds to the coastal State for anxiety concerning its security, the exceptional limitation on passage may be directed only towards that State, but the grounds for withholding customary right from one State must . . . be solid grounds: and by solid grounds I mean more than caprice or morbid suspicion.

Finally, considering whether the absence of diplomatic relations with a State could constitute such solid grounds for refusal to allow the passage of warships in the territorial sea, Sir Eric concluded his remarks in the following way:

> I can quite see that the question of diplomatic relations is material in a question of comity, but the existence of diplomatic relations can by itself have no bearing on the exercise of a general customary right possessed by all States. Otherwise, a State, by breaking off diplomatic relations without any justification, could terminate the customary rights of another State. There are many cases where States, which are most afraid of each other, are in full diplomatic relations, and others where States, which in no way threaten each other, have no diplomatic relations.

A reappraisal of the contentions of the parties shows that the question of who was to judge the existence of exceptional circumstances was at the core of their debate: the coastal State (Albanian thesis) or the flag State (British thesis)?

As stated earlier, the dissenting or individual opinions of some judges consider at length the question of the passage of warships in 'ordinary' territorial waters, although the judgment of the Court reserved any comment on the issue. As had been the case in the pleadings, the opinions of the judges mainly supported or rejected the views of writers.

Judge Azevedo, who made the most lengthy statement on the issue,[53] examined most aspects of the British argument. Agreeing with Hall's principle cited by Albania, and refuting Fauchille's view referred to by Sir Eric Beckett, Judge Azevedo said:

> The right of passage of foreign vessels through the territorial sea is founded on freedom of trade, which presupposes freedom of navigation as the principal means of its accomplishment . . .
> The position is quite different as regards the passage of warships, both as concerns the principle and in many cases its application.
> No doubt, this transit [of warships] is also founded on freedom of navigation; but here the same means serves different ends. And in consequence we arrive at different conclusions. We must mistrust any hasty analogy, and reject explanation such as that of Fauchille, who considered a navy as an accessory to a merchant fleet, just as in the days of corsairs and piracy.[54]

As regards the existence of a customary rule permitting warships to exercise the right of passage in foreign territorial waters, asserted by the British delegate despite the 1930 Hague Final Act and despite the contrary opinion of some writers, Judge Azevedo both agreed and disagreed with the British position.

He agreed that custom prevailed over the views of writers, although Article 38 of the Court's Statute did not establish an order of precedence for the different sources of law. He disagreed on the existence of a custom by stating:

> But it is very doubtful whether a customary practice in this matter can be shown to exist, owing to the vagueness of the precedents. As in the case of possession, these uncertainties are a bar to the causative and confirmative action of time. And the mere lapse of time, according to customary law, does

> not suffice to establish a title by prescription: *in facultativis non datur praescriptio.*[55]

Concluding his comments, Judge Azevedo said:

> To sum up, it is evident that all the arguments invoked are clouded in confusion at any rate sufficiently to bar the recognition of a custom in accordance with traditional requirements . . . In short the passage of warships through territorial waters is subject to a precarious régime which may be modified, in a reasonable manner, by the coastal State.[56]

Expressing his individual opinion, Judge Alvarez, contemplating a perfect world under the umbrella of the United Nations, considered that merchant ships possess an unquestionable right of passage through the territorial sea, since they are discharging a peaceful mission and are contributing to the development of good relations between peoples. Then he stated the following semi-utopian view:

> The position is not the same in the case of warships. As war has been outlawed henceforward, the mission of these ships can only be to ensure the legitimate defence of the countries to which they belong. Therefore, although they may effect an innocent passage through straits . . ., in other cases [i.e. in the territorial seas] the coastal States are entitled to regulate the passage, especially with a view to the protection of their own security or interests but they are not entitled to forbid it. Warships only enjoy an unrestricted right of passage when they are engaged in an international mission assigned to them by the United Nations.

Judge Krylov, on the question of the innocent passage by warships belonging to one State through the territorial waters of another, argued that:

> The Hague Conference of 1930 for the Codification of International Law failed in its efforts to regulate the regime of territorial waters. The practice of States in this matter is far from uniform, and it is impossible to say that an international custom exists in regard to it. We only dispose of scattered sources—suggestions by international associations, doctrines of learned authorities, etc. . . . Accordingly, the right to regulate the passage of warships through its territorial waters appertains to the coastal State.[58]

We are of the opinion that although the International Court reserved the question of passage of warships in the 'ordinary' territorial sea, the pleadings of the parties in the case and the dissenting or individual opinions of some judges could be indicative of probable trends regarding the scope of such a 'right' for warships. If these views are taken into consideration persuasively, the weight of opinion is that warships do not have an independent right of passage in territorial seas but a conditional one, that is, a right whose exercise is subject to coastal State control, through the examination of advance notification or request for authorization which can be accepted or refused. An indicative list of factors which could influence coastal States' judgment in this respect were enumerated by Judge Azevedo when he said:

> insistence on authorisation or prior notification . . . would be justifiable in certain circumstances; for instance in a state of war, which in fact is a great

handicap to the movements of merchant ships as Brüel has mentioned several times.

Then there are the cases of tension between neighbouring countries, to which Gidel alludes, when frontier incidents are constantly occurring; and these may well justify the action of a weaker State, alarmed by the territorial claims of another.

Similarly, absence of diplomatic relations must be recognized as sufficient ground for refusing leave of passage; since this presupposes the existence of good relations.

Bustamante has specially emphasized this point . . . Gidel supports him, in spite of the silence of the Hague Conference on the subject.[59]

The right of innocent passage of warships as seen by the International Law Commission

Taking the *Corfu Channel* case as precedent and the 1930 Codification Conference as a watershed, the International Law Commission, from 1954 onwards, began to debate in earnest the passage of warships in foreign territorial waters.

The Commission adopted Article 12 of the 1930 Hague Codification draft verbatim; the provision became Article 26 of its own draft. Whereas some members considered that the international law in force did acknowledge a right of passage of warships in the territorial seas of a foreign State, others thought that that statement was inaccurate.[60]

Supporting the first view, François, the Special Rapporteur of the Commission said that the replies received from governments by the Preparatory Commission of the 1930 Conference expressed a unanimous view on the subject. Lauterpacht, who shared this view, pointed out that none of the States which had replied to the 1930 Questionnaire had denied the right of foreign warships to pass through the territorial sea. But he did admit that though international custom and usage tended to acknowledge that right, the latter had not been granted in the same unqualified terms for warships as for merchant ships.

Strongly opposing the view that warships enjoy a right of passage in the territorial sea, Mr Zourek, referring to the replies to the 1930 Questionnaires,[61] stated that in those replies many States had also pointed out that they considered themselves fully authorized to regulate the conditions of passage, a statement which implied the possibility of passage being forbidden in certain cases. He added that only some 20 States out of the approximately 60 maritime powers existing at the time had replied to the Questionnaire. Considering the term 'passage' to involve '. . . stopping and anchoring incidental to ordinary navigation . . .', he then wondered how, though justifiable for merchant ships, this could be necessary and logical for warships without any prior knowledge of the coastal State.

At the resumed session of 1955, Mr François observed that Article 26—Article 12 of the Hague Codification—had given rise to a number of observations by governments. One was that the coastal State could, if necessary, temporarily suspend the right of innocent passage in definite areas of its territorial sea. The other was that the coastal State was entitled to require previous authorization or notification not in all cases, but only in exceptional circumstances. However, several governments objected to these two points on the ground that previous authorization or notification was in fact already required by many countries.[62]

As the debate developed, it became clear that more than a matter of drafting was involved. For the Chairman, the Commission had to decide whether in principle the coastal State had the right to forbid passage. In other words, the Commission had to decide whether it would instruct its Drafting Committee to characterize the coastal State's privilege to interfere with the passage of foreign warships as a right or as a mere faculty to be exercised in certain extreme cases. Recalling the 1930 Codification Conference—in the work of which he had participated—the Chairman considered that draft Article 12, which corresponded to Article 26 of the Commission's provisional articles, provided the answer. The first paragraph of Article 12 had read: 'As a general rule a coastal State will not forbid . . .' Consequently, the Conference had merely made a *recommendation* to States not to forbid the passage of foreign warships through their territorial sea in the majority of cases. Had it intended altogether to deny the coastal State the right to prohibit passage, the paragraph would have read: 'The coastal State has no right to forbid . . .' In conclusion, therefore, the Chairman admitted that, as a matter of principle, the coastal State was entitled to prohibit the passage of foreign warships through its territorial sea, although it was recommended that that right be exercised sparingly.[63]

Apparently associating himself with the views of the Chairman, Mr Scelle added that the coastal State did not simply have a *right* to forbid the passage of foreign warships through its territorial sea; it might well have the *duty* to do so in certain circumstances.[64]

Having stated the principle, the Chairman invited Mr Zourek, member of the Commission, to suggest the wording for the question on which the Commission should be asked to vote. The question read: 'Does the coastal State enjoy, in virtue of its sovereignty over the territorial sea, the general right to forbid the passage of foreign warships through its territorial sea—in other words, the right to make such passage subject to previous authorisation or notification?' The Chairman added that if the Commission accepted the principle, it would do so on the clear understanding that the right in question must be construed in the light of international usage and standing practice concerning its exercise. The principle was approved by 6 votes to 3, with 4 abstentions.

Two members of the commission who voted against the principle thought that it had the implication that, in any and all circumstances, the coastal State had the right to prevent *even* the innocent passage of foreign warships through its territorial sea. For these members, the issue was: where passage is permissible, it must be innocent; where the coastal State could forbid it, it cannot be innocent.

For two other members of the Commission, who accepted the principle, any refusal to acknowledge the coastal State's right in the matter would be tantamount to denying to that State the exercise of its sovereignty over its territorial sea.

Considering the views so far expressed, the text of Article 26 as elaborated by the Drafting Committee for study by the Commission in 1956 read as follows:

> The coastal State may make the passage of warships through the territorial sea subject to previous authorisation or notification. Normally it shall grant

innocent passage subject to the observance of the provisions of Articles 19 and 20. Submarines shall navigate on the surface.

In this form, the Article was adopted by 8 votes to 2 with 1 abstention; and its whole text was transmitted to the 1956 session of the Commission for general review and final adoption.[65]

Article 26 relating to the passage of warships became Article 25 at the 1956 session of the Commission.[66] On this occasion, the focus of debate was on Article 26 of the 1955 text which had made it clear that the right of passage of warships was a concession contingent on the consent of the coastal State: hence the justification for the requirement of previous notification and authorization. Criticizing this view, Sir Gerald Fitzmaurice said that it neither accurately enunciated international law nor reflected international practice. He further warned that in a set of articles destined to codify existing law, the Commission should not introduce an innovation which would be in conflict with usage.

Recapitulating remarks made by him in previous sessions, Sir Gerald said that a clear distinction had to be drawn between the visit by a foreign warship to the port of a coastal State and passage through some part of that State's territorial sea. International practice, he went on, was that in the former case notification was always given, whereas in the latter, which involved mere passage, that formality was not required.

Furthermore, as he saw it, the view that previous notification was required resulted from an erroneous conception of both the function of warships in time of peace and of the reasons behind the desire for recognition of the right of innocent passage. In practice, therefore, warships had the right to proceed with their lawful mission, just like any other vessel, and passage of warships through the territorial sea was due to the fact that such a course was the only one available, or that that course was along a normal shipping lane, or that, on account of weather or other special conditions, it was the most practicable highway. In conclusion, Sir Gerald referred to Articles 16 to 19 of the Commission's draft (which dealt with the duties of coastal and flag States during the exercise of the right of innocent passage), which were to apply to all vessels and thus provided adequate safeguards against abuse by warships, including the right to suspend passage under certain conditions. Why then call for previous authorization or notification? In practice, the coastal State would gain nothing by such a provision, which would merely constitute an impediment to navigation.

A series of comments made by the United Kingdom Government and circulated at the time stressed, however, that there was no question of disputing the right of the coastal State to regulate the passage of warships through the territorial sea.[67] In addition, it listed four considerations that should govern the treatment of warships by the Commission. The fourth consideration was connected with the tendency of some countries to claim large expanses of territorial sea.

On the basis of the three-mile limit, the comment conceded, the passage of foreign warships through the territorial sea might be the cause of some apprehension for the coastal State, while there would be none with an extension to 12 nautical miles. Georges Scelle fully endorsed this remark, as did El-Khouri who pointed out that the tendency towards a 12-mile territorial sea would result in most of the maritime highways of the world falling within territorial waters.

Krylov, who led those supporting the 1955 text in opposition against Sir Gerald Fitzmaurice, made reference to Gidel, the statement of Elihu Root in the *North Atlantic Coast Fisheries* arbitration, and to State practice. He also affirmed that, in view of the changed situation brought about by the advent of the Charter of the United Nations—in 1955 Scelle had already made this point—the 1955 draft was an accurate reflection of contemporary conditions. Concerning Fitzmaurice's reference to the navigational aspect of the passage of foreign warships through the territorial sea, Krylov argued that free navigation was a function of merchant ships but not of warships. With the possible exception of cadet training ships, he went on, warships did not navigate ocean waters without top official instructions. They proceeded from one place to another under government orders, which, according to him, was a different matter.

Zourek, who endorsed Krylov's remarks, went on to emphasize what he thought to be the reason for the existence of a special regime, under international law, of innocent passage of warships. He pinpointed the danger the mere presence of a foreign warship in the territorial waters constituted for the coastal State and for the peace of mind of its nationals. A warship was, after all, a combatant unit of the armed forces of a State. As international law prohibited the free entry of foreign land forces into the territory of a State, there was, according to Zourek, every reason to follow the same approach in respect of the passage of warships through the territorial sea, which forms part of the national territory.

Taking the floor once again, Scelle considered that the territorial sea, the contiguous zone and the high seas, though different from the legal standpoint, were, from the practical angle of navigation, all parts of a single element, the sea. Navigation remained navigation, whether the ship was a merchant ship or a warship. Then he invoked the metaphor of the policemen who, fortunately, have the same rights of movement on the highway as ordinary citizens, for otherwise the only persons who would be able to move freely would be brigands. In the same way, warships—the policemen of the seas—had the same normal rights of passage as merchant vessels. To Scelle, Mr Zourek's conception of the purely defensive role of warships would severely restrict their usefulness. Warships could not perform their task if perpetually anchored in their home roadstead. If they were not permitted to pass through territorial waters, they would have no stopover rights ('droit d'escale') and, hence, be unable to circulate freely on the high seas. Regarding the concept of comity in connection with the permission for warships to pass through the territorial sea, Scelle was of the view that international comity, though it had at one time served as a substitute for international law, could not serve as a basis for any rule. Finally, concerning the United Nations Charter, Scelle pointed out that though no agreements had been concluded under Chapter VII, particularly under Article 43, regarding the armed forces to be made available to the Security Council by the members of the United Nations, it was inconceivable that, were there a threat of war, members would not take measures to support the action of the Council. And with the possibility of a sudden invasion, there was no reason to restrict the right of passage of warships.

Following these remarks, some members of the Commission took the floor to counter Scelle's observations. Regarding the reference to Chapter VII of the Charter, Liang, Secretary of the Commission, said that as soon as an international police force would come into being pursuant to Article 43 of the Charter, no notification or authorization would be necessary with respect to warships belonging to that force. This provoked a rejoinder by Zourek who pointed out that, under Article 43 of the United Nations Charter, the placing of armed forces (i.e. an international police force), with assistance and facilities including rights of passage, at the disposal of the Security Council, was not automatic, but conditional on the conclusion of a special agreement or agreements. In any case, Liang added, the 1955 draft text envisaged other, more normal situations which had nothing to do with the application of enforcement measures by the United Nations.

Having consulted the laws and regulations of States at the disposal of the Secretariat, the Secretary of the Commission observed that many countries subjected the passage of warships through their territorial sea to previous authorization or notification. The reasons were, according to him, that for many people the idea of foreign warships was closely associated with that of a display of force; thus, States suspicious of foreign warships had reasons to enact such provisions. Moreover, since warships constituted a far greater threat to the safety of traffic than commercial shipping, previous authorization and/or notification ought to be regarded as a necessary precaution.

However, Liang admitted that the requirement of authorization or notification was subject to two qualifications not open to dispute. The first was the right of warships of a State to enter another State's waters during a storm or other emergency, while the second was the absolute right of passage through straits normally used for international navigation between two parts of the high seas. In other cases, he concluded, previous notification appeared to be called for on grounds of common sense and of general practice.

On the notion of 'droit d'escale', which Scelle invoked in favour of the right of warships to pass in the territorial sea, Zourek observed that that notion was quite different from the right of innocent passage. Furthermore, he continued, there was no rule of international law calling on States to open their ports to warships of other States, though they might of course be admitted in cases of distress.

Dwelling on Scelle's example comparing the right of a policeman and of an ordinary citizen to move on the highway to that of a warship, the policeman of the sea, to be entitled to the same kind of passage as commercial shipping, Amado rejected the idea by using this simple illustration: If an armed foreigner enters a State's territory, the police have a perfect right to ascertain his intentions. Why, therefore, Amado wondered, must a State tolerate the presence of powerful naval units in its territorial waters without even having the right to know the reason for their presence?

As the debate neared completion, Sir Gerald Fitzmaurice once more took the floor and pointed out that there was a tendency to introduce ideological and sociological considerations which were not really germane to the subject. He maintained that under modern conditions, the threat to the security of the coastal State, inherent in the passage of warships through its territorial sea, was totally unreal. He argued that warships could bombard a coast with the utmost accuracy from a distance of 40 miles or more, and aircraft carriers could operate from a distance of 250 miles or more. Thus, there was no need for warships wishing to commit hostile acts to enter the territorial sea and, if they wished to do so, they certainly would not ask for previous authorization. With reference to Zourek's earlier remarks, Sir Gerald acknowledged that he had only established points upon which all were already agreed. There had always been certain reservations regarding the right of innocent passage of warships. The fact remained, he went on, that the practice of States, on which international law was ultimately founded, normally allowed for the passage of foreign warships through the territorial sea without authorization or notification. Indeed, he was prepared to wager that the admiralties of most States equipped with warships, though notifying other States from time to time, did not regard themselves as bound to do so in cases of ordinary passage of warships, without stopping, through the territorial sea. That being the case, and despite Mr Krylov's claims to the contrary, the navigational needs and rights of a warship travelling normally from one point to another are identical with those of a commercial vessel.

Considering the core of the divergence on the 1955 text to be tied to the question of whether the right of innocent passage of warships was subject to previous authorization or notification, Edmonds suggested that a vote be taken on the issue. Spiropoulos stated that he had no strong feelings either way, but was interested in enabling the Commission to reach a solution. In this connection, and considering that the 1930 Codification Conference had approached the question in a much calmer fashion, he suggested that the 1955 text be amended to be in line with Article 12(1) of the 1930 text. This proposal was rejected by 9 votes to 3, with 2 abstentions. Thus, Articles 26 and of course 27 of the 1955 text, which had become Articles 25 and 26, were adopted without change.

After having been processed by the Commission's Drafting Committee, the final text submitted to the General Assembly became Article 24 and read as follows: 'The coastal State may make the passage of warships through the territorial sea subject to previous authorisation or notification. Normally, it shall grant innocent passage subject to the observance of the provisions of articles 17 and 18' (dealing respectively with rights of protection of the coastal State and the duties of foreign ships during their passage).

The commentary which followed that text left no doubt that the tendency was towards a restriction of the innocent passage of warships in territorial waters. It read as follows:

> (1) At its sixth session in 1954, the Commission took the view that passage should be granted to warships without prior authorisation or notification. At its seventh session in 1955, after noting the comments of certain governments and reviewing the question, the Commission felt obliged to amend this Article so as to stress the right of the coastal State to make the right of passage of warships through the territorial sea subject to previous authorisation or notification. Where previous authorisation is required, it should not normally be subject to conditions other than those laid down in Articles 17 and 18. In certain parts of the territorial sea, or in certain special circumstances, the

> coastal State may, however, deem it necessary to limit the right of passage more strictly in the case of warships than in that of merchant ships. The 1955 Article provides a clearer recognition of this right than the 1954 text.
> (2) The Commission reconsidered this matter at its eighth session, in the light of the comments of certain governments, which pointed out that in practice passage was effected without formality and without objection on the part of coastal States. The majority of the Commission, however, saw no reason to change its view. While it is true that a large number of States do not require previous authorisation or notification, the Commission can only welcome this attitude, which displays a laudable respect for the principle of freedom of communications, but this does not mean that a State would not be entitled to require such notification or authorisation if it deemed it necessary to take this precautionary measure. Since it admits that the passage of warships through the territorial sea of another State can be considered by that State as a threat to its security, and is aware that a number of States do require previous notification or authorisation, the Commission is not in a position to dispute the right of States to take such a measure. But so long as a State has not enacted—and duly published—a restriction upon the right of passage of foreign warships through its territorial sea, such ships may pass through those waters without previous notification or authorisation, provided that they do not lie in them or put in at a port. In these latter cases previous authorisation—except in cases of putting in through stress of weather—is always required. The Commission did not consider it necessary to insert an express stipulation to this effect since Article 15, paragraph 4, applies equally to warships.[68]

Finally, the Commission added that '. . . the coastal State may not interfere in any way with the innocent passage of warships through straits normally used for international navigation between two parts of the high seas; hence the coastal State may not make the passage of warships through such straits subject to any previous authorisation or notification'. It also pointed out that 'the Article does not affect the rights of States under a convention governing passage through the straits to which it refers'.

Innocent passage of warships in the (First) Geneva Conference on the Law of the Sea (1958)

At the 1958 Geneva Conference on the Law of the Sea, the United States,[69] the United Kingdom[70] and The Netherlands[71] submitted proposals for the rejection of draft Article 24 of the International Law Commission's final text. Meanwhile, the Soviet Union, Poland, Saudi Arabia and Turkey made representations[72] in support of that Article subjecting the passage of warships to previous notification and/or authorization.

At an early stage of the Conference, in the First Committee, the United States and Britain withdrew their proposals without, however, endorsing the Commission's draft article.

The Dutch delegation stated that it could not accept the text since it was their conviction that, under customary international law, foreign warships had the right of passage through the territorial seas without 'let or hindrance'. As far as the security of the coastal State was concerned, Articles 17 (measures to protect the coastal State) and 25 (right to ask the warship to leave the territorial sea if it refuses to obey the rules on passage) afforded that State sufficient protection.

As a gesture of compromise, the Federal Republic of Germany introduced a proposal[73] whose effect it was to allow coastal States to make the passage of warships through their territorial sea dependent on previous notification without, however, requiring authorization. According to the German delegation,

> mere notification would be quite sufficient to meet the requirements of security. To make warships subject to the long and complicated procedure of obtaining formal authorization would be to place an unnecessary obstacle in the way of navigation.[74]

Lending indirect support to the above proposal, and replying to a British proposal reinstating an absolute right of innocent passage through straits on the basis of the ICJ judgment in the *Corfu Channel* case, the Yugoslav delegation made the following remarks:

> The United Kingdom . . . tended to interpret the judgment in the *Corfu Channel* case somewhat too widely. The Court had admittedly held that warships required no previous authorization, but there was no mention in its judgment of notification.[75] The giving of advance notice was principally a sign of goodwill, but it also enabled the coastal State to give the proposed passage sufficient publicity to prevent alarm among the population.[76]

The Danish representative likewise supported the proposal of the Federal Republic of Germany:

> The solution proposed [by Federal Republic of Germany] satisfied his delegation because it did not preclude the possibility of previous notification being required for passage through the territorial sea and through international straits which were subjected to the same regime but did not admit a requirement of previous authorization.[77]

The Soviet delegation, on the other hand, strongly defended the draft text of the International Law Commission which represented '. . . the fruit of long and careful study . . . and the principle stated therein reflected the practice of many States which considered the passage of warships as a problem apart because of the element of risk involved'.

With regard to the assertion made by The Netherlands and German delegations that requests for authorization might involve onerous procedures and delays on navigation, the Soviet delegate categorically stated: 'The U.S.S.R. delegation could not accept that view, since the paramount interests of a State should not be subordinated to a desire for haste in some other quarter.'[78]

In the First Committee of the Conference, where most of the preliminary debate took place, a vote was taken on the German proposal to delete from the International Law Commission's text the words 'authorization or', leaving only the 'notification'. Although one might think that notification followed by swift rejection to allow passage would have the same final effect as the lack of an authorization to pass, most members of the First Committee were not convinced by this argument. By a vote of 35 to 22, and 8 abstentions, the German proposal was rejected. With minor drafting amendments, the International Law Commission's draft text subjecting the passage of warships to notification and authorization was adopted by a vote of 54 to 5, with only 8 members abstaining.[79]

From the First Committe, the text went to the Plenary Conference for a final debate. Here procedural matters were at the forefront. Predicting that the text of the First Committee would not be adopted, Denmark resurrected the earlier German proposal making the passage of warships subject to previous notification only, with the addition of a direct reference to Articles 15 to 18 dealing with what is or is not innocent passage. In the same spirit, Italy sought a separate vote on the words 'authorization or'. The United Arab Republic and Czechoslovakia opposed the idea of separate votes, and the Soviet Union, seconded by Romania, pointed out that the Danish proposal was in reality not a proposal but an amendment aimed at deleting the words 'authorization or' from the First Committee's text. Consequently, the amendments to that text had to be voted upon before decidiing whether a separate vote should be held on the words 'authorization or'.

For Romania, to consider the Danish text or document as a proposal rather than an amendment to the text of the First Committee would have meant having two separate votes on the same subject:

> It was a mere procedural device intended to enable the opponents of the requirement of prior authorization to secure the deletion of the words 'authoriziation or' by simple majority. If they were not successful in the separate vote, they would have a second bite at the cherry when the Danish document was voted on.[80]

The President of the Conference ruled that the Danish document was considered to be a proposal rather than an amendment because it amounted to another formulation of Article 24 of the First Committee text (in the event of the latter not being adopted). That being the case, the text of the First Committee had to be voted on first, because:

> the Danish document had been submitted as a proposal and not as an amendment, and that the text approved by the First Committee must therefore be voted on first according to the usual practice. After that vote had taken place, the Conference would be free to decide whether or not there should be a vote on the Danish proposal.[81]

The Italian motion for a separate vote on the words 'authorization or' contained in the First Committee draft was put up and adopted by a vote of 50 to 24, with 5 abstentions. The vote on the words 'authorization or', which followed, resulted in 45 votes for its deletion, 27 against, with 6 abstentions.[82]

In explaining the votes for or against the deletion of the words 'authorization or', the Soviet Union said that it had voted for the retention of these words because it considered that in the exercise of its sovereign right every coastal State could claim the right to subject foreign warships wishing to enter its territorial waters to the requirement of prior authorization.

Many of those who shared this view said that they were going to vote against the new Article altogether. On the other hand, among those who supported the deletion of the words 'authorization or' was the United States delegation, which stated: '. . . it was generally recognized, and laid down in many authoritative legal texts, that innocent passage for warships through the territorial waters of other States was admissible in time of peace'. The United States delegate further argued that, in keeping with Article 25, the rights of the coastal State were fully protected by the requirement that warships comply with coastal State regulations. 'The rights of coastal States were fully protected by that Article in accordance with the customary provisions of international law.'[83]

In reply to the United States statement, the Romanian delegate made the following remarks, which must have influenced the voting patterns of the delegations which had earlier considered the 1956 text of the International Law Commission to reflect contemporary international law. He said:

> [Romania] could not agree with the United States representative that the right of a coastal State to security and to the exercise of its sovereign rights was adequately safeguarded by the observance of coastal regulations by a warship which had already entered its territorial waters. The United States representative had cited eminent authorities; but such outstanding jurists as the members of the International Law Commission had seen fit to include Article 24 in their draft rules. The meaning of Articles 24 and 25 taken together was that a warship required authorization to pass into territorial waters and could not thereafter disregard the appropriate regulations of the coastal State.[84]

With the deletion of the words 'authorization or', the new Article 24 was then put to a vote. The result was 43 votes in favour, 24 against, with 12 abstentions. In keeping with the rules of procedures, the new Article was not adopted since it did not secure the qualified majority. However, the provision which followed, i.e. Article 25, dealing with warships' compliance with the *regulations* of the coastal State concerning passage through the territorial sea, was approved without discussion by more than a two-thirds majority (76 for and one abstention). This provision, which became Article 23 of the 1958 Geneva Convention, is the only text in that Convention dealing with warships exercising the 'right' of innocent passage in foreign territorial waters.

Article 23 of the 1958 Convention on the Territorial Sea and the Contiguous Zone runs as follows:

> If any warship does not comply with the regulations of the coastal State concerning passage through the territorial sea and disregards any request for compliance which is made to it, the coastal State may require the warship to leave the territorial sea.

Some writers have commented on this provision. One, G. Tunkin, has gone so far as to read the requirements of authorization and notification into it:

> the clause requiring that foreign warships observe the rules governing passage through territorital waters laid down by the coastal State remains. Such rules can, of course, include a requirement that prior permission be obtained or prior notification of passage given.[85]

Without sharing the above views in any way, Max Sorensen acknowledges that if account is taken of the legislative history of the relevant articles, the above interpretation could be followed by the majority of States, with the United Nations decision-making mechanism taking the blame. Sorensen wrote:

> The Convention as it now stands contains no special provision relating to the innocent passage of warships, but only the general rules applicable to all ships. The actual text of the Convention would therefore warrant the conclusion that warships have the same rights in this respect as other ships, but the proceedings of the Conference leave no room for doubt that this was not the intention of the majority of delegations. Incidentally, this is a typical illustration of the short-comings inherent in the drafting of rules of international law through a process based upon the formalistic rules of procedure and voting of the United Nations.[86]

Whether Article 23 authorizes the coastal State to insist on prior permission (notification and authorization) as an aspect of its regulatory competence, or whether such 'permission' is determined by the uncertain rules of customary international law, was a matter of major concern to subsequent State practice and a key item in the Third United Nations Conference on the Law of the Sea.

Innocent passage of warships in the Third United Nations Conference on the Law of the Sea[87]

At the Third United Nations Conference on the Law of the Sea (Third UNCLOS), the requirements of prior notice and/or authorization for warships intending to exercise the right of innocent passage were revived in a series of proposals aimed ostensibly at harmonizing national legislation with the future Convention on the Law of the Sea.[88] To this effect, at the early stages of the Conference, some draft proposals on navigation through the territorial sea put forward by various delegations contained provisions permitting 'the coastal State to require prior notification and/or authorization by its competent authorities for the passage of warships through its territorial sea, in conformity with the regulations in force in such a State.[89]

Within the Second Committee of the Conference, which had to deal with the problem, a vigorous debate on this issue took place from its 3rd to its 15th meeting.[90] The circle of those who spoke in favour of the requirement extended from China to Spain, with a host of small States. Their arguments included considerations of 'undeniable right of sovereignty' and 'national security'; for one delegate, 'such prior authorization by the coastal State for warships . . . was the prerequisite for the maintenance of peace, good order and security . . . not against States or ships but against intentions and policies'.[91]

Those who opposed the requirement of prior notification and/or authorization included the United Kingdom and the United States. As a justification, the latter invoked the absence of any such requirement from the 1958 Geneva Conventions and pointed out that that requirement 'would not be desirable and would expose coastal States to pressures to which they would not otherwise be subject'.

Furthermore,

> it was unrealistic to entertain proposals which would discriminate against the navigation rights of warships. The exercise of individual and collective defence had been recognized under the United Nations. All nations . . . recognized the importance of maintaining that right for the protection of their vital territorial and political integrity. The maintenance of [navigation] rights for warships . . . was not only consistent with the Charter but was the only policy consistent with global realities and international stability.[92]

The Soviet Union adopted a more ambivalent position which, however, amounted to a departure from the position it had taken at the 1958 Conference. With an increased naval power, the Soviet Union by and large agreed with the United States, except with regard to the passage of foreign warships through its own territorial sea! This interpretation can be deduced from comparing Soviet municipal law on the passage regime in its territorial seas with the statements of the Soviet and allied delegations regarding straits used for international navigation made in the Second Committee of the Conference. Although straits was the main issue covered in the statements, the underlying principle of the passage of warships in foreign territorial seas was also covered. For the Ukrainian Soviet Socialist Republic,

> coastal States must, of course, have some control over navigation through the straits (territorial sea), but such control should be compatible with the interests of international navigation. To grant coastal States absolute power of control did not safeguard equality and justice, since such a step could lead to discrimination against States with which the coastal States did not maintain good relations.
>
> Those advocating the principle of control by the coastal State based their opinion on the increasing threat represented by the strategic interests of the navies of the super-powers. It should, however, be clearly stated that the coastal State's control over the straits (territorial sea) would not prevent an increase in the number of warships, since most countries possessing such fleets did not have to pass through straits (territorial sea) to reach the oceans. That problem could only be solved by adopting the proposal of the Union of Soviet Socialist Republics concerning general and complete disarmament.[93]

Nevertheless, throughout the negotiations, some coastal States presented amendments reintroducing the requirements of prior notification and/or authorization in working documents[94] and counter-proposals.[95]

In a first document issued by the Second Committee, entitled: 'Main Trends', the following three formulae were included:

> Formula A
>
> If any warship does not comply with the regulations of the coastal State concerning passage through the territorial sea and disregards any request for compliance which is made to it, the coastal State may require the warship to leave the territorial sea.
>
> Formula B
>
> [Incorporates verbatim formula A, but adds:] . . . the coastal State may

> suspend the right of passage of such warships and may require (it) to leave the territorial sea by such safe and expeditious route as may be directed by the coastal State.
>
> Formula C
>
> The coastal State may require prior notification to or authorization by its competent authorities for the passage of foreign warships through its territorial sea, in conformity with regulations in force in such a State.[96]

At its 1975 Caracas Session, the Second Committee decided to consolidate the informal working papers into a single working document forming the basis for its future work. The 'Consolidated Text on Innocent Passage',[97] as the new document was called, '*omitted*' formulas A and C above and retained formula B, the predecessor of Article 30 of the 1982 Convention. Part II of the Informal Single Negotiating Text (ISNT 1975), which covered subjects entrusted to the Second Committee, also adopted formula B. Thus, as was the case in the 1958 Geneva Conference, the Committee took a stand which would not be followed by the Plenary later on.

The revision of the ISNT between the 1975 and 1977 sessions of the Conference did not bring any change in formula B. Article 30 of the Informal Composite Negotiating Text (ICNT 1977) contained a requirement to the effect that the warship was to leave the territorial sea '*immediately*'.[98]

At a general debate that took place in the Plenary during the resumed ninth session, many States stressed the less than satisfactory nature of the provisions on warships found in the ICNT.[99] Summarizing the views of these States, the Romanian delegate emphasized that:

> in accordance with existing international law, with the long practice of many States and with national legislation, [the passage of warships in territorial waters] was subject to the prior authorization of, or notification of, the coastal State concerned . . . His delegation was ready to participate in negotiations for the purpose of reflecting that requirement more adequately in the new revision.[100]

An informal proposal was then made by the Philippines, and co-sponsored by Argentina, China, Equador, Madagascar, Pakistan and Peru,[101] to the effect that prior notification and/or authorization was necessary for the passage of warships in the territorial sea. The proposal was to be included in Article 21(1) of the future Law of the Sea Convention, i.e. the provision relating to compliance with the laws and regulations of the coastal State while exercising innocent passage, as a new sub-paragraph (b): 'The navigation of warships, including the right to require prior authorization or notification for passage through the territorial sea.'

In this way, sub-paragraph (a) of Article 21(1), which deals with the safety of navigation and the regulation of maritime traffic, will ensure the 'material security' of vessels, while sub-paragraph (b), which immediately follows, reciprocates as regards the 'security' of the coastal States. The rest of the Article was to be left untouched, except for the consequential re-lettering of the other sub-paragraphs.

The countries which spoke in favour of this proposal included Spain, China, Finland, the Nordic States and many others. The United States and the Soviet Union opposed it. As a result, the text remained unchanged.

At the beginning of the 11th and final session in April 1982, 28 States[102] resurrected and reformulated the Philippine informal proposal of 1980. A similar proposal was put forward by Gabon to complete Article 21 by adding a sub-paragraph granting coastal States the right to regulate the 'navigation of warships, including [the requirement of] notification and/or authorization for passage in territorial seas'.[103]

The proposal of the 28 States, on the other hand, was aimed at adding 'security' to the matters on which, under Article 21(1), coastal States are empowered to adopt laws and regulations.

This addition was to enable coastal States to promulgate laws or regulations subjecting the passage of warships in their territorial sea to prior notification and/or authorization, or to limit the number of warships of one State simultaneously present in their territorial sea on account of security considerations.

In a series of plenary debates which followed, many Latin American and other States reacted favourably to one or the other proposal. However, strong opposition was voiced by the following 16 States: United Kingdom, Netherlands, Italy, Denmark, Belgium, Bahamas, Federal Republic of Germany, Portugal, German Democratic Republic, Bulgaria, Cuba, Chile, Iraq, New Zealand, Soviet Union, United States.[104]

The debates went on as vigorously as ever for and against each of the two proposals. At the final plenary sessions of the Conference, following an appeal by the Conference President stressing the 'package deal'[105] nature of the whole Convention, Gabon withdrew its proposal, whereas the sponsors of the other proposal did not insist on a vote.

The President sought and obtained this result by stating that the delegations concerned

> would, however, like to reaffirm that their decision is without prejudice to the rights of coastal States to adopt measures to safeguard their security interests, in accordance with Article 19 (dealing with the meaning of innocent passage) and Article 25 (dealing with rights of protection of the coastal State) as provided for in the Convention.[106]

Although one may question the legal effect of the entire operation and of the President's statement, it is clear that no true consensus was achieved. Consequently, some States which already require prior notification and/or authorization of warship passage in their national legislation have said that they find no incompatibility between their position and the provisions of the Convention.[107]

Other States even hold that there is implicit recognition for prior notification and/or authorization in the Convention. This latter view was best expressed by Iran at the final session of December 1982. Interpreting the relevant articles in the same spirit as the Conference President, the delegate of Iran said:

> in the light of customary international law, the provisions of Article 21, read in conjunction with Article 19, on the meaning of innocent passage, and Article 25, on the rights of protection of coastal States, recognize, though implicitly, the right of coastal States to take measures to safeguard their security interests,

> including the adoption of laws and regulations regarding, *inter alia*, the requirement of prior authorization for warships willing to exercise the right of innocent passage through the territorial sea.[108]

Referring to the reasons why no vote was taken on the issue in the face of an impossible consensus, and further reaffirming the requirement of notice or consent for the passage of warships in foreign territorial waters, the Maltese delegate said at the signing ceremony:

> As regards . . . the innocent passage of warships through territorial waters, . . . for the sake of general agreement we went along with a compromise contained in a statement by the President of the Conference on 26th April 1982, duly recorded in the annals of the Conference . . . On the eve of the signing of the Convention, we feel that we ought to reaffirm our conviction that it recognizes the right of coastal States to adopt measures to safeguard their security, including the requirement of prior authorization or notice for the innocent passage of warships through territorial waters. My country, therefore, reserves the right, if it deems it necessary, to submit a declaration in this respect at the appropriate time in accordance with Article 310.[109]

The question that ought to be addressed now is: what is the import of such declarations in the context of the Convention? In other words, could these declarations be considered as interpreting the relevant articles of the Convention dealing with the innocent passage of warships, under Article 310, or do they amount to reservations expressly prohibited by Article 309?[110]

Article 310 of the Convention runs as follows:

> Article 309 [the provision prohibiting reservations] does not preclude a State, when signing, ratifying, or acceding to this Convention, from making declarations or statements, however phrased or named, with a view *inter alia*, to the harmonization of its laws and regulations with the provisions of this Convention, provided that such declarations or statements do not purport to exclude or to modify the legal effect of the provisions of this Convention in their application to that State.

Without going into the details of the legality or illegality of unilateral declarations in the framework of multilateral treaties,[111] it is submitted that the statements made at the final session of the Conference and Declarations made upon ratification of the resulting Convention in connection with the innocent passage of warships in territorial waters come within the parameters of Article 310. This is so because in view of the 'constructive ambiguity' of the Convention on the issue, it was quite natural for some States to reiterate positions not decided by a vote. In addition, the declarations do not touch upon the legal effect of any article, for example a provision that would ask coastal States to refrain from requiring notification of, and/or authorization for, the innocent passage of warships.

On the contrary, the declarations in question clarify the 'legal effects' of certain provisions (Articles 19 and 25 principally),[112] which implicity allow coastal States to enact legislation covering these security interests in their territorial sea.

Independently of the above reasoning, what is the fate of innocent passage of warships in a Convention which contains no provision expressly requiring notification and/or authorization, nor any article expressly prohibiting such a requirement?

Grosso modo, the 1982 Convention adopts the format of the 1958 Geneva Convention on the Territorial Sea and the Contiguous Zone. It sets out rules for all ships, which are followed by additional provisions for merchant ships, government commercial or non-commercial ships, and, of course, warships.[113] As regards warships, in particular, the Convention reaffirms the complete immunity of such vessels, establishes the international responsibility of the flag State for injuries caused by them, and, finally and timidly, permits the coastal State to require foreign warships to *immediately* leave its territorial sea if they fail to comply with its laws and regulations and disregard any request for compliance.[114]

An analogy could, at this stage, be made with the rules of diplomatic law. The immunities enjoyed by warships and diplomatic missions are similar. Fairly similar remedies are applied in cases of abuses of those immunities. As the warship in the circumstance is required *immediately* to leave the territorial sea, so the host State has an ultimate remedy to 'call for *immediate* closure of the offending mission'.[115] The immediacy required in complying with the measure is the utmost that can be done and nothing more. Primarily because of this, diplomatic missions need the consent of the host State to be within its territory. For analogous reasons, it seems appropriate that warships should be required to notify and/or be authorized before they can enter foreign territorial seas.

As no provision of the 1982 Convention expressly allows or prohibits such a requirement as far as warships are concerned, reference could be made to the Preamble of that Convention. The Preamble explicitly refers to customary international law on unsettled issues such as the passage of warships in foreign territorial sea by stating that: '. . . matters not regulated by this Convention continue to be governed by the rules and principles of general international law . . .' That being the case, reliance has to be placed on the State practice emerging from domestic legislation.

(b) Some municipal law provisions on the exercise of the right of innocent passage by warships

Many States have adopted laws requiring prior notification and/or authorization for foreign warships to exercise the right of innocent passage in their territorial seas. Thus, it is not surprising to note that, despite the absence of such a requirement from the 1982 Convention, 'approximately 50 States had supported the right of coastal States to require prior notification or authorization or had incorporated prior notice or consent requirements in their domestic laws relating to warship transit before completion of the 1982 Convention'.[116] Even some coastal States which favoured the deletion of the requirement of prior authorization and/or notification from the Convention continue to have national legislation with provisions on the passage of warships in their territorial seas akin to subjecting such passage to notification if not prior authorization.[117]

To illustrate this point, a representative cross-section of domestic legislation will be examined hereafter. In this connection, some 'important maritime' nations of each region will be considered.

The Soviet Union

The Law on the State Boundary of the U.S.S.R. (1982)[118] provides, in the last paragraph of Article 13 (Innocent Passage through Territorial Waters), that:

> Foreign warships, and also submarine means of transport, shall effect innocent passage through the territorial waters of the U.S.S.R. *according to the procedure established by the U.S.S.R. Council of Ministers*. In so doing, submarines and other submarine means of transport shall navigate on the surface and under their own flag.[119]

The People's Republic of China

A Declaration presented to the United Nations Secretary General by the Permanent Representative of China on 22 November 1979 provides the passage of foreign warships in Chinese territorial waters in the following terms:[120]

> The Government of the People's Republic of China declares: . . . No foreign vessels for military use and no foreign aircraft may enter China's territorial sea and the air space above it without the permission of the Government of the People's Republic of China.
> While navigating Chinese territorial sea, every foreign vessel must observe the relevant laws and regulations laid down by the Government of the People's Republic of China.

Denmark

A Danish Ordinance of 27 February 1976 Governing the Admission of Foreign Warships to the Danish Territorial Sea in Time of Peace[121] states that:

> Foreign warships shall enjoy the right of passage through the territorial sea subject to advance notification being given through diplomatic channels . . . For simultaneous passage of the territorial sea of more than three warships of the same nationality, advance permission, obtained through diplomatic channel, is required.

Brazil

Decree No. 56.515 of 28 June 1965 Establishing the Rules Governing Visits by Foreign Warships to Brazilian Ports and Territorial Waters in Time of Peace[122] assimilates 'visits' to passage and prescribes:

> Notice of Visit: Advance notice of any visit shall be given by the government of the State to which the visiting ship belongs.

> . . . Limitation on number and length of stay: Unless special authorization is granted, not more than three warships of the same nationality may be present simultaneously in Brazilian . . . territorial waters.

The United States

The spirit of the laws of the United States on the rights of warships in foreign territorial waters can be adequately deduced from a National Policy Declaration made by the President of the United States on 10 March 1983, and a Communication transmitted to the Permanent Missions of States members of the United Nations on 10 July 1985.

In substance, the President declared, on navigational issues generally, that

> the United States is prepared to accept and act in accordance with the balance of interests relating to traditional uses of the oceans—such as navigation and overflight. In this respect, the United States will recognize the rights of other States in the waters off their coasts, as reflected in the Convention, so long as the rights and freedoms of the United States and others under international law are recognized by such coastal State.
> . . . The United States will exercise and assert its navigation and overflight rights and freedoms on a worldwide basis in a manner that is consistent with the balance of interests reflected in the Convention. The United States will not, however, acquiesce in unilateral acts of other States designed to restrict the rights and freedoms of the international community in navigation and overflight and other related high sea uses.[123]

Succinctly the Communication transmitted to the Permanent Missions of the States members of the United Nations at the request of the United States representative concerning US policy on innocent passage of all ships, including warships, was as follows:

> first, the right of innocent passage is one that under long-standing principles of international law may be exercised by all vessels whether or not engaged in commercial service; second, international law does not permit a coastal State to limit innocent passage of vessels . . . to certain periods of time; third, under long-standing principles of international law, the coastal State may not claim to condition the right of innocent passage upon prior notification to it.[124]

These statements, illustrative of the assertive United States policy since the Second World War, counteract the general trend of many other States on the matter. Whether it temporarily prevents prior notification or authorization for the exercise of innocent passage by warships crystallizing as customary international law requirements is debatable.[125] However, the United States pronouncements should also be interpreted within the context of an inevitable behaviour congenial to a major sea power.

Sudan

The Sudanese Territorial Waters and Continental Shelf Act of 1970 states in its Article 8(3) that:

> The passage of military vessels in the territorial waters shall be subject to previous permission, and the Government may take all necessary action against ships committing any breach, and submarines shall navigate on the surface and shall show the flag of the nation to which they belong.[126]

Some special cases of simple notification only

Egypt: Upon Ratification, the Government of Egypt, under the provisions of Article 310 of the 1982 U.N. Convention on the Law of the Sea, made the following Declaration concerning the passage of warships in its territorial sea:

> [With reference to the provisions of the Convention relating to the right of the coastal State to regulate the passage of ships through its territorial sea:] Warships shall be ensured innocent passage through the territorial sea of Egypt, subject to *prior notification*.[127]

India: The Indian Territorial Waters . . . and other Maritime Zones Act, 1976, provides in its Article 4(2) thus:

> Foreign warships including submarines and other underwater vehicles may enter or pass through the territorial waters after giving *prior notice to the Central Government*.[128]

Yugoslavia: The following Declaration was made by Yugoslavia before she ratified the 1982 Convention:

> Proceeding from the right that State parties have on the basis of Article 310 of the United Nations Convention on the Law of the Sea, the Government of the Socialist Federal Republic of Yugoslavia considers that a coastal State may, by its laws and regulations, subject the passage of foreign warships to the requirement of *previous notification* to the respective coastal State and limit the number of ships simultaneously passing, on the basis of the international customary law and in compliance with the right of innocent passage (articles 17–32 of the Convention).[129]

Conclusion

By and large, it is fair to say that, whatever the content of national provisions or policy statements, there is a strong tendency in State practice in favour of subjecting the passage of foreign warships in territorial waters to prior notification and/or authorization (unless there is an express coastal State legislation to the contrary).[130] If this is a reflection of the inherent 'dangerous' character of warships, does the same situation prevail for other dangerous vessels? It is not uncommon to consider as 'dangerous' submarines and nuclear-propelled ships as well as vessels carrying nuclear or other noxious substances. Is their exercise of the right of innocent passage to be restricted on account of this characteristic?

3. The exercise of the right of innocent passage by foreign nuclear-powered ships and by ships carrying nuclear weapons or other dangerous substances

It was in the (First) Conference on the Law of the Sea in 1958 that, for the first time, mention was made of the possibility of enacting provisions on the exercise of the right of innocent passage by what was then simply termed 'ships carrying any kind of nuclear weapons', instead of including them in the blanket expression 'warships', thus distinguishing such vessels from warships.

When the 1958 Conference discussed what then was Article 24 of the Provisional Articles on Territorial Sea, dealing with previous authorization and/or notification for warships to exercise the right of innocent passage, Yugoslavia proposed to complete it by a paragraph allowing coastal States to deny the exercise of this 'right to any ship carrying any kind of nuclear weapons'.[131]

In justifying the need for this new paragraph, the Yugoslav representative explained to the Second Commission that such a provision '. . . reflected his Government's belief that nuclear energy should be applied solely to peaceful ends and that international law did not authorize its utilization for military purposes'.[132]

However, in order to except cases of peaceful transportation, the proposal was amended, before being put to a vote, to cover only warships carrying nuclear weapons. The Second Commission, however, rejected the proposal by a vote of 33 against, 7 in favour, and 22 abstentions.[133] Accordingly, the Plenary of the 1958 Conference had no opportunity to consider the exercise of the right of passage by warships carrying nuclear weapons and other noxious substances.

At the Third United Nations Conference on the Law of the Sea, a similar but more comprehensive proposal was put forward by four States in a draft text on navigation in the territorial seas.

Article 8 of that Draft, dealing with the navigation of ships with special characteristics, including nuclear-powered ships or ships carrying nuclear weapons, provided the following:

1. The coastal State may regulate the passage through its territorial sea of the following:
   (a) Nuclear-powered ships or ships carrying nuclear weapons;
   (b) Marine research and hydrographic survey ships;
   (c) Oil tankers and chemical tankers carrying harmful or noxious liquid substances in bulk;
   (d) Ships carrying nuclear substances or materials.
2. The coastal State may require prior notification to or authorization by its competent authorities for the passage through its territorial sea of foreign ships mentioned in subparagraph (a) of paragraph 1.
3. The coastal State may require prior notification to its competent authorities for the passage through its territorial sea, except along designated sealanes, of foreign ships mentioned in sub-paragraph (b) of paragraph 1.
4. The coastal State may require the passage through its territorial sea along designated sealanes of foreign ships mentioned in sub-paragraphs (c) and (d) of paragraph 1, in conformity with Article 7.[134]

As it stood, the proposal purported not only to subject the passage of such vessels to previous authorization and/or notification, but also envisaged the possibility of denying passage. After a lively debate in the Second Committee, a revised draft was produced and included verbatim in the 1982 Convention. The resulting provision permits coastal States to stop and check the files of such vessels and even to supervise their movement:

> Foreign nuclear-powered ships and ships carrying nuclear or other inherently dangerous or noxious substances shall, when exercising the right of innocent passage through the territorial sea, carry documents and observe special precautionary measures established for such ships by international organizations.[135]

In explaining its preference for the above formulation, rather than for the original draft article, the delegation of Fiji[136] pointed out that as far as measures to prevent pollution were concerned, the 1973 International Convention for the Prevention of Pollution from Ships adequately covered those risks. Regarding the other risks inherent in the presence of such vessels in foreign coastal waters, the delegation of Fiji demonstrated that it was superfluous to enumerate further powers of the coastal State in these provisions since they were covered in other articles of the Convention and thus did not require further elaboration.

As will be seen in the next chapter, Article 21 of the 1982 Convention, relating to the laws and regulations which may be adopted by coastal States in connection with innocent passage, empowers the latter, *inter alia*, to enact legislation on the safety of navigation and the preservation of the environment; as noted earlier, Article 25 entitles the coastal State to take necessary steps in its territorial sea to prevent passage which is not innocent. If the provisions of the Convention are read together, it may be concluded, therefore, that nuclear-powered ships and nuclear-armed ships are subject to the same prior notification and/or authorization regime as warships in foreign territorial seas. This is even more true if the warship is carrying nuclear weapons.

The situation is less clear concerning nuclear-powered or nuclear-armed submarines. Issues of this nature were brushed aside at the Third United Nations Conference on the Law of the Sea which, it was contended, was not the proper forum for such a topic. Consequently, the 1982 Convention is silent on the regime governing the innocent passage of nuclear-propelled or nuclear-armed submarines.

The contemporary international Law of the Sea subsumes nuclear-powered or nuclear-armed submarines under the general rules applicable to submarines so far as the right of innocent passage in foreign coastal waters is concerned. Thus, little or no weight is given to the nuclear characteristics of such submarines. Consequently, neither Article 23 nor the related provisions of the 1982 Convention are applicable to such vessels. Thus, the implied requirement of prior notification and/or authorization only applies[137] to warships *ipso facto*.

Be that as it may, underwater vehicles or submarines, armed or unarmed, nuclear-propelled or not, are subject to certain conditions short of prior notification and/or authorization.

4. The exercise of the right of innocent passage by submarines

Before the invention of the submarine, at the beginning of this century, most navigational rules and regulations envisaged only surface navigation through the territorial sea. Consequently, it was only natural that such underwater vehicles, as they entered foreign territorial waters in exercise of the right of innocent passage, would be required to travel on the surface.

In the 1920s, the arguments for prescribing emerged passage for submarines included considerations relating to the safety of navigation and the verification of the innocent character of passage. These considerations are still valid today.

Thus Article 12, embodied in the Final Act of the 1930 Hague Codification Conference which dealt with warships navigating in coastal waters, contained a paragraph prescribing that '. . . submarines shall navigate on the surface'. No matter how innocuous the sentence may have seemed at the time, the message conveyed was quite clear. There was a legal obligation for submarines to navigate on the surface while in foreign territorial seas. Otherwise, their passage was deemed to be non-innocent.

At the International Law Commission, where the Hague Draft Articles on the Territorial Sea were prominent in the debates between 1952 and 1956, the requirement for foreign submarines to travel on the surface while in the territorial sea was one of the very few proposals unanimously agreed upon. The final Draft of the International Law Commission in 1956[138] likewise prescribed that 'submarines are required to navigate on the surface'. Furthermore, the 1956 Draft inserted this rule in the Article dealing with the definition of innocent passage rather than in a provision on warships—a solution which would have encouraged the idea that submarines fall automatically into the category of warships. In a commentary, the Commission stated that the transfer of the rule to the general rules on innocent passage was aimed at embracing commercial submarines if and whenever they would be introduced.

The sentence 'submarines are required to navigate on the surface and to show their flag' is found in Article 14(6) of the 1958 Geneva Convention on the Territorial Sea and the Contiguous Zone in the framework of rules applicable to all ships while exercising the right of innocent passage. This sentence has been interpreted in two ways.

Some authors are of the opinion that the *innocence* of passage by submarines is not made dependent on the compliance with this condition.[139] In other words, a submarine could be presumed to be exercising the right of innocent passage even if it were doing so in a submerged state. The supporters of this interpretation rely on the context of Article 14(6), particularly paragraph 5 of that Article. They point out that that paragraph specifies the conditions under which foreign fishing vessels 'shall not be considered innocent'; the absence of parallel specific language that failure to surface 'shall not be considered innocent' in the case of submarines 'undercuts any assumption that such a behaviour is clearly non-innocent'.[140]

A contrary opinion, which crystallized during the Third United Nations Conference on the Law of the Sea, is that navigation on the surface is a prerequisite of innocence for submarines. Within the Second Committee of that

Conference, only the United States delegation expressed the opinion that, since submarines were equipped to travel submerged, that was the safest way for them to exercise the right of innocent passage.[141] For most other delegations, in particular that of Spain, 'the regime of innocent passage applied strictly to navigation on the surface, and had nothing to do with the secret passage of submerged vessels . . .'.[142]

The 1982 Convention by and large reproduces, in an independent Article 20, the rule of the 1958 Convention by providing that: 'In the territorial sea, submarines and other underwater vehicles are required to navigate on the surface and to show their flag.'[143]

On the basis of this Article, read together with other provisions of the Convention, it is argued that the innocence of passage is dependent on the compliance with the requirement of navigation on the surface.[144] Inasmuch as Article 21 of the 1982 Convention provides in its paragraph 1 that the coastal State may adopt laws and regulations relating to the safety of navigation and the regulation of maritime traffic, and in its paragraph 4 that foreign vessels shall comply with all such laws, it is rightly thought that, despite the language of Article 20 cited above, there is a strong presumption of non-innocence for submerged passage if the coastal State laws prohibit such passage.[145]

In sum, under the present conventional and customary Law of the Sea, submarines and other underwater vehicles are required to navigate on the surface and to show their flag while in the territorial seas of other coastal States.

One can suppose, in addition, that whenever such underwater vehicles have the characteristics of a warship, described in Article 29 of the 1982 Convention, they are required to notify and/or be authorized by the coastal State before exercising the right of innocent passage in that State's territorial sea.[146]

5. Conclusion

The above analysis of the right of innocent passage by different types of sea-going vessels, be they nuclear-powered or nuclear-propelled ships, warships or submarines, leads to the conclusion that that right is not as independent as it looks but is subordinated, to a very large degree, to the sovereignty of the coastal State over its territorial sea. But this sovereignty is, in turn, subordinated to the right of innocent passage.

Thus, it seems possible to maintain, in view of this mutual relationship, that the exercise of sovereignty and the exercise of the right of innocent passage on the territorial sea are a reciprocal bundle of rights and obligations, of risks and responsibilities.

Notes

1. 1982 Convention, Article 32; 1958 Geneva Convention, Articles 22–23; 1926 Brussels Convention Concerning the Immunity of State-Owned Ships, Article 3. See also T.K. Thommen, *Legal Status of Government Merchant Ships in International Law*, The

Hague, Nijhoff, 1962, pp. 3–8. Immunity in this context means that public vessels used for public purposes can never be subjected to coastal State jurisdiction, unlike merchant ships. For public vessels used for private (commercial) purposes, there remains a controversy as to whether they enjoy immunity. It is fairly generally accepted in international law and State practice that the immunity of a foreign State is restricted to its public acts (*jure imperii*) and does not extend to its private (commercial) activities (*jure gestionis*).

2. Articles 1 and 2 assimilate 'sea-going vessels owned or operated by States' for commercial purposes to privately owned merchant vessels and thus subject them to the same obligations and rules regarding the jurisdiction of tribunals. Article 3(1) provides: 'The provisions of [Articles 1 and 2] shall not be applicable to ships of war, government yachts, patrol vessels, hospital ships, auxiliary vessels, supply ships, and other craft owned or operated by a State and used at the time a cause of action arises exclusively on governmental and non-commercial service, and such vessels shall not be subject to seizure, attachment or detention by any legal process, nor to judicial proceedings *in rem*.' Hudson, M.O. (ed.), *International Legislation*, vol. III (1922–1927), Washington, DC, Carnegie Endowment for International Peace, 1931, p. 1837.
3. LON Doc. C.230 M.117.1930.V., p. 6.
4. Ibid., at p. 9.
5. The 1952 Brussels Convention on the Arrest of Sea-Going Ships deals with 'sea-going ships' generally and with their liability to arrest in respect of a 'maritime claim' (Article 2). Article 3 allows arrest of any sister ship owned by the same 'person', and 'person' is defined to include 'Governments, their Departments and Public Authorities' (Article 1(3)). In ratifying the Convention, most States, however, reserved their right not to apply it to 'warships or to vessels owned by or in the service of a State'.
6. ILC, *Yearbook* 1954, vol. I, p. 158.
7. Ibid.
8. ILC, *Yearbook* 1955, vol. I, p. 141.
9. ILC, *Yearbook* 1956, vol. II, p. 276.
10. See generally Thommen, op. cit., note 1; Vitanyi, B., 'L'immunité des navires d'Etat', *Netherlands International Law Review*, vol. 10, 1963, pp. 33–61, 156–77.
11. Rovine, A.W., *Digest of United States Practice in International Law 1974*, Washington, Department of State Publications, p. 259.
12. Although, of course, the trend is that, for State-owned vessels operated for commercial purposes, unlike merchant vessels, a distinction is made between jurisdiction in the sense of court proceedings resulting in a judgment to which the ship can be subjected, and immunity from execution in the sense of measures to enforce judgment for which the consent of the flag State is always required. cf. J. Crawford, 'Execution of Judgments and Foreign Sovereign Immunity', *AJIL*, vol. 75, 1981, pp. 820–69. At p. 862, however, Crawford says that: 'If international law allows a State to exercise civil jurisdiction over matters arising out of the commercial use of a State-owned trading ship, then it seems likely that it also allows that jurisdiction to be enforced by the arrest of and execution against such a ship. This would be so irrespective of whether any more general immunity from execution is required or recognized.' Note, however, that the procedure of interim attachment ('saisie conservatoire') of State trading ships, particularly those on innocent passage, is illegal even if the related claim pertains to the use and ownership rights of the ship (or a sister ship) as the case may be. (Interview with Mr Balanda, member of the United Nations International Law Commission, July 1985.)
13. Unlike merchant ships, warships belong to the armed or naval forces of a State. They are placed under the command of a duly commissioned officer and manned by a crew

which is submitted to regular armed forces discipline. cf. the 1958 Convention on the High Seas (Article 8(2)) and the 1982 Convention (Article 29). Consequently warships, like State vessels used for non-commercial purposes, are immune from the jurisdiction of the coastal State while exercising the right of innocent passage. However, unlike other public vessels, their right to enjoy the right of passage is contested.

14. A list of the latest writings on the subject includes: Froman, F.D. 'Uncharted Waters: Non-Innocent Passage of Warships in the Territorial Sea', *San Diego Law Review*, vol. 21, 1984, pp. 625–89; Oxman, B.H., 'The Regime of Warships under the United Nations Convention on the Law of the Sea', *Virginia Journal of International Law*, vol. 24, 1984, pp. 809–63; Lucchini L., 'Les opérations militaires en mer en temps de paix', *Revue générale de droit international public*, vol. 88, 1984, pp. 9–45; O'Connell, D.P., 'Innocent Passage of Warships', *Thesaurus Acroasium*, vol. 7, 1977, pp. 405–451. See generally, O'Connell, D.P., *The Influence of Law on Sea Power*, Manchester, Manchester University Press, 1975.
15. O'Connell, D.P., *The International Law of the Sea*, vol. I, Oxford, Clarendon Press, 1982, pp. 274–5.
16. Ibid.
17. Ibid., p. 275.
18. Froman, op. cit., note 14, p. 632.
19. *The North Atlantic Coast Fisheries* arbitration, Hackworth, *Digest of International Law*, vol. 1, Washington, DC, Government Printing Office, 1940, pp. 646ff.
20. Ibid., but quoted from Jessup, P.C., *The Law of Territorial Waters and Maritime Jurisdiction*, New York, Jennings and Co., 1924, p. 20.
21. LON, Doc. C.196.M.70.1927, p. 72.
22. IDI, *Annuaire* 1928, Projet de Règlement Relatif à la Mer Territoriale, p. 627, at p. 659.
23. Quoted in *AJIL*, vol. 23, 1929, Special Supplement, p. 376.
24. ILA, Report of the 34th Conference held at Vienna, 1926, Draft Convention on Laws of Maritime Jurisdiction in Time of Peace, p. 101 (Article 10).
25. Quoted in the *AJIL* op. cit., note 23, p. 372.
26. Ibid., pp. 328–9.
27. Jessup, op. cit., note 20, p. 20.
28. Rosenne, S., (ed.), League of Nations, *Conference for the Codification of International Law (1930)*, Dobbs Ferry, NY, vol. II, Oceana, 1975, pp. 250–93.
29. Ibid.
30. Ibid., p. 293.
31. Ibid.
32. Op. cit., note 28, vol. IV, pp. 1260–78.
33. In a proposal presented by France, the following wording for a future provision was stated: 'A coastal State is bound to allow foreign ships, *other than ships belonging to naval forces*, a right of innocent passage through its territorial waters, it being understood that fishing vessels will not actually engage in fishing and that commercial submarines will not be entitled to make use of this right of passage except on the surface.' Ibid., at p. 185.
34. Ibid., at p. 1261.
35. Ibid., at p. 1265.
36. LON Doc. G.230.M.117 1930.V, p. 10.
37. Ibid.
38. For example, Guggenheim, although implicitly, in ICJ, *Case Concerning Right of Passage over Indian Territory* (Portugal v. India), Pleadings, Oral Arguments, Documents, vol. IV, p. 95.
39. Gidel, G., *Le droit international public de la mer*, Paris, Sirey, 1932–34, vol. 3, p. 284.

40. Ibid., at pp. 283–4.
41. Bustamante y Sirven, A.S., *The Territorial Sea*, New York/Oxford, Oxford University Press, 1930, pp. 115–16.
42. *Corfu Channel* case (Merits), ICJ, *Reports* 1949, p. 3, at p. 28.
43. Ibid., at p. 30.
44. Ibid.
45. ICJ, *Corfu Channel* case, Pleadings, Oral Arguments, Documents, vol. I, 1949, p. 43.
46. Ibid., vol. II, pp. 129ff.
47. Ibid., pp. 288ff., at pp. 289–90.
48. Ibid., vol. III, pp. 378–80.
49. Op. cit., note 45, vol. III, pp. 377–82.
50. Fauchille, P., *Traité de droit international public*, vol. I, Part II (*Peace*), Paris, A. Rousseau, 1925, pp. 506ff.
51. Spiropoulos, P., *Traité théorique et pratique de droit international public*, Paris, Librairie générale de droit et de jurisprudence, 1933, pp. 153ff.
52. Op. cit., note 45, vol. IV, pp. 542ff.
53. *Corfu Channel* case (Merits), op. cit., note 42, pp. 98–104.
54. Ibid., p. 98.
55. Ibid., p. 99.
56. Ibid., p. 101.
57. Ibid., pp. 46–7.
58. Ibid., p. 74.
59. Ibid., p. 102.
60. Those in support included MM. François and Lauterpacht, those who thought otherwise included MM. Zourek and Amado. cf. ILC, *Yearbook* 1954, vol. I, pp. 154–61.
61. Rosenne, op. cit., note 28, pp. 322–412.
62. ILC, *Yearbook* 1955, vol. I, pp. 143–50, particularly p. 143.
63. Ibid., p. 146.
64. Ibid., p. 147.
65. Ibid., pp. 260–1.
66. ILC, *Yearbook* 1956, vol. I, pp. 211–16.
67. Ibid., vol. II, pp. 80–8, at p. 86.
68. ILC, *Yearbook* 1956, vol. II, pp. 276–7.
69. (First) UNCLOS, Official Records, vol. III, p. 222 (United States proposal, Doc. A/CONF.13/C.I/L.43).
70. Ibid., p. 218 (United Kingdom proposal, Doc. A/CONF.13/C.I/L.37).
71. Ibid., p. 224 (Netherlands proposal, Doc. A/CONF.13/C.I/L.51).
72. Ibid., pp. 127–32.
73. Ibid., p. 224 (Doc. A/CONF.13/C.I/L.48).
74. Ibid., p. 128.
75. In its judgment of 9 April 1949 in the *Corfu Channel* case, the International Court of Justice said: 'It is, in the opinion of the Court, generally recognized and in accordance with international custom that States in time of peace have a right to send their warships through straits used for international navigation between two parts of the high seas without the previous authorization of a coastal State, provided that the passage is innocent. Unless otherwise prescribed in an international convention, there is no right for a coastal State to prohibit such passage through straits in time of peace.'
76. Op. cit. note 65, p. 129.
77. Ibid., p. 130.
78. Ibid., pp. 129–30.
79. Ibid., p. 131.

80. (First) UNCLOS, 1958, vol. II, p. 66.
81. Ibid., p. 67.
82. Ibid.
83. Ibid., p. 68.
84. Ibid.
85. G. Tunkin, 'The Geneva Conference on the Law of the Sea', *International Affairs* (Moscow), vol. 7, 1958, pp. 47–52, at p. 49.
86. Sorensen, Max, 'Law of the Sea', *International Conciliation*, No. 516, pp. 193–256, at p. 235.
87. For some recent articles, see, *inter alia*, Oxman, B.H., 'The Regime of Warships under the United Nations Convention on the Law of the Sea', *Virginia Journal of International Law*, vol. 24, 1984, pp. 809–63; Froman, F.D., 'Uncharted Waters: Non-innocent Passage of Warships in the Territorial Sea', *San Diego Law Review*, vol. 21, 1984, pp. 625–89.
88. Between 1957 and 1973 some of the States which had enacted national legislation subjecting the innocent passage of warships to prior notification and/or authorization included the Soviet Union, Sweden, Denmark, Brazil, the Dominican Republic, Algeria and Sudan. Those to follow between 1973 and 1977 comprised India and Pakistan. See United Nations, National Legislation and Treaties Relating to the Law of the Sea, Doc. ST/LEG/SER.B/15, 16 and 19; respectively on pp. 254–70, 55–8, 142–50.
89. See, for example, Article 15 of Doc. A/CONF.62/C.2/L.16, Third UNCLOS, Official Records, vol. III, p. 192 (Malaysia, Morocco, Oman and Yemen: Draft Articles on Navigation Through the Territorial Sea, Including Straits Used for International Navigation.
90. Third UNCLOS, Official Records, vol. II, pp. 99–142.
91. Ibid., p. 142.
92. Ibid., p. 135.
93. Ibid., p. 140.
94. See Renate Platzöder (ed.), *Third UNCLOS: Documents*, Dobbs Ferry, NY, Oceana, 1982, pp. 224, 242 and 260–1, and ibid., vol. IV, 1983, at p. 27.
95. See, e.g. UN Doc. A/CONF.62/L.97 and A/CONF.62/L.117. The most 'popular' amendment was included in Doc. A/CONF.62/C.2/Informal Meeting/58; it was co-sponsored by Argentina, China and 30 other coastal States.
96. Third UNCLOS, Official Records, vol. III, p. 114. In an introductory statement relating to this document, it was stated, *inter alia*, that: 'The inclusion of these formulations does not imply any opinion on the degree of support they have commanded either in the preparatory stage or in the proceedings of the Caracas Session of the Conference. The inclusion . . . does not necessarily imply that there are no other opinions concerning these questions or that all or most delegations agree on the necessity for such a provision.' Ibid., p. 109.
97. UN Doc. A/CONF.62/C.2/Blue Paper No. 14, 7 May 1975, Platzöder, op. cit. note 94, vol. IV, at p. 153.
98. Doc. A/CONF.62/WP.10 and Add. 1, Third UNCLOS, Official Records, vol. VIII, p. 9.
99. The debate can be found in Third UNCLOS, Official Records, vol. 14, pp. 15–81.
100. Ibid., p. 18.
101. See Doc. C.2/Informal Meeting/58, 20 March 1980, reprinted in Platzöder, op. cit. note 94, vol. V, at p. 62.
102. Doc. A/CONF.62/L.117 of 13 April 1982, co-sponsored by Algeria, Bahrain, Benin, Cape Verde, China, Congo, Egypt, Guinea-Bissau, Djibouti, Iran, Libya, Malta, Morocco, Oman, Pakistan, Papua New Guinea, Philippines, Syria, North Korea,

Romania, São Tomé and Príncipe, Sierra Leone, Somalia, Sudan, Surinam, Uruguay, and both Yemens, Third UNCLOS, Official Records, vol. XVI, p. 225.

103. Doc. A/CONF.62/L.97 of 13 April 1982 in Third UNCLOS, Official Records, vol. XVI, p. 217.

104. In a letter to the President of the Conference, the representative of the United States of America even stated: '. . . the United States firmly opposes any substantive changes to the delicate balance that has been so painstakingly achieved. Particularly as regards the navigation and overflight provisions, any destabilizing change would make it impossible for the United States to participate in the Convention. Special emphasis of our opposition is made to those formal amendments which address Articles 21, 39 and 410, or any amendment that would permit reservations to the navigation and overflight provisions. Such amendments would compromise the very foundation upon which the *negotiating package* rests, and would in turn compromise the character of the resultant provisions, both within the context of the Conference and without.' Doc. A/CONF.62/L.130, Third UNCLOS, vol. XVI, p. 235.

105. In order to achieve universal acceptance of the Convention as a whole, decision making in the Third UNCLOS was by consensus. Intricately linked to this was the idea of a *package deal*. The underlying principle of this concept was that in view of the different priorities of different States, each State would bargain for provisions in the Convention that were most desirable and at the same time accept the demands of another on a different issue. A typical example of this comprising of a liberal navigational status in foreign coastal waters *vis-à-vis* an international seabed mining regime. The whole compromise put together would consist of one huge bundle. By picking and choosing portions of the Convention at this moment, the question could be asked whether this may not amount to eliminating the 'quid' of another State's 'quo'? i.e. the tendency to reject Part XI of the 1982 Convention by some States may amount to defeating the interpretation of the provisions which could have acted as a compromise on navigations as far as this Convention is concerned. For details on the notion of package deal, see Caminos, H. and Molitor, R.M., 'Progressive Development of International Law and the Package Deal', *AJIL*, vol. 79, 1985, pp. 871–90.

106. Third UNCLOS, Official Records, vol. XVI, p. 132 (176 meeting). At the closing session of Conference in Jamaica (December 1982), some supporters of the Gabonese proposal referred to the President's statement to substantiate their view that the requirement of notification and/or authorization for warships to exercise the right of innocent passage was recognized, albeit indirectly, in the Convention. A typical instance of this was the statement made by the Romanian delegate to the effect that: 'Concerning passage of foreign warships through territorial seas . . . coastal States . . . (have) the right to adopt national regulations concerning passage of such ships through the territorial sea. The right to adopt such measures is fully in keeping with the provisions of Articles 19 and 25, and this is clear also from the statement made by the President of UNCLOS . . . on 26 April 1982, as well as from other provisions on the status of the territorial sea. Under these regulations, the territorial sea is an integral part of the national territory and is under the full sovereignty of the coastal State. That is why nothing could prevent the coastal State from adopting national regulations to protect its security interests.' Ibid., vol. XVII, p. 72.

107. This is the position of the Baltic States, particularly Sweden and Finland, where a 'special regional rule' is said to exist.

108. Third UNCLOS, Official Records, vol. XVII, p. 106. Somewhat similar statements were made by at least eight other delegations at the signing ceremony.

109. Ibid., p. 123.

110. Article 309 states that no reservations or exceptions may be made to the Convention

unless expressly so provided for in the relevant articles; which is not the case regarding the passage of warships.

111. For further details on this complex issue, see in particular McDorman, T.L., 'Reservations and the Law of the Sea Treaty', *Journal of Maritime Law and Commerce*, vol. 13, 1982, pp. 481–591; McRae, D.M., 'The Legal Effect of Interpretative Declarations', *BYBIL*, vol. 49, 1978, pp. 155–73.
112. Article 19 specifically excludes as non-innocent any passage prejudicial to the security of the coastal State, whereas Article 25 expressly provides that a coastal State 'may take the necessary steps in its territorial sea to prevent passage which is not innocent'. The best minimum precaution to be taken by the coastal State is, of course, the requirement of notification and/or authorization for the passage of warships.
113. 1982 Convention, sub-section A, Articles 17–26; sub-section B, Articles 27–28; sub-section C, Articles 29–32, respectively.
114. Ibid., Articles 32, 31 and 30.
115. Case concerning *United States Diplomatic and Consular Staff in Tehran* (United States v. Iran), ICJ, *Reports* 1980, p. 40.
116. Froman, op. cit. note 87, p. 642.
117. e.g., by restricting the number of warships passing at one time, or by suspending, in principle 'temporarily' but in fact indefinitely, the passage of ships under Article 25(3) for security reasons.
118. Found in Simmonds, K.R. (ed.), *New Directions in the Law of the Sea*, Dobbs Ferry, NY, Oceana, 1983, pp. 9–26; Butler, W.E. (ed.), *The USSR Eastern Europe and the Development of the Law of the Sea*, Dobbs Ferry, NY Oceana, 1983, p. 8.
119. Referring to the 1960 Rules (on Notices to Mariners), a weekly publication of the USSR Ministry of Defence, W.E. Butler states: 'Under the 1960 Rules, consent for the passage of foreign warships into Soviet territorial waters must be requested through diplomatic channel thirty days prior to the proposed visit. The request must specify the number, class, and name of the ship, . . . the purpose of the passage, . . . the rank and name of the commander . . . Not more than three ships may enter any one area of territorial waters at the same time . . . These provisions also apply to naval auxiliary vessels and armed vessels for the protection of fisheries. Foreign warships carrying heads of State or heads of diplomatic representations accredited to the Government of the U.S.S.R. follow a procedure of notification rather than authorization. These Rules do not apply to foreign warships seeking refuge because of damage or distress of storm; however, compulsory pilotage regulations do apply in all instances.' The 1960 Rules are still in force. cf. 'Rules for Navigation and Sojourn of Foreign Warships in the Territorial Waters (Territorial Sea) of the U.S.S.R. and the Internal Waters and Ports of the U.S.S.R.', in *International Legal Materials*, vol. XXIV, 1985, p. 1715, particularly Articles 4, 8, 12 and 15.
120. United Nations Doc. A/34/712.S/13640, 23 November 1979, reprinted in Nordquist, M.H. and Park, C.H. (eds), *North America and the Asian Pacific and the Development of the Law of the Sea Treaties and National Legislations*, Dobbs Ferry, NY, Oceana, 1981, p. 6. For a current official Chinese perspective see Shao Jin, 'The Question of Innocent Passage of Warships: After UNCLOS III', *Marine Policy*, vol. 13, no. 1, January 1989, pp. 56–67.
121. Reprinted in United Nations Legislative Series, ST/LEG/SER.B/19, p. 133.
122. United Nations Legislative Series, ST/LEG/SER.B/16, p. 55.
123. Reprinted in Simmonds, op. cit. note 118, p. 314.
124. *Law of the Sea Bulletin*, No. 6, October 1985, p. 40.
125. Bernhardt, R., 'Custom and Treaty in the Law of the Sea' (*Recueil des Cours*) *Collected Courses of the Hague Academy of International Law*, 1987, vol. 5, pp. 251–330, particularly p. 329.

126. Op. cit. note 122, p. 30.
127. *Law of the Sea Bulletin*, No. 3, March 1984, p. 13.
128. op. cit. note 121, p. 48.
129. *Law of the Sea Bulletin*, Special Issue I, March 1987, p. 8.
130. See, for example, British practice as found in an extract of a Parliamentary Debate in *BYBIL*, vol. 55, 1984, p. 549.
131. Op. cit. note 69, p. 214, Doc. A/CONF.13/C.1/L.21 (Yugoslavia: Proposal on Article 24). The proposal was as follows:
1. The text of the present article to become paragraph 1.
2. After the new paragraph 1 add the following new paragraph 2: "2. The coastal State may deny the exercise of the right of innocent passage through its territorial sea to any ship carrying any kind of nuclear weapon."
132. Ibid., p. 129.
133. Ibid., p. 146.
134. Third UNCLOS, Official Records, vol. III, p. 192, Doc. A/CONF.62/C2/L.16 (Malaysia, Morocco, Oman and Yemen: Draft Articles on Navigation Through the Territorial Sea). In introducing these Draft Articles, the delegate of Oman made it clear, however, that oil tankers and chemical tankers would not be subject to authorization and/or control. Ibid., vol. II, pp. 135–6.
135. 1982 Convention, Article 23.
136. Third UNCLOS, Official Records, vol. II, p. 137.
137. In other words, the suspicion that a vessel carries nuclear weapons would not be a sufficient ground for requiring prior notification and/or authorization, were it not for the fact that they are considered warships passing through the territorial sea.
138. ILC, *Yearbook* 1956, vol. II pp. 272–3.
139. cf. Fitzmaurice, G., 'Some Results of the Geneva Conference on the Law of the Sea', *International and Comparative Law Quarterly*, vol. 8, 1959, p. 98.
140. Froman, op. cit. note 116, p. 663.
141. According to some submarine commanders, it is preferable to go through congested waters in a submerged condition because there is less likelihood of collision. A submarine on the surface lies low in the water and sometimes is not all that easy to see. Per Johnson, D.H.N., in Report of the 58th Conference of the *International Law Association*, Manila, 1978 (Proceedings of the Law of the Sea Commitee), pp. 248–338, at p. 337.
142. Third UNCLOS, Official Records, vol. II, p. 137.
143. As an independent article, it covers all types of underwater vehicles, be they nuclear submarines, warships, etc.
144. W. Riphagen comes to the same conclusion: '. . . la règle de conduite stipulée pour les sous-marins à l'article 20 du texte de 1982 (article 14(6) du texte de 1958) a pour but d'exiger la manifestation du caractère inoffensif du passage. Ceci conduit à la conclusion que la non-observation de cette règle ôte le caractère inoffensif au passage.' *Perspectives du droit de la mer à l'issue de la 3e Conférence des Nations Unies*, Société française pour le droit international, Colloque de Rouen, Paris, Pedone, 1984, p. 199.
145. Some authors are of the opinion that in this connection a distinction must be made between non-innocent passage and violations of coastal State laws and regulations, on the basis of the sanctions available to meet each breach. They say that ships in non-innocent passage could be treated legally as though they were passing through the coastal State's internal waters, whereas the more limited sanction of warning and expulsion would apply, for example, to warships breaching some pertinent coastal State laws and regulations. The characterization of a breach as one rendering passage non-innocent or as merely violative of a coastal State law is quite misleading here, for two reasons. First, a proper reading of the Convention would warrant the proposition

that some violations of pertinent coastal State laws would automatically deprive the ship or vessel of the right of innocent passage. Otherwise such laws and regulations would not have been placed in Part II, section 3, dealing with the right of innocent passage in the territorial sea. Secondly, the milder sanction of expulsion, applied, for example, to warships breaching coastal State laws, is not due to the type of breach contemplated but to the immunity such vessels should enjoy even when they violate rules pertaining to the exercise of the right of innocent passage. It is of course contradictory to envisage, as is done in Article 31 of the 1982 Convention, that a ship, and a warship for that matter, can still be presumed in innocent passage while at the same time engaging the international responsibility of the flag State for any loss or injury to the coastal State resulting from non-compliance with the laws and regulations of the coastal State. cf. Froman, op. cit. note 116, p. 664.

146. Referring to this type of submarine, D.P. O'Connell asserts: 'Most submariners will agree that submergence in the territorial sea . . . may be adopting a belligerent posture *vis-à-vis* the coastal State . . . and that presence there in these circumstances would not amount to innocent passage.' 'International Law and Contemporary Naval Operations', *BYBIL*, vol. 44, 1970, pp. 57–8.

Chapter 6

Rights and obligations of the coastal State and the flag State connected with the exercise of the right of innocent passage in coastal waters

1. The Rights and obligations of the coastal State

The coastal State has rights and obligations towards sea vessels exercising the right of innocent passage. Whereas the obligations of the coastal State are essentially preventive, its rights are of a prescriptive and a punitive nature. Unlike the merely jurisdictional prerogatives *in rem* and *in personam* described in Chapter 4, the rights to be examined below clearly show the precarious autonomy enjoyed by the right of innocent passage *vis-à-vis* the sovereignty of coastal States over their territorial waters.

(a) Rights of the coastal State over foreign vessels exercising the right of innocent passage

The prescriptive or punitive rights exercised by the coastal State over vessels in their territorial seas are numerous, irrespective of the fact that these vessels may be exercising or planning to the exercise the right of innocent passage. However, some of these rights are strictly subsidiary or superfluous[1] because they are already contained in other rights, as will be seen below. Others are of a more substantial character because they give the coastal State enforcement power. We shall examine three of these rights, in order to illustrate their effects on the autonomy of the right of innocent passage in coastal waters. These rights are:

(1) the right to suspend innocent passage;
(2) the right to enforce anti-pollution measures; and
(3) the right of hot pursuit.

The right to suspend innocent passage

That the coastal State has the right to suspend innocent passage in certain portions of its territorial sea, even temporarily, suggests that the right to such passage is subordinated to the sovereignty of the coastal State over these waters.[2] Despite the conditions on which suspension is made dependent in the relevant Article of the 1982 Convention, it has been recognized since 1954, when a draft text on this point was first examined by the International Law Commission, that the suspension depends on the coastal State's initiative.

Although no text was proposed at the 1930 Hague Codification Conference regarding the possibility for the coastal State to suspend innocent passage in certain portions of its territorial sea,[3] this possibility was supplied in Article 5 embodied in the Final Act. Article 5 stated that:

> The right of passage does not prevent the coastal State from taking all necessary steps to protect itself in the territorial sea against any act prejudicial to the security, public policy or fiscal interests of the State . . .

Apparently extrapolating that Article, a member of the International Law Commission, considering that in some instances even innocent passage could constitute a danger, and that a State had a right, on security grounds, to forbid even the innocent passage of foreign ships through its territorial sea, proposed a new provision specifically to cover these concerns. The proposed new provision read:

> The coastal State may suspend temporarily and in definite areas of its territorial sea the exercise of the right of innocent passage on the ground that it is necessary for the maintenance of public order. In this case the coastal State is bound to give due publicity to the suspension.[4]

In a commentary which followed the above provision, it was stated that:

> In exceptional cases even a temporary suspension of the right of innocent passage is permissible, if compelling reasons connected with public order or general security so require. Although it is arguable that this power was in any case implied. The Commission consider it desirable to mention it expressly . . . (and) that only a temporary suspension in definite areas is permissible. The Commission is of the opinion that the article states the international law in force.[5]

In the following sessions of the International Law Commission and up to the adoption of a final text on the territorial sea by that body in 1956, the provision on temporary suspension of the right of innocent passage was constantly reaffirmed. However, the term 'public policy', embodied in the 1954 text as one of the grounds justifying suspension, was eliminated. Commenting on this elimination, the Commission explained that 'the term "public policy" used in Article 20 of the 1954 draft being interpretable in different ways, the Commission preferred a text containing no mention of it . . .'.[6]

Of course, the expression 'public policy' is so broad that a coastal State would be entirely at liberty to suspend indefinitely in unspecified areas the right of innocent passage, under the flimsiest pretexts. Subsequent texts thus provided for the suspension of innocent passage if it was 'essential for the protection of the *security* of the coastal State'.

At the (First) Conference on the Law of the Sea held in 1958, various attempts were made to limit the geographical scope of any possible suspension, despite general consensus on the security considerations which could serve as a justification. In this regard, an amendment was proposed at the level of the Second Committee, to the effect that innocent passage could not be suspended in international straits for security reasons. Another amendment was also proposed, which partly innovated on the *Corfu Channel* principle and prohibited the 'suspension of the innocent passage of foreign ships through straits which are used for international navigation between . . . high seas . . . or the territorial sea of a foreign State'. Both proposals were adopted[7] and became paragraphs (3) and (4) of Article 16 of the 1958 Geneva Convention on the Territorial Sea and the Contiguous Zone.

Article 16(3) and (4) runs as follows:

> Subject to the provisions of paragraph 4, the coastal State may, without discrimination amongst foreign ships, suspend temporarily in specified areas of its territorial sea the innocent passage of foreign ships if such suspension is essential for the protection of its security. Such suspension shall take effect only after having been duly published.
> There shall be no suspension of the innocent passage of foreign ships through straits which are used for international navigation between one part of the high seas and another part of the high seas or the territorial sea of a foreign State.

At the Third United Nations Conference on the Law of the Sea, in addition to the 'security' considerations that could justify the exercise of the right of temporarily suspending the right of innocent passage, another security-based consideration was included. This consideration involves weapons exercises to which the coastal State is directly or indirectly a party. Although weapon exercises may be considered as being covered by the reference to the coastal State's security, the inclusion of an express stipulation seems to have been motivated by concerns relating to existing military alliances.[8]

In view of the special treatment given to straits in the 1982 Convention, the latter emphasizes that the coastal State cannot exercise the right of suspension of innocent passage in straits.[9] As regards the territorial sea, Article 25(3) of the 1982 Convention provides that

> the coastal State may, without discrimination in form or in fact among foreign ships, suspend temporarily in specified areas of its territorial sea the innocent passage of foreign ships if such suspension is essential for the protection of its security, including weapons exercises. Such suspension shall take effect only after having been duly published.

Consequently, under contemporary trends the right of suspension granted to the coastal State is subject to important qualifications. At the same time, the determination of how essential the suspension is, and of what does constitute the security of the coastal State, is left to that State. It remains to be seen whether the restrictions placed on the exercise of the coastal State's right of suspension adequately limit the discretion of that State, particularly in preventing it from permanently suspending innocent passage.

The coastal State's right to suspend innocent passage is subordinated to the following conditions:

(1) It must be non-discriminatory as between foreign ships: in principle, *all* foreign vessels must be banned from the suspension areas. If this condition were to be applied strictly, 'joint manoeuvres' involving foreign vessels in the portion of the territorial sea where passage is suspended would lead to discrimination against third States. The reference to weapons exercises

contained in Article 25(3) could, however, serve as a defence against a plea of discrimination since such exercises may well involve non-national vessels. Furthermore a special relationship between two States could justify the granting of special rights in the suspension areas, and other States could not invoke these rights as a ground for claiming similar treatment.

(2) The suspension must be temporary and thus not involve the permanent closure of portions or of the entire territorial sea. In the absence of any indication as to what constitutes temporary suspension, successive notifications of suspension of innocent passage in alternative portions of the territorial sea could in effect permanently deprive foreign vessels from traversing these waters, without any perceived violation of the rule by the coastal State. In practice, of course, this is the accepted trend, as acknowledged by Tullis Treves in Chapter 15 of a recent collective publication.[10]

(3) The third condition for the suspension of innocent passage is that that suspension may only cover specified areas of the territorial sea. This carries the implication that the suspension should at no time cover the entire territorial sea. However, it is common practice, due to geopolitical considerations, for a suspension to go beyond the limits of the security requirements that prompted it in the first place.[11]

(4) The fourth condition is that the suspension should be essential for protection of coastal State security, including weapons exercises. The suspension must be essential and not just one among several options open to the coastal State. Who decides whether suspending innocent passage is merely convenient or the only option? Given the sensitivity of States to security issues, the necessity of a suspension of innocent passage is too subjective a matter for referring to any standards other than those set by the coastal State itself. In the same vein, protection of security might involve much more than could be anticipated in the legislative history of the rule. As will be seen in the pages ahead, an apparently lesser concern in terms of security, such as marine pollution, could and has been used to justify the suspension of the right of innocent passage in portions of the territorial sea of a coastal State. Thus, passage might also be suspended in order to construct artificial islands, installations, deepwater ports, etc., which might facilitate rather than restrict the exercise of the right of innocent passage.

(5) The last condition for the coastal State legitimately to suspend innocent passage is for the suspension to be published before it becomes effective. Of course, this is also a prerequisite for all coastal State laws and regulations concerning navigations in the territorial sea.

Be this as it may, the conditions enumerated above do not significantly diminish the scope of the unilateral initiative of the coastal State and the obvious danger this represents for the right of innocent passage as an independent institution. Nevertheless, the legality of each suspension would in the final analysis be based on 'reasonableness' viewed in the light of all the circumstances rather than on the ambivalent concept of 'security considerations'.

The right to enforce anti-pollution measures

As far as maritime pollution[12] is concerned, the tradition has always been that vessel-source pollution was an exception. Where such pollution occurred, pre-1982 conventions generally subjected anti-pollution law enforcement to the flag State under whose authority a particular ship operated.

Under the 1982 Convention, the power to enforce marine pollution standards is extended to the port State, in the case where a ship has entered the port of a foreign State, and to the coastal State within whose waters a ship may be exercising the right of innocent passage.

The exercise of jurisdiction and the enforcement of marine pollution standards have always been based on the assumption that it is the flag State and not the coastal State that has competence. Consequently, agreements prior to the 1982 Convention assigned coastal States the secondary role of investigating alleged pollution offences and of supplying the flag State with the necessary evidence for purposes of prosecution.[13] Thus, a coastal State affected by pollution due to a ship exercising the right of innocent passage had no power to investigate the ship itself (e.g. its 'operations' or its anti-pollution equipment, if any). This lack of competence was exacerbated by the fact that, despite acknowledged coastal State sovereignty, there had been no direct reference in ealier conventions to any coastal State power to enforce anti-pollution measures in its territorial sea.

By implication at least, it could be said that the 1958 Geneva Convention on the Territorial Sea and the Contiguous Zone did make some reference to the competence of the coastal State to enforce anti-pollution legislation in its territorial sea.[14] If there were still doubts on whether the coastal State should be able to enforce pollution standards against ships exercising the right of innocent passage, these doubts were dispelled by the 1982 Convention. Article 21 granting the coastal State the right to establish and enforce laws for the control of pollution from ships exercising the right of innocent passage in the territorial sea provides the following:

> 1. The coastal State may adopt laws and regulations, in conformity with the provisions of this Convention and other rules of international law, relating to innocent passage through the territorial sea, in respect of . . . (f) the preservation of the environment of the coastal State and the prevention, reduction and control of pollution thereof.
> 2. Such laws and regulations shall not apply to design, construction, manning of equipment of foreign ships unless they are giving effect to generally accepted international rules or standards.
> 4. Foreign ships exercising the right of innocent passage through the territorial sea shall comply with all such laws and regulations and all generally accepted international regulations relating to the prevention of collision at sea.

Furthermore, the coastal State's right in this field is confirmed in Article 211(4) on pollution from vessels, where it is stated:

> Coastal States may, in the exercise of their sovereignty within their territorial sea, adopt laws and regulations for the prevention, reduction and control of

marine pollution from foreign vessels, including vessels exercising the right of innocent passage.

Can the coastal State, in preventing, reducing and controlling marine pollution by enactments and enforcement measures, deny or disturb the right of innocent passage through its territorial sea? In other words, could the coastal State in enforcing anti-pollution standards, go beyond the standards inscribed in international conventions and adopt more exacting laws and regulations, thus impairing the right of innocent passage? Although the legislative history of the Articles cited above shows that there was majority support for the view that coastal States could impose higher standards within the territorial sea where special circumstances so warrant, or where the waters were exceptionally vulnerable to pollution, no provision directly envisions this possibility. Instead, to pinpoint a limit to coastal State prerogatives in this regard, it is clearly stated in Article 21(2) cited earlier that coastal State laws and enforcement measures shall not apply to the design, construction, manning and equipment of vessels unless they are giving effect to (i.e. are not more stringent than) generally accepted international standards. Understandably, this was to avoid extreme disparities between coastal State laws, making it difficult for the ship and its flag State to comply with all laws. Nevertheless, for purposes of navigational 'safety', requirements such as speed limits, traffic lanes, tolerated oily residue on ships, etc., in the exercise of the right of innocent passage, are placed under exclusive coastal State jurisdiction. Furthermore,the coastal State has the power, in enforcing anti-pollution standards, to react to special acts of 'wilful and serious pollution contrary to this Convention' as in that case the passage would no longer be 'innocent' but 'prejudicial to the peace, good order or security of the coastal State'.[15] This could be true, in particular, for pollution by dumping which, under the pertinent provision of the 1982 Convention, cannot be carried out without the express prior consent of the coastal State 'which has the right to permit, regulate and control such dumping . . .'.[16]

Finally, independently of whether a ship is exercising the right of innocent passage, in cases of accidents or maritime casualties, the coastal State may invoke Article 221 of the 1982 Convention which allows that State to take protective measures 'pursuant to international law, both customary and conventional'. In this regard, States can rely on a broad range of intervention/enforcement measures pursuant to the doctrines of self-preservation or self-help.

The right of hot pursuit

Another right with which the coastal State is endowed by virtue of its sovereignty over the territorial sea, a power superior to the right of innocent passage, is the right of hot pursuit. Unlike the two coastal State rights analysed above, namely, the right to suspend innocent passage and the right to enforce anti-pollution measures, the right of hot pursuit allows the coastal State to 'effectively administer justice'. In other words, by recognizing the principle of hot pursuit, the international Law of the Sea acknowledges 'the need for protection of certain essential interests of the State by developing customary rights of a jurisdictional character. Where such customary rights exist the legality of State action needs no further justification . . .'.[17]

The right of hot pursuit is one of the oldest remedies in the customary international Law of the Sea. And even if it may apply in other areas of international law, it is mainly the right of the coastal State to arrest a vessel that was once in the territorial sea and, if found guilty of wrong-doing, to punish the vessel according to its laws.[18]

All the Laws of the Sea conventions have granted the right of hot pursuit to the coastal State, despite the potential danger it may present for what is left of the right of innocent passage. Article 111 of the 1982 Convention, which reproduces Article 23 of the 1958 Geneva Convention on the High Seas, and which in turn codifies the customary international law on the subject,[19] succinctly prescribes the following:

> The hot pursuit of a foreign ship may be undertaken when the competent authorities of the coastal State have good reason to believe that the ship has violated the laws and regulations of that State. Such pursuit must be commenced when the foreign ship or one of its boats is within the internal waters, the archipelagic waters, the territorial sea or the contiguous zone of the pursuing State, and may only be continued outside the territorial sea or the contiguous zone if the pursuit has not been interrupted.
>
> The right of hot pursuit ceases as soon as the ship pursued enters the territorial sea of its own State or of a third State.
>
> Hot pursuit is not deemed to have begun unless the pursuing ship has satisfied itself by such practicable means as may be available that the ship pursued or one of its boats or other craft working as a team and using the ship pursued as a mother ship is within the limits of the territorial sea . . .
>
> Where a ship has been stopped or arressted outside the territorial sea in circumstances which do not justify the exercise of the right of hot pursuit, it shall be compensated for any loss or damage that may have been thereby sustained.

Considering the few conditions in the above text, it could be argued that *vis-à-vis* vessels exercising the right of innocent passage, the coastal State can easily frustrate that right.

In determining whether to undertake hot pursuit, the coastal State is given the discretion to decide whether or not it 'has good reason to believe' that a ship has violated its laws. Thus the coastal State is absolved from any error of judgment that might prevent the foreign vessel from exercising the right of innocent passage. This is particularly the case if the pursuit began and stopped within the territorial sea of the coastal State.

Be that as it may, the restrictions placed on the exercise of the right of hot pursuit—cessation of that right as soon as the ship enters a foreign territorial sea, or that of its flag State; duty to pay compensation for any abusive exercise of the right of hot pursuit—do not sufficiently guarantee the right of innocent passage as an independent regime of international navigations in coastal waters.

Despite the frustrating effect the various coastal State rights outlined above could have on foreign vessels in the territorial sea, the coastal State is, nevertheless, subject to certain obligations towards vessels exercising the right of innocent passage. An analysis of the various draft projects and Law of the Sea conventions shows, however, that these obligations placed on the coastal State are preventive against any abuses rather than 'positive'.

(b) Obligations of the coastal State

By virtue of its sovereignty over its territorial sea, a coastal State enjoys the rights and carries the obligations imposed by international law on any territorial sovereign. Towards foreign ships exercising the right of innocent passage, the coastal State is bound to observe specific obligations. But these duties scarcely counterbalance the rights the coastal State exercises over foreign vessels on innocent passage.

When a foreign vessel is in innocent passage, the coastal State is subjected to two obligations: abstention and information.

The duty of abstention

This was the first and only duty acknowledged at the 1930 Hague Codification Conference. Article 4 embodied in the Final Act provided that 'a coastal State may put no obstacles in the way of the innocent passage of foreign vessels in the territorial sea'.

This call for self-restraint was aimed at limiting the powers which other parts of the Draft Articles gave the coastal State to protect itself in the territorial sea. Thus, the coastal State, when exercising its legislative powers or its economic rights through anti-pollution measures or the building of structures in the territorial seas, was to ensure first and foremost that the rights of other States to use the sea for navigation were respected.

In the International Law Commission, this duty of abstention was given the shape of a positive obligation. The Final Draft on the territorial sea provided in Article 16(1) that:

> The coastal State must not hamper innocent passage through the territorial sea. It is required to use the means at its disposal to ensure respect for innocent passage through the territorial sea and must not allow the said sea to be used for acts contrary to the rights of other States.

In the commentary accompanying this paragraph it was explained:

> If they hamper innocent passage, installations intended for the exploitation of the seabed and subsoil of the territorial sea must not be sited in narrow channels or in sealanes forming part of the territorial sea and essential for international navigation.[20]

At the 1958 Geneva Conference on the Law of the Sea, a majority of coastal States considered this positive obligation unwarranted and expressed preference for the 1930 formulation.[21] By requiring the coastal State 'to use the means at its disposal to ensure respect for innocent passage' (i.e. to act as a benevolent policeman for foreign vessels in its territorial sea), the coastal State was being burdened by international responsibilities which had not been contemplated before.

The 1958 Geneva Convention on the Territorial Sea and the Contiguous Zone reverted to the 1930 solution in this regard. Article 15(1) of that Convention simply states, as had been the case at The Hague, that 'the coastal State must not hamper innocent passage through the territorial sea'.

Article 24(1) of the 1982 Convention reads as follows:

> The coastal State shall not hamper the innocent passage of foreign ships through the territorial sea except in accordance with this Convention. In particular, in the application of this Convention or of any laws or regulations adopted in conformity with this Convention, the coastal State shall not:
> (a) impose requirements on foreign ships which have the practical effect of denying or impairing the right of innocent passage; or
> (b) discriminate in form or in fact against the ships of any State or against Ships carrying cargoes to, from or on behalf of any State.

The duty of information

The coastal State's duty to inform other States, by way of publicity, of any inherent dangers to navigation within its territorial sea was confirmed by the International Court of Justice in 1949 in the *Corfu Channel* case between the United Kingdom and Albania. As we saw in Chapter 4, the essential fact of the case was that British warships exercising the right of innocent passage struck contact mines moored in Albanian territorial waters immediately after the Second World War. In its judgment, the Court held that, independently of Albania's conduct after the explosions, the dilatory nature of its diplomatic notes, and the legal existence of a situation of war in the area, there was a *duty to inform* vessels of the existence of mines in its territorial sea,[22] since there was an overwhelming presumption that Albania knew of the mines, in view of the circumstances, and since Albania had exercised great diligence in watching over this portion of its territory.

The duty to inform others of real or possible dangers in the territorial sea has subsequently been included in all the Law of the Sea conventions. The draft article of the International Law Commission, its Final Draft, the 1958 Geneva Convention on the Territorial Sea and the Contiguous Zone, and, of course, the 1982 Convention contain the following provision on this point: 'The coastal State shall give appropriate publicity to any danger to navigation, of which it has knowledge, within its territorial sea.'[23]

Conclusion

These obligations of abstention and information do not mean that the coastal State must incur extra expenditures to ensure the safety of vessels exercising the right of innocent passage. In other words, the obligations in question do not involve positive measures such as dredging the territorial seas or internal waters, erecting lighthouses or removing wrecks from the navigational channels. However, as regards dangers to navigation which are created by the coastal State itself (building offshore installations and structures of artificial islands, etc.), that State is under a duty to mark clearly any navigational hazards so created, to maintain warning devices and, of course, to file appropriate notice to vessels likely to exercise the right of innocent passage. But, with regard to dangers to navigation in the territorial sea not caused by the coastal State (for example a shipwreck), it is the flag State (of the wrecked ship in our example) that is responsible for any claims, although the coastal State does have the right—but not the obligation!—to remove such wrecks in its territorial sea.

A fine distinction is sometimes made between the dangers to navigation and the difficulties of navigation.[24] The notion of difficulties of navigation is said to cover situations in which the ship, its cargo or its passengers are threatened due to stress of weather or to the special characteristics of particular channels which normally require the designation of sealanes and/or the prescription of traffic separation schemes.[25] Under these circumstances, if a foreign ship exercising the right of innocent passage is damaged, the coastal State in principle bears no obligation. Nonetheless, the question can still be asked as to what happens, if, before the accident, the coastal State was aware of these difficulties? In sum, regardless of whether one is faced with dangers to, or with difficulties of, navigation, the coastal State is obliged to give appropriate publicity or information, if it has knowledge thereof,[26] in order to escape responsibility.

2. The rights and obligations of foreign vessels and/or flag State

(a) Rights of foreign vessels/flag State

To a certain degree the rights and obligations of the coastal State towards a vessel exercising the right of innocent passage are respectively the obligations and rights of a foreign vessel while in a coastal State's territorial sea. However, in view of the coastal State's sovereignty over its territorial sea, foreign vessels in this part of the sea are subjected to more obligations than rights independently of the right of innocent passage.

The main right enjoyed by foreign vessels in foreign territorial seas is the right of innocent passage, which forms the object of this study. That is, wherever a merchant ship is not endangering and will not endanger a coastal State's security and other interests, or wherever a warship is given consent to navigate in those coastal waters, general international law acknowledges that these vessels have a right to navigate in them.

(b) Obligations of foreign vessels/flag State

Vessels exercising the right of innocent passage, like aircraft flying over a foreign sovereign airspace, must observe the local laws regardless of the fact that they are exercising an independent right. The situation would be different if these vessels were availing themselves of this independent right extra-territorially and in a 'no-man's land' such as the high seas. Exercising the right in sovereign coastal waters means submission to the main laws and regulations of that coastal State. Although by and large foreign vessels remain under the jurisdiction of their flag State, they nevertheless have duties towards the coastal State while exercising the right of innocent passage.

The obligations of foreign vessels in innocent passage were embodied in Article 6 of the Final Act of the 1930 Hague Codification Conference. Article 6 ran as follows:

> Foreign vessels exercising the right of passage shall comply with the laws and regulations enacted in conformity with international usage by the coastal State, and, in particular, as regards:
> (a) the safety of traffic and the protection of channels and buoys;
> (b) the protection of the waters of the coastal State against pollution of any kind caused by vessels;
> (c) the protection of the products of the territorial sea;
> (d) the rights of fishing, shooting and analogous rights belonging to the coastal State.
>
> The coastal State may not, however, apply these rules or regulations in such a manner as to discriminate between foreign vessels of different nationalities, nor, save in matters relating to fishing and shooting, between national vessels and foreign vessels.[27]

A corresponding provision was inserted as Article 18 in the Final Draft of the International Law Commission. This rule modified the 1930 provision and stated simply:

> Foreign ships exercising the right of passage shall comply with the law and regulations enacted by the coastal State in conformity with the present rules and other rules of international law and, in particular, with the laws and regulations relating to transport and navigation.[28]

In the commentary appended to Article 18, the Commission cited *in toto* the observations which had followed Article 6 of the Final Act of the 1930 Conference, including examples of the laws foreign vessels must obey. The commentary ran as follows:

> '(1) International law has long recognized the right of the coastal State to enact, in the general interest of navigation, special regulations applicable to ships exercising the right of passage through the territorial sea.
>
> (2) Ships entering the territorial sea of a foreign State remain under the jurisdiction of the flag State. Nevertheless, the fact that they are in waters under the sovereignty of another State imposes some limitation on the exclusive jurisdiction of the flag State. Such ships must comply with the laws and regulations enacted by the coastal State in conformity with the present rules and other rules of international law and, in particular, with the laws and regulations relating to transport and navigation. At its seventh session, the Commission though it useful to give the following examples:

(a) The safety of traffic and the protection of channels and buoys;
(b) The protection of the waters of the coastal State against pollution of any kind caused by ships;
(c) The conservation of the living resources of the sea;
(d) The rights of fishing and hunting and analogous rights belonging to the coastal State;
(e) Any hydrographical survey.

(3) At the 8th session, a proposal was made for the addition of the following to this list:
— use of the national flag,
— use of the route prescribed for international navigation,
— and observance of rules relating to security and of customs and health regulations.

The Commission considered that such a list, which could not be exhaustive, would be somewhat arbitrary and preferred to mention these cases in the commentary without including them in the body of the Article'.[29]

Article 18 of the Draft of the International Law Commission was reproduced verbatim in Article 17 of the 1958 Geneva Convention on the Territorial Sea and the Contiguous Zone. However, in the Third United Nations Conference on the Law of the Sea, it was rightly thought that the 1930 provision, except for possible incompleteness of the enumeration of areas where coastal State legislation is permissible, was preferable to the open-ended Article 17, which referred vaguely to 'laws and regulations . . . in conformity with these Articles and other rules of international law . . . and, in particular . . . laws and regulations relating to transport and navigation'.

After enumerating exhaustively the laws and regulations a coastal State may enact relating to innocent passage, Article 21 of the 1982 Convention, in its paragraph 4, formulated the duties of foreign ships in coastal waters in the following way:

> Foreign ships exercising the right of innocent passage through the territorial sea shall comply with all such laws and regulations and all generally accepted international regulations relating to the prevention of collisions at sea.[30]

Furthermore, unlike any earlier treaty before it, the 1982 Convention also establishes additional obligations for foreign nuclear-powered ships or ships carrying nuclear or other inherently dangerous or noxious substances. It provides that when exercising the right of innocent passage these types of vessels must *carry documents* and observe special *precautionary measures* instituted for such vessels by international agreements.[31]

3. Effects of non-compliance with obligations relating to the exercise of the right of innocent passage

As can be deduced from the comparison of the rights and obligations of the coastal State and foreign ships, it would seem that while the coastal State is *duty bound vis-à-vis* every other State to avoid disrupting the exercise of the right of innocent passage by foreign vessels in its coastal waters, foreign vessels for their part are *required* to obey coastal State laws and regulations. Consequently whereas the Convention expressly provides for sanctions following non-compliance with coastal State laws by at least some vessels, nothing of the sort befalls a coastal State disrupting arbitrarily the right of innocent passage, except of course the unpleasantness of being called an unfriendly State.

The failure of a foreign ship exercising the right of innocent passage to discharge its obligations towards the coastal State would in many instances result in the passage being non-innocent. One type of violation of such obligations is the non-compliance with the coastal State laws and regulations mentioned in Article 21 of the 1982 Convention. Another is the failure to pay charges levied for services rendered to the ship by the coastal State. Do these types of non-compliance amount to measures restricting the right of innocent passage? And does the international responsibility incurred by the flag State or the coastal State interfere with the right of innocent passage? These issues will be briefly considered below.

(a) The foreign ship's non-compliance with coastal State laws and regulations

Innocence of passage and compliance with coastal State laws and regulations are directly linked.[32] This direct connection is exemplified in many instances, in the 1982 Convention, by the almost identical provisions in Article 19 on the meaning of innocent passage and in Article 21 on the laws and regulations of the coastal State relating to innocent passage.[33]

This overlapping of coastal State laws and regulations with what would constitute prejudice to the peace, good order or security of the coastal State to render passage non-innocent covers warships and submarines, merchant, fishing and research vessels alike. In spite of this overlap between Articles 19 and 21, does non-compliance with coastal State laws and regulations automatically render passage non-innocent? This is not very clear. The provision obliging foreign ships to comply with coastal State laws and regulations states that: 'Foreign ships *exercising the right of innocent passage* . . . shall comply with all laws and regulations and all generally accepted international regulations . . .'[34]

The wording of this provision in some respect envisages a separation of the right of innocent passage from compliance with coastal State laws and regulations, on the one hand, and from compliance with accepted international regulations, on the other. If this is correct, the exercise of the right of innocent passage would be considered an independent primary and main rule of the Article. Consequently, compliance with coastal State laws and regulations would be subsidiary to the prevailing idea of 'exercising the right of innocent passage'.[35] Thus, treating the two notions as mutually exclusive or almost hierarchical would of course mean that innocent passage and compliance with coastal State laws and regulations are governed by different standards. Naturally violations would call for appropriate sanctions, but not for the refusal of passage. Thus, the violation of coastal State laws and regulations would not necessarily render passage non-innocent. In other words, there could be a right of innocent passage which is not in compliance with coastal State laws and regulations.

A contrary view can be asserted as well. The above-cited provision, in spite of its wording, does not envisage any separation between innocent passage and compliance with coastal State laws. Rather, it envisages the duty of foreign ships, even if exercising another right, to comply with coastal State laws and regulations: while foreign vessels *not* exercising the right of innocent passage in foreign coastal waters must comply with the laws and regulations of the territorial sovereign; even foreign ships exercising that right are subject, a priori, to the coastal State laws and regulations.

This interpretation is further strengthened by the fact that Article 21(4) not only exhorts the foreign vessel exercising the right of innocent passage to comply with coastal State laws, but, on account of the words 'shall comply', obliges it to do so.

Thirdly, as adumbrated earlier, the connection between the activities prejudicial to the peace, good order or security of the coastal State (Article 19(2)) and the issues that could be covered by coastal State laws and regulations (Article 21(1)) requires a joint reading of both and common sanctions. The logical extrapolation of this is the near impossibility of conceiving of non-innocent passage which is at the same time in compliance with coastal State laws and regulations.

A truly genuine exercise of the right of innocent passage ought not to be in violation of coastal State laws and regulations. More so if these laws and regulations do not go beyond the parameters of Article 21 of the 1982 Convention. Where these laws and regulations do not directly affect navigation in coastal waters, the foreign ship's right of innocent passage is not affected. Be this as it may, the only viable position, in our view, remains that foreign ships which do not comply with 'appropriate' coastal State laws and regulations deprive themselves of the genuine exercise of the right of innocent passage and may be considered in non-innocent passage. Innocent passage in compliance with all coastal State laws and regulations is the generally accepted form of co-existence in coastal State territorial waters.

(b) The foreign ship's failure to pay coastal navigational charges

A foreign vessel about to exercise or exercising the right of innocent passage is supposed to pay charges for services rendered to it. This is expressly provided for in Article 26 of the 1982 Convention, which in its first paragraph cautions: 'No charge may be levied upon foreign ships by reason only of their passage through the territorial sea'.

The question to be asked here is whether failure by the foreign ship to pay for a service rendered by the coastal State does not affect the innocent passage right as such. One school of thought has it that failure to pay the charges for services rendered in connection with passage through the territorial sea does not affect the 'innocent' nature of such passage. The protagonists of this position hold that it is only proper that the right of innocent passage remains intact while the coastal

State makes claims through other channels for the payment of the charges arising out of the services rendered.

Another school of thought takes the view that Article 26 of the 1982 Convention, which covers this issue, is placed in Section 3 of Part II of the 1982 Convention, which exhaustively regulates the right of innocent passage in the territorial sea. Thus it is argued that there must be a positive relationship between innocent passage and the charges which foreign ships may be held to pay in appropriate circumstances to the coastal State.

This latter opinion is quite tenable when the legislative history of the provision is considered. The 1982 Convention follows verbatim the provision inserted in the Final Act of the 1930 Hague Codification Conference. *Inter alia*, the 1930 text stated: 'Charges may only be levied upon a foreign vessel passing through the territorial sea as payment for specific services rendered to the vessel. These charges shall be levied without discrimination.'[36] The observations attached to this Article were the following:[37]

> The object of this article is to exclude any charges in respect of general services to navigation (light or conservancy or buoyage dues, etc.), and to allow payment to be demanded only for special services rendered to the vessel (pilotage, towage, etc.). These latter charges must be made on a basis of strict equality and with no discrimination between one vessel and another.
>
> The provision of the first paragraph will include the case of compulsory anchoring in the territorial sea, in the circumstances indicated in Article 3, last paragraph.[38]

A joint reading of the Article and the observations justify the interpretation that in appropriate circumstances no foreign vessel could escape these charges. Thus, a ship which fails to pay the dues could by the same token forfeit the right of innocent passage. Apart from aiming at excluding charges in respect of general services, the provision empowers the coastal State to withhold the service in the event of non-payment and thus to frustrate the right of innocent passage.

That this situation was conceivable results from the deliberations of the International Law Commission. In the Commission a proposal was made that the following clause be added to the provision on charges to be levied upon foreign ships:

> The right of the coastal State to demand and obtain information on the nationality, tonnage, destination and provenance of passing vessels in order to facilitate the levying of charges is reserved.[39]

Although the Commission became reluctant to insert such a paragraph later for fear it might seriously interfere, if injudiciously applied, with the passage of ships, they agreed, nevertheless, that it was 'an indisputable fact that, in certain circumstances, the coastal State may be entitled to ask for the above-mentioned information'.[40]

When discussing another point, however, the Commission appeared divided on whether those charges were conditions that could affect the right of innocent passage. The final text of the Commission's Draft eliminated from Article 19 the phrase: 'These charges shall be levied without discrimination.'

In explaining this alteration, the commentaries of the Commission stated *inter alia* that:

> As a general rule, these charges should be levied on terms of equality . . . by omitting this paragraph, the Commission did not mean to imply that it does not contain a general, established rule of international Law. The Commission considers, however, that cases may occur in which special rights granted by one State to another given State may be fully justified by the special relationship between the two States, and that in the absence of treaty provisions to the contrary, the grant of such rights cannot be invoked by other States as a ground for claiming similar treatment. The Commission prefers, therefore, that this question should continue to be governed by the general rules of law.[41]

At the First Geneva Conference of 1958 on the Law of the Sea, this omission was considered unjustified. The non-discrimination clause was thus reinserted in the relevant portion of Article 18 of the 1958 Geneva Convention on the Territorial Sea and the Contiguous Zone. By so doing, the drafters of that Convention recognized the fact that there could be no special rights in the framework of the general obligation to pay charges to the coastal State for specific services rendered to foreign vessels. In other words, the payment of charges, whenever necessary, and the exercise of the right of innocent passage were phenomena which could not be divorced one from the other.

The 1982 Convention has followed the 1958 and the 1930 texts and, hence, has adopted this interpretation. Thus, in appropriate circumstances, the non-payment of charges levied by the coastal State could be prejudicial to the exercise of the right of innocent passage.

(c) International responsibility and the right of innocent passage

With the growing tendency to look upon a ship flying a particular State's flag as having a *sui generis* status between being a national and the State itself, it may be assumed that, in appropriate circumstances, the flag State may be internationally responsible towards the coastal State for the conduct of ships exercising the right of innocent passage. So also can the coastal State bear international responsibility towards flag States in similar circumstances.[42]

However, there are no express provisions in the 1982 Convention for the international responsibility of the coastal State towards flag States on account of the latters' vessels using its territorial sea. A United Kingdom proposal along these lines, submitted in the early stages of the Third United Nations Conference on the Law of the Sea, was categorically rejected.[43] Similarly rejected was a proposal made at the same Conference by some delegations to the effect that:

> If a ship exercising the right of innocent passage does not comply with the laws and regulations concerning navigation and any damage is caused to the coastal State, the coastal State shall be entitled to compensation for such damage.[44]

Nevertheless, the responsibility of the flag State for the unlawful activities of its official vessels is *expressis verbis* referred to in the 1982 Convention.

It was in the course of the Third United Nations Conference on the Law of the Sea that a series of draft proposals suggested a provision on State responsibility for government ships exercising the right of innocent passage.[45]

Succinctly, the proposal was stated thus:

> If, as a result of . . . government ship operated for non-commercial purposes . . ., any damage is caused to the coastal State (including its environment and any of its facilities, installations or other property, or to any ships flying its flag), international responsibility shall be borne by the flag State of the ship causing the damage.[46]

This proposal, after some rephrasing, became Article 31 of the 1982 Convention.

Thus, unlike the 1958 Geneva Convention on the Territorial Sea and the Contiguous Zone, Article 31 of the 1982 Convention recognizes the international responsibility of the flag State for any loss or damage to the coastal State resulting from non-compliance by a warship or other government ships operated for non-commercial purposes with the laws and regulations of the coastal State concerning passage through the territorial sea or with the provisions of the Convention or other rules of international law. This responsibility is borne by the flag State notwithstanding the immunities of warships and other government ships operated for non-commercial purposes.

Nonetheless, even as regards merchant ships, the flag State can still be responsible *via* the general rules of State responsibility.[47] So also can the coastal State.[48]

Our concern in this context is the effect the attribution of international responsibility to the flag State may have on the exercise of the right of innocent passage. It is quite inconceivable that, once the responsibility of a foreign vessel is engaged regarding the exercise of a right, that right remains unaffected by that responsibility. No matter how independent the right of innocent passage, that right cannot be separated from international responsibility when incurred by a foreign vessel in a foreign territorial sea. Thus, once a foreign vessel causes damage to the coastal State when exercising the right of innocent passage, that State can legitimately deprive the ship from continuing to exercise that right at least on the same voyage.

In spite of the extensive rights and obligations of the coastal State and the flag State, and the serious consequences of non-compliance with coastal State laws and regulations by a foreign vessel, practice reveals a reluctance to acknowledge non-innocent passage on the part of coastal States; and this for two extraneous factual considerations. In the first place, many coastal States do not have the operative capacity to identify violations of applicable regulations relating to passage in their territorial seas, let alone the appropriate method of response. Secondly, for political reasons most coastal States prefer to look the other way. Similarly, some flag States prefer to avoid unnecessary 'fights' to protect their right of passage.

However, it is not in all circumstances that the above scenario comes into play. Where the presumption of non-innocent passage is acknowledged, what options are open to the coastal State, short of complacency? On the other hand, what are the options for a foreign vessel or a flag State, whose exercise of the right of innocent passage is hampered, denied or impaired? These are the final issues we shall consider. In view of the close link between substantive rules and the disputes settlement system, our investigation will take the form of analysing the disputes settlement mechanism concerning the exercise of the right of innocent passage as provided mainly in the 1982 Convention.

Notes

1. Among these are, for example, the right of the coastal State 'to take the necessary steps to prevent any breach of the conditions to which admission of . . . ships to internal waters or such a call [as a port] is subject' (1982 Convention, Article 25(2)); and the right to take the necessary steps in the territorial sea to prevent passage which is not innocent (1982 Convention Article 25(1)).
2. '. . . Le droit de l'Etat côtier de suspendre ce droit de passage inoffensif est typiquement un "droit résiduel" [residual right] résultant de sa souveraineté "territoriale" . . . la réservation même temporaire d'un espace déterminé . . . [par] . . . l'Etat côtier en incluant juridiquement toute autre activité telle que le passage inoffensif dans cet espace . . . [est] . . . typiquement l'exercice d'une souveraineté territoriale.' Per Riphagen, *W.*, *Perspectives du droit de la mer à l'issue de la 3e Conférence des Nations Unies*, Société française pour le droit international, Colloque de Rouen, Paris, Pedone, 1984, p. 192.
3. But, at the Conference, the United States delegate had made the following statement: 'It is quite a common practice for the coastal State to close a portion of the territorial waters for a particular time . . . in principle, the right of the coastal State, when it is necessary for national purposes to use a portion of the territorial sea either on the surface or the subsoil, is superior to the right of innocent passage.' Doc. C.351(b).M.145(b).1930.V, in Rosenne, Sh. (ed.), *League of Nations, Conference for the Codification of International Law*, Dobbs Ferry, NY, Oceana, 1975, vol. 4, p. 1260.
4. ILC, *Yearbook* 1954, vol. II, p. 150.
5. Ibid.
6. ILC, *Yearbook* 1955, vol. II, p. 39.
7. (First) UNCLOS, Official Records, vol. III, pp. 99–100.
8. The original Belgian proposal was meant to cover artillery exercises of the coastal State.
9. 1982 Convention, Articles 44 and 45.
10. This distinguished member of the Italian delegation to the Third UNCLOS affirms that: 'La condition que la suspension ne soit que temporaire n'est pas suivie de manière stricte dans la pratique, où l'on voit des suspensions permanentes du droit de passage inoffensif dans des zones de mer donnant sur des bases ou des chantiers navals.' Voir Dupuy, R.-J. and Vignes, D. (eds), *Traité du nouveau droit de la mer*, Paris, Economica/Bruxelles, Bruylant, 1985, at pp. 775–6. See also Churchill, R. and Lowe, A.V., *The Law of the Sea*, Manchester, Manchester University Press, 1983, p. 68.
11. Dupuy and Vignes, loc. cit., note 10.
12. Typical maritime pollution in our context are the dumping at sea, by ships exercising the right of innocent passage, of harmful waste other than that derived from a ship's normal operations or from land-based sources. Another type could be pollution threatening to cause serious harm to coastal State's interests and deriving from shipping accidents, for example the Amoco Cadiz incident. cf. Lucchini, L., 'A

propos de l'Amoco Cadiz—La lutte contre la pollution des mers: Evolution ou révolution du Droit international', *AFDI*, vol. 14, 1978, pp. 721–71.

13. cf. International Convention for the Prevention of Pollution from Ships of 1973, particularly Article 4(2) and (3), *International Legal Materials*, vol. 12, 1972, p. 1319ff. But consider the exception in the case of dumping resulting from Article VII(2) of the International Convention on the Prevention of Marine Pollution by Dumping of Wastes and Other Matters at Sea, *International Legal Materials*, vol. 11, 1972, p. 1294.
14. Article 17 of that Convention provides: 'Foreign ships exercising the right of innocent passage shall comply with the laws and regulations enacted by the coastal State in conformity with these Articles and other rules of international law and, in particular, with such laws and regulations relating to transport and navigation.'
15. 1982 Convention, Article 19(2) (h), read in conjunction with Articles 21(1), 25(1) and 211(4), might allow coastal States to apply higher standards than those set in international treaties.
16. 1982 Convention, Article 210(5). Although dumping will also be outside the notion of innocent passage since, in accordance with Article 19(2) (i) of the same Convention, dumping is an activity not having a direct bearing on passage.
17. Bowett, D.W., *Self-Defence in International Law*, Manchester, Manchester University Press, 1958, pp. 33ff., particularly p. 86.
18. A current writer defines the right of hot pursuit as: '. . . the right of the coastal State to continue outside the territorial sea, the contiguous zone, or certain adjacent areas, the pursuit of a foreign vessel which—while within the internal waters or the territorial sea, the contiguous zone, or certain adjacent areas of the pursuing State—has violated the laws and regulations of this State, provided, however, that the pursuit has commenced immediately after the offence and has not been interrupted.' Poulantzas, N.M., *The Right of Hot Pursuit in International Law*, Leiden, Sijthoff, 1975, p. 39.
19. See, for an earlier case law on the subject: *S.S. I'm Alone* (Canada v. United States), in *United Nations, Reports of International Arbitral Awards*, vol. III, pp. 1609–18.
20. ILC, *Yearbook* 1956, vol. II, p. 266.
21. 'In considering the duties of the coastal State, the question was whether that State should play an active or a passive role in ensuring innocent passage through its territorial sea . . . It was clear . . . from the judgment of the International Court of Justice in the *Corfu Channel* case, that a coastal State should play an *active* role in ensuring the safety of navigation in its territorial sea'. A proposal to this effect by the Yugoslav delegate, as a reinforcement of Article 16, was rejected by 17 votes to 11, with 43 abstentions. See (First) UNCLOS, Official Records, vol. III, pp. 114–15.
22. 'The obligations . . . in notifying (i.e. duty to inform) . . . are based . . . on certain general and well-recognized principles, namely: elementary considerations of humanity, even more exacting in peace than in war; the principle of maritime communications; and every State's obligation not to allow knowingly its territory to be used for acts contrary to the rights of other States.' The *Corfu Channel* case (merits), *ICJ*, 1949, p. 22.
23. 1982 Convention, Article 24(2), 1958 Geneva Convention Article 15(2), or Final Draft of the International Law Commission (1956), Article 16(2).
24. Awal El Mor, 'The Regime of Passage in Straits', *Revue égyptienne de droit international*, vol. 37, 1981, pp. 13–83, at p. 66.
25. Ibid.
26. Knowledge of the circumstances is what is important. This knowledge cannot simply be presumed. The International Court of Justice made this point clear when it stated: '. . . it cannot be concluded from the mere fact of the control exercised by a State over its territory and waters that that State necessarily knew, or ought to have known . . .

This fact, by itself and apart from other circumstances, neither involves *prima facie* responsibility nor shifts the burden of proof . . .' *Corfu Channel* case, op. cit. note 22, p. 18.

27. LON, Doc. C.230.M.117.1930,V, pp. 6ff, at p. 7.
28. ILC, *Yearbook* 1956, vol. II, pp. 273ff.
29. Ibid.
30. 1982 Convention, Article 21(4).
31. Ibid. Article 23. For further details, see Henry, C.E., *The Carriage of Dangerous Goods by Sea*, London, Frances Pinter, 1985, pp. 92–122.
32. Attempts were made in the 1958 Conference to separate the two notions and to minimize the importance of these laws and regulations. See (First) UNCLOS, Official Records, vol. III, pp. 80ff, 96ff. A Mexican proposal (Doc. A/CONF.13/C.1/L/45), to the effect that: 'Foreign ships exercising the right of [innocent] passage shall comply, in conformity with the present rules and other rules of international law, with laws and regulations enacted by the coastal State, and, in particular, with those relating to transport and navigation', was narrowly adopted by a vote of 33 in favour, 30 against and 10 abstentions. Ibid., p. 101. Speaking in favour of the Mexican amendment, the Soviet Union stated: '. . . foreign ships exercising their right of passage would be obliged to comply, first with the present rules; second, with other rules of international law; and third, with the laws and regulations of the coastal State . . .'. Ibid., p. 97. In clear opposition to the amendment, the United Kingdom considered that: '. . . there would be no limitation whatsoever on the laws which the coastal State could enact. The Mexican amendment, far from making the enactment of laws and regulations by the coastal State subject to their conformity with the rules of international law . . ., imposed the obligation only on foreign ships exercising their right of passage.' Ibid., p. 97.
33. See the following 'couples' in the 1982 Convention: Article 19(2) (a) ('any threat or use of force . . .') and Article 21(1) (a) ('the safety of navigation . . .'); Article 19(2) (9) ('acts . . . contrary to the customs, fiscal, immigration or sanitary laws and regulations') and Article 21(1) (h) ('. . . infringement of the customs, fiscal, immigration or sanitary laws and regulations'); Article 19(2) (h) ('. . . any act of wilful and serious pollution . . .') and Article 21(1) (f) ('the preservation of the environment . . . and control of pollution . . .'); Article 19(2) (i) ('any fishing activities') and Article 21(1) (d) ('the conservation of the living resources of the sea'); Article 19(2) (j) ('the carrying out of research or survey activities') and Article 21(1) (g) ('marine scientific research and hydrographic surveys'); and, finally, Article 19(2) (k) ('interfering with . . . communication or any other facilities or installations . . .') and Article 21(1) (b) ('the protection of navigational aids and facilities and other . . . installations') or (c) ('the protection of cables and pipelines').
34. 1982 Convention, Article 21(4).
35. This view is strengthened by Article 24 of the 1982 Convention where it is stated that coastal State laws and regulations may not hamper, deny, or impair innocent passage, nor discriminate in form or in fact against foreign ships on the basis of the flag or the State of destination.
36. LON, op. cit. note 27, p. 8.
37. Ibid.
38. Here as in subsequent provisions, passage is defined to include stopping and anchoring if these are incidental to ordinary navigation or are rendered necessary by *force majeure* or by distress.
39. ILC, *Yearbook* 1956, vol. II, p. 274.
40. Ibid.
41. Ibid.

42. See, generally, Smith, B.D., *State Responsibility and the Marine Environment: The Rules of Decision*, Oxford, Clarendon Press, 1988, particularly pp. 185–215.
43. The United Kingdom Draft: 'Article 18, paragraph 5: The coastal State shall ensure that the application, in form and in fact, of its laws and regulations upon foreign ships exercising the right of innocent passage is in conformity with the provisions of this convention. If the coastal State acts in a manner contrary to the provisions of this chapter and loss or damage to a foreign ship results, the coastal State shall compensate the owners of the ship for that loss or damage.' cf. Article 18(5), Doc. A/CONF.62/C.2/L.3, Third UNCLOS, Official Records, vol. III, p. 183.
44. Proposal of Malaysia and Others, Doc. A/CONF.62/C.2/L.16 in Third UNCLOS, Official Records, vol. III, p. 193.
45. One of these proposals was the United Kingdom Draft Articles on the Territorial Sea, Article 28, Doc. A/CONF.62/C.2/L.16 in Third UNCLOS, Official Records, vol. III, p. 183.
46. Ibid, at p. 185.
47. On the general rules of State responsibility, see ILC, *Yearbook* 1978, vol. II, Part. II, pp. 75–94, particularly pp. 78 and 79.
48. But can the coastal State also be responsible to an injured third State for the dangerous acts of a foreign merchant ship exercising the right of innocent passage, despite the fact that unlike other actors within the territorial sovereignty, the ship had no permission of that coastal State to be there? One author suggests in this respect that: 'Responsibility should follow (thereof) only from the coastal State's failure to exercise *diligently* the authority it does possess to prescribe and enforce laws, stopping short of prohibition, designed to prevent injuries arising out of the ultrahazard (such as environmental pollution). If it has not, the coastal State will stand responsible, together with any other States in breach (e.g. the flag State) to the injured State.' (per Smith, B.D., op. cit. note 42, pp. 214–15.) Any other solution in this respect would be an undue generalization of the regime of strict responsibility in a case of severe circumscribed capacity of intervening on the part of the coastal State to prevent the damage without prohibiting innocent passage.

Chapter 7

Disputes settlement procedure involving the exercise of the right of innocent passage

1. Introduction

Foreign vessels in the territorial sea considered by the coastal State to be on non-innocent passage could legally be considered to be sojourning in the coastal State's internal waters. Against such an intrusion the coastal State has a right of protection or of self-preservation. This right of self-protection could involve persuasive or forceful measures against the flag State or the foreign vessel, as the case may be. On the other hand, if the flag State or foreign vessel considers the coastal State's characterization of the passage as 'non-innocent' to be an abuse of right,[1] then the flag State has the option of persuasion or use of force to protect the right of innocent passage.

However, the resort to measures of force by either the coastal State or the flag State in the relevant instances is strongly prohibited by all international instruments regulating the conduct of international intercourse.

The United Nations Charter provisions require members to 'settle their international disputes by peaceful means in such a manner that international peace and security, and justice, are not endangered'.[2] It also prohibits members 'from the threat or use of force against the territorial integrity or political independence of any State, or in any other manner inconsistent with the Purposes of the United Nations'.[3] Inspired by such exhortations, the 1982 United Nations Law of the Sea Convention also requires settlement 'by peaceful means'[4] of any dispute concerning the Convention's interpretation or application and reproduces *verbatim* the Charter provision on the non-use of force against the territorial integrity and political independence of States.[5]

Unlike the optional and ineffectual dispute settlement provisions and procedure of the 1958 Geneva Conventions or any similar earlier instruments,[6] and of course unlike the largely consensual jurisdiction found in the Statute of the International Court of Justice,[7] the compulsory features embodied in the judicial and arbitration disputes settlement procedures of the 1982 Convention on the Law of the Sea clearly set the latter instrument apart.[8] To appreciate the place of the right of innocent passage in the framework of disputes settlement, the inquiry will refer essentially to the 1982 Convention.

Part XV of the 1982 Convention, which deals with the settlement of disputes, first requires parties to a dispute to 'proceed expeditiously to an exchange of views regarding its settlement by negotiation or other peaceful means'.[9] The Convention then envisages the possibility of a deadlock produced by optional methods of settlement. In this event, the next step, according to Part XV, is for the parties to 'proceed expeditiously to an exchange of views'.[10] Thereafter, subject to certain exceptions of direct interest to this study, any party to the dispute may initiate a compulsory and binding dispute resolution procedure.[11] If these optional, flexible and compulsory disputes settlement procedures were also applicable in all cases involving the exercise of the right of innocent passage, that right could still withstand the assaults of the coastal State and thus be judged an 'independent' right despite the fact that it is exercised in sovereign territorial seas.

However, such an eventuality is substantially eroded by certain limitations and exceptions to compulsory procedure, mostly for the benefit of the coastal State. Two areas of the conventional provisions on dispute settlement that minimize flag States' or foreign vessels' claims for such a settlement as assertion of the right of innocent passage will be examined. These limitations will be considered in the light of the extent of the compulsion to accept mandatory third-party settlement and secondly the 'military activity' exceptions.

Before proceeding to these limitations, it may be necessary to consider the question of the capacity to sue. The right of innocent passage belongs to all States, i.e. the international community. In case of an alleged infringement of that right by the coastal State, does the claimant in disputes settlement proceedings have to be the flag State, or can it be any other State Party to the Law of the Sea Convention and acting on behalf of the world community at large? In other words: does the Convention allow for an *actio popularis* on innocent passage issues? Dismissing such an eventuality as far as the 1982 Convention is concerned, Riphagen points out that:

> en principe, le rapport juridique entre un Etat côtier et un Etat du pavillon est un rapport [bilatéral], aussi en ce sens que l'Etat côtier n'est autorisé à exercer ses pouvoirs que dans son *propre intérêt*; la défense légitime collective n'est nullement prévue, ce qui pose d'ailleurs des problèmes en cas de coopération intime sur le plan régional.[12]

This view can be substantiated by referring to the *voluntary* nature of international adjudication[13] generally and the options for compulsory settlement of disputes provided in the Convention. Moreover, the International Court of Justice has on several occasions denied standing to third States if they cannot show that an interest of their own has been infringed. In its advisory opinion in the *South West Africa* cases, the Court denied:

> that [it] should allow the equivalent of an *actio popularis*, or right resident in any member of a community to take legal action in vindication of a public interest. But although a right of this kind may be known to certain municipal systems of law, it is not known to international law as it stands at present: nor is the Court able to regard it as imported by the 'general principles of law' referred to in Article 38, paragraph 1(c), of its Statute.[14]

However, a few years after making the above statement, the Court accepted the possibility of an *actio popularis* in certain circumstances:

> an essential distinction should be drawn between obligations of a State towards the international community as a whole, and those arising vis-à-vis another State . . . By their very nature, the former are the concern of all States. In

> view of the importance of the rights involved, all States can be held to have a legal interest in their protection; they are obligations *erga omnes*.
> Such obligations derive, for example, in contemporary international law, from the outlawing of acts of aggression, and of genocide, as also from the principles and rules concerning the basic rights of the human person . . .[15]

Although admitting *actio popularis* by the examples given, the Court only contemplated extremely serious infringements. An infringement of the right of innocent passage by the coastal State can hardly have that degree of seriousness. It would therefore seem that although the right of innocent passage belongs to the international community, the legal interest of vindicating it lies with each individual State. In other words, the claimant State ought to be able to show that it has an interest of its own that the coastal State has injured. When this can be done, can the coastal State be compelled to submit the dispute to the compulsory settlement proceedings of the 1982 Convention?

2. Scope of the obligation of the coastal State to submit to the settlement of disputes on innocent passage

The extent of the obligation to submit innocent passage disputes to arbitration or judicial settlement procedures represents a compromise between, on the one hand, the coastal State's concern to be free from constant harassment by being summoned by those who are seeking to challenge its regulatory and enforcement powers in the territorial seas, and, on the other, the flag State's concern with the abuse of its rights by the coastal State.

Although there are no express exclusions regarding the recourse to binding disputes settlement procedures in connection with the territorial sea, archipelagic waters or internal waters, where foreign States could exercise the right of innocent passage, the provisions of the 1982 Convention may be interpreted to imply such exclusions. Express reference to 'limitations' on binding settlement procedures in the Convention are concerned mainly with the exclusive economic zone[16] and the continental shelf,[17] where the coastal States enjoy 'sovereign rights or jurisdiction' and not 'sovereignty' as is the case with the territorial sea[18] or archipelagic waters.[19]

Article 297 of the 1982 Convention guarantees binding dispute settlement procedures between coastal States and the flag State or foreign ship, as the case may be, on issues concerning sovereign rights and navigational freedoms, thus excluding issues of sovereignty[20] involving areas such as the territorial sea. The pertinent provisions of Article 297 read as follows:

> 1. Disputes concerning the interpretation or application of this Convention with regard to the exercise by a coastal State of its sovereign rights or jurisdiction provided for in this Convention shall be subject to the procedures provided for in section 2 (on compuslory procedures entailing binding decisions) in the following cases:
>   (a) When it is alleged that a coastal State has acted in contravention of the provisions of this Convention in regard to the freedoms *and rights*

of navigation, overflight or the laying of submarine cables and pipelines, or in regard to other internationally lawful uses of the sea specified in article 58;

(b) When it is alleged that a State exercising the aforementioned freedoms, rights or uses has acted in contravention of this Convention or of laws or regulations adopted by the coastal State in conformity with this Convention and other rules of international law not incompatible with this Convention. (emphasis added)

It can be argued that by not emphasizing the necessary guarantees for the application of compulsory disputes settlement procedures in an area where the coastal States have sovereignty (i.e. the territorial sea) but in an area where they have sovereign *rights* (i.e. the exclusive economic zone), the drafters of the 1982 Convention intended to limit the binding disputes settlement provisions to portions of the seas not placed under coastal State's full sovereignty. In other words, in the absence of an express clause on compulsory settlement procedures concerning the territorial sea, where coastal States' possessory and regulatory rights are absolute, the applicability of such procedures cannot be presumed.[21]

There is, however, the reference to 'rights of navigation' in Article 297(1) (a) (emphasized in the above quotation). In this connection, Quéneudec points out:

> Ce qui est ainsi visé, ce n'est pas seulement la navigation dans la zone économique, qui est régie par un principe de liberté; c'est aussi la navigation, sous forme de droit de passage, dans la mer territoriale, et c'est pourquoi le texte fait ici référence au droit de navigation.[22]

But then a simple rule of interpretation warrants that the specific should govern the general; and thus, since paragraph 1 of Article 297 speaks only of 'disputes concerning . . . sovereign rights or jurisdiction', and enumerates mostly rights and freedoms common to areas beyond the territorial sea, an argument can be made that that latter zone was not contemplated.

Article 297 goes on to emphasize its preoccupation mainly with areas where coastal States exercise sovereign *rights* by providing in paragraph 2 that:

> (a) [for compulsory procedures entailing binding decisions for disputes concerning the interpretation or application of the provisions of this Convention] except that the coastal State shall not be obliged to accept the submission to such settlement of any dispute arising out of:
> (i) the exercise by the coastal State of a right or discretion [concerning maritime scientific research in the exclusive economic zone and on the continental shelf]; or
> (ii) a decision by the coastal State to order suspension or cessation of a research project [in the areas where she exercises sovereign rights].

Paragraph 3 of the same Article enumerates measures of the coastal State in fisheries matters, which are not subject to compulsory dispute resolution procedures, stating that:

> (a) . . . the coastal State shall not be obliged to accept the submission to such settlement of any dispute relating to its sovereign rights with respect to the

living resources in the exclusive economic zone, or their exercise, including its discretionary powers for determining the allowable catch, its harvesting capacity, the allocation of surpluses to other States and the terms and conditions established in its conservation and management laws and regulations.

Finally, even where Article 297 tries to restrict the coastal State's discretion in providing, by way of compromise, for compulsory recourse to conciliation,[23] it specifies that 'in no case shall the conciliation commission substitute its discretion for that of the coastal State'.[24]

On account of the emphasis thus placed on disputes connected with the extension and protection of discretionary rights in areas where coastal States enjoy sovereign rights rather than sovereignty (i.e. the exclusive economic zone), an argument could be made that there was no intention to impose on the coastal State a duty to submit to compulsory settlement disputes relating to the seas placed under territorial sovereignty.[25]

In spite of the above argument, the phrase 'rights of navigation' referred to in Article 297(1) (a) must have some significance. Quéneudec's view expressed earlier is, in our opinion, authoritative. More so, since he is credited to have made the proposal for the insertion of this clause in the whole article. Otherwise, the question could be asked: what were these rights of navigation which, of course, are themselves different from the freedoms of navigation? Although there is clearly an insufficiently precise reference in that Article as to matters within the territorial seas, bearing in mind the maxim *ut magis valeat quan pereat* [that the thing may rather have effect than be destroyed], it may be acknowledged, *in arguendo*, that among the rights covered in Article 297(1) (a), for purposes of compulsory third-party disputes settlement, is the right of innocent passage.

Obviously, subjecting innocent passage disputes to compulsory third-party settlement would best reflect the fair and equitable nature of the concept of 'package deal' that characterized the 1982 Convention. However, some current State practice of selecting and rejecting portions of that Convention eliminates this equilibrium, legitimizing the avoidance of compulsory jurisdiction by coastal States on issues concerning areas where they exercise sovereignty. This does not mean of course that there is a complete lack of judicial settlement on these matters. Relying on the 1982 Convention, parties are advised to exhaust local remedies regarding disputes concerning the interpretation or application of the Convention.[26] Innocent passage disputes can squarely fall within this provision.

Independently of the Convention, it is an accepted State practice to refuse a disputes settlement[27] mechanism resulting in binding decisions, particularly when the vital interest means territorial sovereignty on the coastal waters. This practice would become uncompromising if consideration were given to the possibility, provided for by the Convention, of entities other than States (like ship-owners) being able to have standing before a dispute settlement forum *vis-à-vis* a State.[28]

In sum, therefore, a dispute involving the exercise of the right of innocent passage would more likely have to be resolved either by recourse to the domestic court of the respondent coastal State or subjected to the application of the non-compulsory procedures of Articles 279 to 284 of the 1982 Convention.[29]

3. The optional exception relating to military activity and its impact on the right of innocent passage

Article 298, paragraph 1, of the 1982 Convention contains 'optional exceptions' concerning military and law enforcement activities which directly affect the resolution of disputes on innocent passage. This paragraph states:

> When signing, ratifying or acceding to this Convention or at any time thereafter, a State may, . . . declare in writing that it does not accept any one or more of the [compulsory] procedures provided for in section 2 with respect to one or more of the following categories of disputes:
> (a) (i) [sea boundary delimitations or those involving historic bays or titles].
> (b) disputes concerning *military activities*, including military activities by government vessels and aircraft engaged in non-commercial service, and disputes concerning law enforcement activities in regard to the exercise of sovereign rights or jurisdiction excluded from the jurisdiction of a court or tribunal under Article 297, paragraph 2 or 3.
> (c) [disputes submitted to the Security Council].

This paragraph aims at allowing the coastal State to withdraw from the compulsory settlement procedures of national jurisdictional issues and issues placed before the United Nations Security Council. That any compulsion to submit to disputes settlement procedures could be rendered meaningless by States through reservations on delicate issues of territorial sovereignty could be traced to the origin of the provision.[30] Article 298(1) constitutes a recognition of the possibility conferred on coastal States to exclude disputes arising out of the exercise of discretionary rights of sovereignty, except where this could lead to an abuse of power with resultant damage to other States.[31]

The military activity exception clause included in paragraph 1(b) of Article 298 is the second of three exceptions which may be made to compulsory disputes settlement procedures. Unlike other exceptions, military activity exceptions to general rules, particularly those on the Law of the Sea, can easily cut both ways, sometimes favouring the coastal States, or sometimes shielding foreign naval war vessels from the coastal State.

However, thorough analysis of the whole Convention calls for caution in this respect. If the exception applies at all to the territorial sea, its application would be centred on the circumstances where the right of innocent passage has been exceeded by military acitvities. Nevertheless, military activities, normally implying military manoeuvres, exercises, and weapons practice, are by definition excluded from the meaning of innocent passage.[32] In addition, the coastal State is empowered to suspend the exercise of the right of innocent passage on account of weapons exercises warranted by its security[33] (by virtue of the right of military protection and other rules of international law). Therefore, the military activity exception in Article 298(1) (b) could be said to be open only to the coastal State, at least in the territorial sea. If it were otherwise, despite the consent which coastal States would give *via* prior notification and authorization for a foreign military vessel to pass through the territorial sea, the use by third States of this exception 'would subject the less powerful coastal States to the whims of their more powerful neighbours, who could, by exercising the exception, gain licence to conduct military activities in the territorial seas of other States in violation of the [consented] right of innocent passage with virtual impunity.[34] Virtual impunity because in addition to the exception which would withdraw the activities of the foreign military vessel in the territorial sea from compulsory dispute settlement, the traditional doctrine of sovereign immunity prohibits the coastal State from taking any action against the foreign warship without the consent of the flag State.[35].

Some scholars are of the view that the provisions of Article 298(1) (b) eliminating recourse to mandatory dispute settlement apply only to military activities and law enforcement measures connected with the exercise of sovereign rights within the exclusive economic zone and on the continental shelf of coastal States.[36] Others take the view that States could apply the exception to naval activities in the territorial sea.[37] An analysis of the context of the exclusion clause points directly to the former view. First, as stated earlier, the right of innocent passage exercised in the territorial seas does not include military activities. Second, the exclusion clause mentions aircraft, which are not entitled to the exercise of the right of innocent overflight. Finally, the exclusion clause, in its second part, refers to 'disputes concerning law enforcement activities in regard to the exercise of *sovereign rights or jurisdiction* . . .' and to the limitations of Article 297)2) and (3). Within these legal parameters, the spirit and intent of the 1982 Convention limits the expression 'sovereign rights and jurisdiction' of the coastal States to the exclusive economic zone and the continental shelf. Furthermore, paragraphs 2 and 3 of Article 297, cited in Article 298, concern marine scientific research and fisheries, that is, activities permitted in the economic zone and continental shelf but not in coastal waters subject to a regime of innocent passage.

However, if recent trends can be taken as a guide, it can be said that the military exclusion clause is intended to operate broadly.[38] This would mean that the coastal State could avail itself of the clause to restrict, deny, impair and hamper with impunity the exercise of the right of innocent passage in its territorial sea. Thus, regardless of the interpretation given to the military exclusion clause, as regards naval operations in the territorial seas, that clause has the effect of removing possible disputes concerning naval vessels from the purview of third-party settlement.[39]

A compulsory disputes settlement mechanism would have helped to strengthen the independence of the right of innocent passage. The optional nature of resorting to disputes settlement in this respect, and the existence of exclusion clauses favourable to the coastal State are, however, elements strengthening the supremacy of coastal State sovereignty over the right of innocent passage in the territorial sea. It should be added, however, that if a coastal State elects to use the exclusion clause, this could be detrimental to its interests in the long run, since it is, according to Article 298(3), subject to reciprocity:

> A State Party which has made a declaration under paragrah 2 shall not be entitled to submit any dispute falling within the excepted category of disputes to any procedure in this Convention as against another State Party, without the consent of that party.

Notes

1. The 1982 Convention provides in its Article 300 that: 'State Parties shall fulfil in good faith the obligations assumed under this Convention and shall exercise the rights, jurisdiction and freedoms recognized in this Convention in a manner which would not constitute an abuse of right.'
2. United Nations Charter, Article 2(3).
3. Ibid., Article 2(4).
4. 1982 Convention, Article 279.
5. Ibid., Article 301.
6. cf. Sohn, L.B. 'Settlement of Disputes Arising Out of the Law of the Sea Convention', *San Diego Law Review*, vol. 12, 1975, pp. 495–524, at pp. 516–17.
7. Statute of the International Court of Justice, Article 36.
8. For further details, see, generally, Schallawitz, R., *Settlement of Disputes in the Law of the Sea Convention*, thesis, IUHEI, 1986.
9. 1982 Convention, Article 283(1). What is important for us in this respect is the obligation to use voluntary means of peaceful settlement. This unlimited latitude of choice of ways and means short of war to settle differences could also involve non-judicial or diplomatic means which would result in the setting aside of rules of international law. The mechanism contemplated therefore in the first Section of this Part XV gives States flexible choices of modes of settlement, ranging from the most informal non-compulsory procedures with non-binding decisions on issues where coastal State sovereignty and immunity are involved, to the most formal and compulsory settlement procedures entailing binding decisions for other issues. However, the classic statement made in the *Mavrommatis* case by Judge Pessôa remains valid: '. . . the mere fact that negotiations have taken place between the two Governments does not suffice to bring a question within the jurisdiction of the Court; it is further indispensable that either the conflict from its very nature cannot be settled by negotiation or else that negotiations shall have failed. The fact of requiring such negotiation is . . . a tribute to the sovereignty of nations; the principle is that all disputes shall be settled between the nations concerned themselves. The Court can only interpose its authority when such solution is recognized as impossible.' Dissenting opinion of Judge Pessôa, The *Mavrommatis Palestine Concessions*, PCIJ, Series A, No. 2 (1924), at p. 91.
10. 1982 Convention, Article 283, para. 2.
11. Ibid., Article 286. This Article is included in Section 2 of Part XV dealing essentially with dispute settlement by compulsory procedures involving binding decisions which results from submission to arbitration and/or judicial settlement.
12. Riphagen, W., *Perspective de droit de la mer à l'issue de la 3e Conférences des Nations Unies*, Société française pour le droit international, Colloque de Rouen, Paris, Pedone, 1984, p. 207.
13. Lord Finlay had this to say in this respect in the *Mavrommatis* case: 'The jurisdiction of the Permanent Court [or of any international court] rests upon consent, and without consent there is no jurisdiction over any State.' The *Mavrommatis Palestine Concessions*, op. cit. note 9, p. 42.
14. *South-West African* cases (Second Phase), ICJ, *Reports* 1966, p. 47. See also case concerning the *Northern Cameroons* (Cameroon v. United Kingdom), Preliminary Objections, ICJ, *Reports* 1963, pp. 15–196, at 100ff.
15. Case concerning the *Barcelona Traction, Light and Power Company, Limited* (Second Phase), ICJ, *Reports* 1970, p. 4, at p. 32.
16. 1982 Convention, Article 56(1).
17. Ibid., Article 77(1).

18. Ibid., Article 2(1).
19. Ibid., Article 49(1).
20. The Convention specifically uses the words 'sovereign rights' to refer to material or economic benefits to the coastal State, consequently less than full sovereignty. On this point, Treves has the following to say: '. . . il y a certaines dispositions qui sont indéterminées par omission, du fait qu'elles ne sont pas là. Tel est notamment le cas au sein de l'article 297 relatif aux limitations à la juridiction obligatoire pour le règlement des différends. Il y est dit qu'il n'y a de juridiction obligatoire que dans trois cas en ce qui concerne l'exercice par un Etat côtier de ses droits souverains ou de sa juridiction, c'est-à-dire dans sa zone économique. On ne dit rien quant à la possibilité de soumettre à une juridiction des différends ayant trait aux activités dans la mer territoriale. Il y a là un point qu'on a voulu laisser de côté, parce que, si on l'avait mentionné, les opinions auraient été extrêmement divergentes.' Per Treves, T., in *Perspectives du droit de la mer à l'issue de la 3e Conférence des Nations Unies*, Société française pour le droit international, Colloque de Rouen, Paris, Pedone, 1984, p. 239.
21. This interpretation is strengthened by the fact that the various proposals made in the Informal Group on the Settlement of Disputes at the beginning of the UNCLOS negotiations and leading to the adoption of the Informal Negotiating Text on Settlement of Disputes (Doc. A/CONF.62/WP.9 of 21 July 1975) contained functional approaches to settlement of disputes on issues of fisheries, pollution and scientific research and nothing on navigational 'rights' which could have also thus concerned the exercise of the right of innocent passage. See *International Legal Materials*, vol. 14, 1975, pp. 778–80.
22. *Perspectives du droit de la mer à l'issue de la 3e Conférence des Nations Unies*, op. cit. note 20, p. 240.
23. Article 297(3) (b) provides that 'where no settlement has been reached by recourse to [other methods not involving compulsory procedures entailing binding decisions] a dispute shall be submitted to conciliation under Annex V, Section 2 . . . [dealing with compulsory submission to conciliation procedure]'.
24. Article 297(3) (c).
25. One author takes the view that the absence of provision regarding binding disputes resolution procedures in the territorial sea is due to the fact that, with a surface area over fifteen times that of the territorial sea, the exclusive economic zone held a much higher potential for conflict among users. Consequently, the absence of provisions should be interpreted to mean that the Convention's binding dispute settlement procedures also apply to disputes involving the abuse or infringement of rights of passage in the territorial sea. Froman, D.F., 'Uncharted Waters: Non-Innocent Passage of Warships in the Territorial Sea', *San Diego Law Review*, vol. 21, 1984, pp. 625–89, at pp. 669–70.
26. 1982 Convention, Article 295. The exhaustion of local remedies as a precondition for international proceedings will require, in our context, that the coastal State would have primary jurisdiction over disputes involving the abuse or infringement of the right of innocent passage. See Adede, A.O., 'Settlement of Disputes Arising under The Law of the Sea Convention', *AJIL*, vol. 69, no. 4, 1975, pp. 798–818, at p. 815.
27. cf. Dissenting opinion of Lauterpacht in the case of *Certain Norwegian Loans* (France v. Norway), ICJ, Report 1957, p. 34, particularly pp. 57–8.
28. Sohn, op. cit. note 6, pp. 495ff.
29. This same conclusion is shared by one writer when he admits that: 'Coastal States sought protection from harassment through international tribunals . . . However, the rights and freedoms of the other States would be meaningless if they had no mechanism by which to challenge arbitrary and capricious behaviour. The Convention

appears to have resolved the question in favour of the coastal States.' Gaertner, M.P., 'The Dispute Settlement Provisions of the Convention on the Law of the Sea: Critique and Alternatives to the International Tribunal for the Law of the Sea', *San Diego Law Review*, vol. 19, 1982, pp. 577–97, at p. 586.

30. In a paper presented to the Working Group on Disputes Settlement by Professor Andrés Arambúru of Peru, the phrasing was as follows: 'When ratifying the present Convention or expressing in another manner its consent to be considered as bound under this convention, any State will be entitled to declare that it does not accept any of the proceedings for the solution of controversies, specially provided for in this Convention, to be applied to those raised as a consequence of events that took place in areas subject to its sovereignty and/or jurisdiction, such as the territorial sea . . .' Reprinted from Adede, op. cit. note 26, at p. 814.
31. See the *Corfu Channel* case, ICJ, *Reports* 1949, pp. 4ff., but particularly the *Trail Smelter* arbitration (United States and Canada), *AJIL*, vol. 35, 1941, pp. 684ff., where the Arbitral Tribunal declared: 'No State has the right to use or permit the use of its territory in such manner as to cause injury . . . in or to the properties of persons therein . . .' Although this arbitration concerned ecological damage in the United States resulting from fumes emanating from Canada, the *ratio decidendi* goes beyond matters such as pollution to cover issues of damage to other States resulting from an exercise of sovereign rights.
32. The 1982 Convention, Article 19(2) (b) and (f).
33. Ibid., Article 25(3).
34. Froman, op. cit. note 25, p. 673.
35. The general doctrine of sovereign immunity in this case is that '. . . warships remain under the exclusive jurisdiction of the flag State during entry and stay in foreign ports and waters. No legal proceedings can be taken against it, either for recovery of possession or for damages for collision or for a salvage reward, or for any other cause, and no official of the territorial State is permitted to board the vessel against the wishes of its commander'. Per Colombos, J.C., *The International Law of the Sea*, 4th edn, London, Longmans, 1961, at p. 227.
36. See, for example, Gaertner, op. cit. note 29, pp. 593–4.
37. Janis, M.W., 'Dispute Settlement in the Law of the Sea Convention: the Military Activities Exception', *Ocean Development and International Law*, vol. 4, 1977, pp. 51–65 at pp. 56 and 62. See also Adede, op. cit. note 26, pp. 814–15.
38. See Froman, op. cit. note 25, p. 671.
39. Janis, op. cit. note 37, p. 62.

Chapter 8

Conclusion: General evaluation of the right of innocent passage in coastal waters in the light of contemporary law and practice

The object of this book was to determine the nature and content of the right of innocent passage as well as the context within which this right does or does not guarantee international navigation in coastal waters.

To this end, we have considered, among other issues, the historical evolution of that right in the light of the changing legal status of coastal waters, its evolving definition, its derivative significance in other zones under coastal jurisdiction, and the jurisdictional consequences *vis-à-vis* different types of vessels. The work has centred on identifying the phenomenon of shared 'use' allocated by international law to coastal States having sovereignty over these seas, and to third States exercising 'independent' navigational rights.

Viewed in a customary international law perspective as a derogation from the sovereignty of the coastal State, or as a corollary of the right to trade, or as a right derived from the freedom of navigation on the high seas, the right of innocent passage can no longer be completely seen as the outcome of a balancing process seeking to accommodate navigational needs in coastal waters. It appears today as a vestige of history under the constant assault of an ever-expanding notion of sovereignty.

The apparently absolute nature of sovereignty in this respect should be no surprise. The creation, in the first place, of the territorial sea was aimed at protecting the sovereignty of coastal States within their territories.

Although recognizing the right of innocent passage of foreign vessels in foreign coastal State waters, the 1982 Convention also grants sovereignty over these waters to the coastal State.[1] If past judicial pronouncements can still be considered lessons for the present, the temptation to consolidate 'newly' acquired sovereignty to the detriment of international navigation could reflect modern trends. The International Court of Justice has affirmed the classical rule that: 'Between independent States, respect for territorial sovereignty is an essential foundation of international relations.'[2] Max Huber had stated earlier in the *Island of Palmas* award that 'the exclusive competence of the State in regard to its own territory' is 'the point of departure in settling most questions that concern international relations'.[3] This statement is based on an earlier assertion in the *North Atlantic Coast Fisheries* case, to the effect that '. . . one of the essential elements of sovereignty is that it is to be exercised within territorial limits, and that, failing proof to be contrary, the territory is co-terminous with the sovereignty . . .'.[4]

Nevertheless, the right of innocent passage in coastal waters, based as it is on the notion of *jus communicationis*, is not seen as a violation of coastal State sovereignty over those waters, but as a limitation created by sovereignty itself.

Since the 1970s, nonetheless, the contours of the rules relating to the right of innocent passage have given way to the renewed resilience of coastal State sovereignty in coastal waters. Independently of the determination of most coastal States at the Third Law of the Sea Conference to give primacy to their interests, even in areas beyond 12 nautical miles, two other reasons are advanced for this change in the regime of international navigation in immediately adjacent coastal seas.

First, the change is thought to result from a decrease of flag-State influence, based on the fact that the control exercised by the traditional maritime nations over international shipping has diminished.[5] The conferment of national character upon ships regardless of any genuine link is very pertinent in this respect. By allowing shipowners to use flags of convenience, these nations have separated economic and diplomatic control from control over safety and navigation, thus weakening the principle of flag-State jurisdiction.[6]

Second, international navigational regimes and objectives were largely formulated by the traditional maritime nations alone—hence the focus on minimal interference with international shipping by authorities other than those of the flag State.[7] In the Third United Nations Conference on the Law of the Sea, however, these regimes and objectives have had to include the prevention of pollution[8] and, in particular, the safeguarding of essential economic, political, and security interests of coastal States.

International navigation in coastal waters was one of the main pawns on the chessboard of the 'package' characterizing the negotiation of the 1982 Convention. Navigation in these areas is geographically zone-specific, tailored to various types of vessels and their manner of locomotion. From the jurisdictional viewpoint, this, inevitably, led to a new blend of flag-State and coastal-State jurisdiction. The objective was to reconcile the claims and counter-claims of individual States and the international community's navigational needs.

The right of innocent passage in the 1982 Convention, as a regime of international navigation in coastal waters, is exercisable not only in the territorial sea, as has been the case before, but also in international straits, in archipelagic waters and in certain internal waters. This zonal expansion of the right of innocent passage has altered the structure and the scope of that right. Structurally, the right of innocent passage has been split into a non-suspendable right when exercised in international straits, and a suspendable right when exercised in other areas.

As far as the territorial sea proper is concerned, its maximum breadth of 12 nautical miles is accepted almost globally. With this development, there have been increases in the rights, responsibilities and risks of coastal States, and of the ships exercising the right of innocent passage.

One of these increases is that possession of this maritime zone is not optional, nor dependent upon the will of the coastal State, but compulsory.[9] Another consequence is that, in its territorial sea, the coastal State enjoys increased authority over ships in innocent passage. These ships are in principle not allowed to roam freely in the territorial seas of other States. A coastal State is empowered to establish roads in the form of sealanes and traffic separation schemes in the territorial sea whereto innocent passage can be restricted.[10] Furthermore, the coastal State has the right to adopt laws and regulations pertaining to innocent passage, and the freedom to take appropriate steps to prevent passage which is not innocent.[11]

With the acceptance of the archipelagic State concept in the 1982 Convention, conceding sovereignty in the enclosed seas to the coastal State, innocent passage applies *mutatis mutandis* as it does in the territorial sea. Within archipelagic waters, the archipelagic State may designate sealanes and traffic separation schemes as in the territorial sea. However, contrary to the territorial sea, in these roads, the new and more liberal right of archipelagic sealanes passage is exercisable. Furthermore, such sealanes and traffic separation schemes have to conform to generally accepted international regulations. Reference is made to the relevant rules of the International Maritime Organization which can be useful for other zones as well.

In straits used for international navigation, either the right of innocent passage or the right of transit passage may be exercised. With the extension of the maximum breadth of the territorial sea to 12 nautical miles, areas located within such straits which were considered to be part of the high seas come under the regime of territorial waters. This had led to a need to reconcile the new rules with the previous regime of international straits. The right of innocent passage may be exercised in straits formed by an island of a State bordering the strait and its mainland, provided there exists seaward of the island a convenient route through the high seas or through the exclusive economic zone (Article 38(1) of the 1982 Convention). It is also exercisable in straits connecting a part of the high seas or an exclusive economic zone with the territorial sea (Article 45(1) (b)). Due to a lack of appropriate criteria for determining what constitutes 'straits used for international navigation', it may be necessary to draw up an internationally acknowledged list of such straits.

Finally, since the 1951 judgment in the *Fisheries* case, where judicial recognition was given to the use of straight baselines to enclose portions of the seas within the internal waters, innocent passage has been the guaranteed passage regime in these waters.

Within the areas of internal waters, archipelagic waters, international straits and the territorial sea, the right of innocent passage figures very prominently. However, in some of these areas, there are competing rights of transit passage and archipelagic sealanes passage. Despite the perceptible differences between those rights and the right of innocent passage as concerns overflight,[12] and the legal quibble over what is the 'normal' mode of passage, it is submitted that, but for their geographically specific area of operation, the differences between these three regimes are mainly of a political and pyschological nature.

Considering the right of innocent passage, it is worth noting that, in spite of the often acclaimed independent nature of that right, coastal States are empowered to suspend that right, albeit temporarily, and to adopt laws and regulations circumscribing it. And, as if this were not enough, various Law of the Sea conventions expressly provide for specific ways of exercising that right by certain types of vessels (i.e. surface navigation for submarines), or prohibit other similar objects from exercising that right (i.e. absence of a right of innocent overflight).

Notwithstanding the comprehensive international rules on navigation contained on the 1982 Convention, the right of innocent passage for all ships is still controversial in many respects, as it was in the era of early codification attempts. This is particularly the case with the definition of acts constituting *non*-innocent passage, the recognition of the possibility of reservations/declarations, the innocent passage of warships or other similar 'special' sea vessels, and the practice of coastal States policing the exercise of this right. In a laudable effort to limit—and thus to render objective the definition of—prohibited acts, by withdrawing their appreciation from the discretion of the coastal State, the 1982 Convention enumerates, apparently exhaustively, 12 proscribed types of activities, among which one finds 'any threat or use of force . . . or any other manner in violation of the principles of . . . the Charter . . .' and 'any other activity not having a direct bearing on passage' (Article 19(2)). Almost all of the acts enumerated in the above Article fall in the ambit of one or both of these categories. These 'catch-all' phrases reintroduce a subjective determination of the meaning of innocent passage.

Contrary to expectations, within the letter of the provisions of the Convention, coastal States can still decide alone whether or not passage is innocent and the appropriate measures to be taken.[13]

Article 309 of the 1982 Convention prohibits the formulation of reservations or exceptions, except where expressly allowed. However, the next provision, Article 310, permits States, when signing the Convention, to make declarations or statements aimed at harmonizing their national laws with the Convention. On this basis, some States have already made declarations with consequences touching upon the right of innocent passage (i.e. emphasizing their sovereignty over the territorial sea and over other coastal seas). It has not yet been decided whether such declarations are in fact reservations because of their 'legal effects'. But, whatever characteristics such declarations may have, the negative impact of these on the right of innocent passage is inevitable.

This brings us to the exercise of the right of innocent passage of warships. Although the International Court of Justice, in the *Corfu Channel* case of 1949, acknowledged the right of States 'in time of peace to send their warships through *straits* . . . without previous authorization of the coastal State, provided that the passage is *innocent*', the application of this principle in the territorial sea, in archipelagic waters, and in straits has not been accepted by all States. Judging from the lawful assertions of exclusive competence of the coastal State to regulate navigation through the territorial sea by virtue of Articles 25(1) and 19 of the 1982 Convention, in view of that State's responsibility for dangers for ships in transit generally, and in view of its intimate knowledge of the conditions prevailing in its coastal seas, it is clearly desirable for that State to subject the passage of warships in coastal waters to prior notification and/or authorization. The practice of most States thoroughly accords with such a policy. Contrary to what was the case in the 1940s and 1950s, the sophistication of contemporary warships in terms of size (large aircraft carriers), purpose (projection of power ashore), etc., makes it desirable for most coastal States not only to require prior notification and/or authorization, but to prohibit such passage altogether in some instances.

Therefore, with the growing and categorical assertion of the sovereignty of coastal States in coastal waters, the right of innocent passage is being slowly emptied of its legal substance. The extension of coastal State jurisdictional and judicial competences are not the least indicators of this trend. Although the general prescriptions of the 1982 Convention for the allocation of jurisdiction (civil, criminal and administrative) over ships in innocent passage are phrased in terms of territorial impact, in practice where the coastal State relinquishes competence, this is not because of its incompetence, but because of its disinterest.

Despite the broad options opened in the 1982 Convention for flexible but compulsory settlement of disputes, it can be argued that the right of innocent passage, which was supposed to be expressly covered by such stipulations, is not so included. In so far as compulsory proceedings would remove dispute resolution from the realm of force and foster the determinacy of right, the absence of such direct reference to procedures for the right of innocent passage disputes would weaken the protection and independence of that right. The express possibility given to coastal States to refuse compulsory settlement for disputes concerning military activities, manoeuvres, etc. (Article 298(1) (b)), completes the chain of restrictions on an independent right of innocent passage. Pursuant to that stipulation, a coastal State may use its warships or coast guard vessels to board, search or arrest a foreign merchant ship in its territorial sea without being subject to compulsory, third-party settlement on grounds of 'unlawful' interference with the right of innocent passage. However, if Elihu Root's assertion made in 1908[14] is still valid today, the 'right' of innocent passage, even if considered a mere tolerance, should be subjected to some form of disputes settlement beyond the wishes and options of the coastal State.

In sum, whether viewed as an imperfect right, or a mere tolerance or comity,[15] the right of innocent passage establishes and maintains a set of prescriptions for protecting all who use the coastal seas. Thus, it attempts to establish stability, certainty and uniformity in the expectations of States across State frontiers and between States and, at the same time, to promote vital ocean commerce. But for these considerations, the right of innocent passage today represents a vestige of the old principle of coastal State servitude. This principle has given way to a firmer assertion of coastal State sovereignty in the coastal seas. The 1982 Convention has irreversibly altered the meaning and significance of the right of innocent passage in favour of coastal States. The continuous survival and respect of this right will depend on the good faith of coastal States and on the perception of their sovereignty and security in these coastal waters. With the modern development of giant tankers, ships carrying dangerous substances, sophisticated warships, nuclear powered vessels, etc., one wonders how it could be otherwise.

> The right of a State to adopt the course which it considers best suited to the exigences of its security and to the maintenance of its integrity, is so essential a right that, in case of doubt, [treaty] stipulations cannot be interpreted as limiting it, even though these stipulations do not conflict with such an interpretation.[16]

However, considering the fact that coastal States could be flag States in other circumstances, the dictates of reciprocity and the interest of international intercourse necessitate a reasonable interpretation of sovereignty in this context and a lesser inclination to consider the right of innocent passage as a mere gesture of friendship of the coastal State to passing foreign ships.

Notes

1. The relevant provisions of the 1982 Convention are Articles 2, 34 and 49, dealing with the territorial sea, straits used for international navigations, and archipelagic waters.
2. The *Corfu Channel* case (Merits), ICJ, *Reports* 1949, p. 35.
3. *The Island of Palmas* arbitration (1928), United Nations, *Reports of International Arbitral Awards*, vol. II, p. 829, at p. 838. 'Sovereignty in relation to a portion of the surface of the globe is the legal condition necessary for inclusion of such portion in the territory of any particular State.'
4. The *North Atlantic Coast Fisheries* arbitration (1910), Scott, J.B. (ed.), *The Hague Court Reports*, New York, 1916, p. 141, at p. 157.
5. Slot, P.J., 'The International Legal Regime for Navigation', *Ocean Development and International Law*, 1985, vol. 15, pp. 89–99, at p. 93.
6. For further details on this point, see Tache, S.W., 'The Nationality of Ships: The Definition Controversy and Enforcement of Genuine Link', *The International Lawyer*, 1982, vol. 16, pp. 301–12.
7. Op. cit. note 5, p. 93.
8. cf. Smith, B.D., *State Responsibility and the Marine Environment: The Rules of Decision*, Oxford, Clarendon Press, 1988.
9. See Dissenting Opinion of Sir Arnold McNair, *Fisheries* case (United Kingdom v. Norway), ICJ, *Reports* 1951, p. 160.
10. The 1982 Convention, Article 22(1).
11. Ibid., Articles 21 and 25(1).
12. One wonders why the 1982 Law of the Sea Convention grants a right of overflight over sovereign spaces, whereas the appropriate air law instruments do not.
13. The 1985 case of the 'Greenpeace' ship present in the waters surrounding the Mururoa atoll is illuminating in this respect. See '*Le Monde*' of 15 October 1985, p. 15.
14. 'There are no international controversies so serious that they cannot be settled peaceably if both parties really desire peaceable settlement, while there are few causes of dispute so trifling that they cannot be made the occasion of war if either party really desires war. The matters in dispute between nations are nothing; the spirit which deals with them is everything.' *AJIL*, 1914, vol. 8, Part I, p. 134.
15. In this sense, comity is viewed neither as a matter of absolute obligation, nor as one of mere courtesy and good will of the coastal State, but something in between the two notions.
16. Dissenting opinion of judges Anzilotti and Huber in the case '*Wimbledon*', PCIJ, Series A, No. 1, p. 1, at p. 37 (1923).

Appendix

Relevant extracts of the 1982 United Nations Convention on the Law of the Sea

Section 3. Innocent passage in the territorial sea

Subsection A. Rules applicable to all ships

Article 17. Right of innocent passage

Subject to this Convention, ships of all States, whether coastal or land-locked, enjoy the right of innocent passage through the territorial sea.

Article 18. Meaning of passage

1. Passage means navigation through the territorial sea for the purpose of:
   a) traversing that sea without entering internal waters or calling at a roadstead or port facility outside internal waters; or
   b) proceeding to or from internal waters or a call at such roadstead or port facility.
2. Passage shall be continuous and expeditious. However, passage includes stopping and anchoring, but only in so far as the same are incidental to ordinary navigation or are rendered necessary by *force majeure* or distress or for the purpose of rendering assistance to persons, ships or aircraft in danger or distress.

Article 19. Meaning of innocent passage

1. Passage is innocent so long as it is not prejudicial to the peace, good order or security of the coastal State. Such passage shall take place in conformity with this Convention and with other rules of international law.
2. Passage of a foreign ship shall be considered to be prejudicial to the peace, good order or security of the coastal State if in the territorial sea it engages in any of the following activities:
   a) any threat or use of force against the sovereignty, territorial integrity or political independence of the coastal State, or in any other manner in violation of the principles of international law embodied in the Charter of the United Nations;
   b) any exercise or practice with weapons of any kind;
   c) any act aimed at collecting information to the prejudice of the defence or security of the coastal State;
   d) any act of propaganda aimed at affecting the defence or security of the coastal State;

e) the launching, landing or taking on board of any aircraft;
f) the launching, landing or taking on board of any military device;
g) the loading or unloading of any commodity, currency or person contrary to the customs, fiscal, immigration or sanitary laws and regulations of the coastal State;
h) any act of wilful and serious pollution contrary to this Convention;
i) any fishing activities;
j) the carrying out of research or survey activities;
k) any act aimed at interfering with any systems of communications or any other facilities or installations of the coastal State;
l) any other activity not having a direct bearing on passage.

Article 20. Submarines and other underwater vehicles

In the territorial sea, submarines and other underwater vehicles are required to navigate on the surface and to show their flag.

Article 21. Laws and regulations of the coastal State relating to innocent passage

1. The coastal State may adopt laws and regulations, in conformity with the provisions of this Convention and other rules of international law, relating to innocent passage through the territorial sea, in respect of all or any following:
   a) the safety of navigation and the regulation of maritime traffic;
   b) the protection of navigational aids and facilities and other facilities or installations;
   c) the protection of cables and pipelines;
   d) the conservation of the living resources of the sea;
   e) the prevention of infringement of the fisheries laws and regulations of the coastal State;
   f) the preservation of the environment of the coastal State and the prevention, reduction and control of pollution thereof;
   g) marine scientific research and hydrographic surveys;
   h) the prevention of infringement of the customs, fiscal, immigration or sanitary laws and regulations of the coastal State.
2. Such laws and regulations shall not apply to the design, construction, manning or equipment of foreign ships unless they are giving effect to generally accepted international rules or standards.
3. The coastal State shall give due publicity to all such laws and regulations.
4. Foreign ships exercising the right of innocent passage through the territorial sea shall comply with all such laws and regulations and all generally accepted international regulations relating to the prevention of collisions at sea.

Article 22. Sea lanes and traffic separations scheme in the territorial sea

1. The coastal State may, where necessary having regard to the safety of navigation, require foreign ships exercising the right of innocent passage through its territorial sea to use such sea lanes and traffic separation

schemes as it may designate or prescribe for the regulation of the passage of ships.

2. In particular, tankers, nuclear-powered ships and ships carrying nuclear or other inherently dangerous or noxious substances or materials may be required to confine their passage to such sea lanes.
3. In the designation of sea lanes and the prescription of traffic separation schemes under this article, the coastal State shall take into account:
   a) the recommendations of the competent international organization;
   b) any channels customarily used for international navigation;
   c) the special characteristics of particular ships and channels; and
   d) the density of traffic.
4. The coastal State shall clearly indicate such sea lanes and traffic separation schemes on charts to which due publicity shall be given.

Article 23. Foreign nuclear-powered ships and ships carrying nuclear or other inherently dangerous or noxious substances

Foreign nuclear-powered ships and ships carrying nuclear or other inherently dangerous or noxious substances shall, when exercising the right of innocent passage through the territorial sea, carry documents and observe special precautionary measures established for such ships by international agreements.

Article 24. Duties of the coastal State

1. The coastal State shall not hamper the innocent passage of foreign ships through the territorial sea except in accordance with this Convention. In particular, in the application of this Convention or of any laws or regulations adopted in conformity with this Convention, the coastal State shall not:
   a) impose requirements on foreign ships which have the practical effect of denying or impairing the right of innocent passage; or
   b) discriminate in form or in fact against the ships of any State or against ships carrying cargoes to, from or on behalf of any State.
2. The coastal State shall give appropriate publicity to any danger to navigation, of which it has knowledge, within its territorial sea.

Article 25. Rights of protection of the coastal State

1. The coastal State may take the necessary steps in its territorial sea to prevent passage which is not innocent.
2. In the case of ships proceeding to internal waters or a call at a port facility outside internal waters, the coastal State also has the right to take the necessary steps to prevent any breach of the conditions to which admission of those ships to internal waters or such a call is subject.
3. The coastal State may, without discrimination in form or in fact among foreign ships, suspend temporarily in specified areas of its territorial sea the innocent passage of foreign ships if such suspension is essential for the protection of its

security, including weapons exercises. Such suspension shall take effect only after having been duly published.

Article 26. Charges which may be levied upon foreign ships

1. No charge may be levied upon foreign ships by reason only of their passage through the territorial sea.
2. Charges may be levied upon a foreign ship passing through the territorial sea as payment only for specific services rendered to the ship. These charges shall be levied without discrimination.

Subsection B. Rules applicable to merchant ships and government ships operated for commercial purposes

Article 27. Criminal jurisdiction on board a foreign ship

1. The criminal jurisdiction of the coastal State should not be exercised on board a foreign ship passing through the territorial sea to arrest any person or to conduct any investigation in connection with any crime committed on board the ship during its passage, save only in the following cases:
   a) if the consequence of the crime extend to the coastal State;
   b) if the crime is of a kind to disturb the peace of the country or the good order of the territorial sea;
   c) if the assistance of the local authorities has been requested by the master of the ship or by a diplomatic agent or consular officer of the flag State; or
   d) if such measures are necessary for the suppression of illicit traffic in narcotic drugs or psychotropic substances.
2. The above provisions do not affect the right of the coastal State to take any steps authorized by its laws for the purpose of an arrest or investigation on board a foreign ship passing through the territorial sea after leaving internal waters.
3. In the cases provided for in paragraphs 1 and 2, the coastal State shall, if the master so requests, notify a diplomatic agent or consular officer of the flag State before taking any steps, and shall facilitate contact between such agent or officer and the ship's crew. In cases of emergency this notification may be communicated while the measures are being taken.
4. In considering whether or in what manner an arrest should be made, the local authorities shall have due regard to the interests of navigation.
5. Except as provided in Part XII or with respect to violations of laws and regulations adopted in accordance with Part V, the coastal State may not take any steps on board a foreign ship passing through the territorial sea to arrest any person or to conduct any investigation in connection with any crime committed before the ship entered the territorial sea, if the ship, proceeding from a foreign port, is only passing through the territorial sea without entering internal waters.

Article 28. Civil jurisdiction in relation to foreign ships

1. The coastal State should not stop or divert a foreign ship passing through the territorial sea for the purpose of exercising civil jurisdiction in relation to a person on board the ship.
2. The coastal State may not levy execution against or arrest the ship for the purpose of any civil proceedings, save only in respect of obligations or liabilities assumed or incurred by the ship itself in the course or for the purpose of its voyage through the waters of the coastal State.
3. Paragraph 2 is without prejudice to the right of the coastal State, in accordance with its laws, to levy execution against or to arrest, for the purpose of any civil proceedings, a foreign ship laying in the territorial sea, or passing through the territorial sea after leaving internal waters.

Subsection C. Rules applicable to warships and other government ships operated for non-commercial purposes

Article 29. Definition of warships

For the purpose of this Convention, 'warship' means a ship belonging to the armed forces of a State bearing the external marks distinguishing such ship of its nationality, under the command of an officer duly commissioned by the government of the State and whose name appears in the appropriate service list or its equivalent, and manned by a crew which is under regular armed forces discipline.

Article 30. Non-compliance by warships with the laws and regulations of the coastal State

If any warship does not comply with the laws and regulations of the coastal State concerning passage through the territorial sea and disregards any request for compliance therewith which is made to it, the coastal State may require it to leave the territorial sea immediately.

Article 31. Responsibility of the flag State for damage caused by a warship or other government ship operated for non-commercial purposes

The flag State shall bear international responsibility for any loss or any damage to the coastal State resulting from the non-compliance by a warship or other government ship operated for non-commercial purposes with the laws and regulations of the coastal State concerning passage through the territorial sea or with the provisions of this Convention or other rules of international law.

Article 32. Immunities of warships and other government ships operated for non-commercial purposes

With such exceptions as are contained in subsection A and in articles 30 and 31, nothing in this Convention affects the immunities of warships and other government ships operated for non-commercial purposes.

Bibliography

Cases

The *Fisheries* case (UK v. Norway), ICJ *Reports* 1951, pp. 116–206.

The *Corfu Channel* case (UK v. Albania), ICJ *Reports* 1949, pp. 4–169.

The *Island of Palmas* arbitration, 1928. Reports of International Arbitral Awards, Vol. II UN Publications, 1949, pp. 829–71.

The *North Atlantic Coast Fisheries* arbitration (Great Britain v. United States), Scott J.B. (ed.), The Hague Court Reports, New York, University of Oxford Press (1916), pp. 141–225.

The *Case concerning the right of passage over Indian Territory* (Portugal v. India), ICJ *Reports* (1960), pp. 6–144.

The *S.S. Wimbledon*, Permanent Court of International Justice, ser. A No. 1 (1923) pp. 1–47.

USS-'Pueblo' case. United States Department of State Bulletin, Vol. 60, January 6th, 1968, pp. 1–3.

The League of Nations and United Nations Publications and Related Texts

A. United Nations

– Geneva Convention on the Territorial Sea and the Contiguous Zone, April 29th 1958, UN Treaty Series, vol. 516, pp. 205–218

– The United Nations Conventions on the Law of the Sea (1982) with Index and Final Act of the Third UN Conference on the Law of the Sea, UN Publications, New York, 1983, 224 pp.

– Law and Regulations on the Regime of the Territorial Sea: UN Legislative Series, New York, 1959, ST/LEG SER. B/8.

– Laws and Regulations on the Regime of the Territorial Sea, UN Legislative Series, 1975, ST/LEG/SER. B/6.

– The United Nations Conference on the Law of the Sea, 1974–1982, Official Doc. vol. 1–14.

– 'Sea Law: Highlights', UN Chronicle, Vol. XIX No. 6, June 1982.

– Second UN Conference on the Law of the Sea, March 17th–April 26th, 1960. Official Documents: Summary Records of Plenary Meetings of the Committee of the Whole; A/CONF. 19/8.

– (First) UN Conference on the Law of the Sea, Febr. 24th–April 27th, 1958. Official Documents vol. 1–7, especially

(i) Official Records vol. 1, Preparatory Documents: A/CONF. 13/37, in particular: Kennedy R.H., 'A Brief Geographical and Hydrographical Study of Straits which Constitute Routes for International Traffic', pp. 114–64.

(ii) Official Records vol. 3, First Commitee (Territorial Sea and Contiguous Zone). A/CONF. 13/C. 1/SRI–SR 66.
(iii) Official Records, vol. 4: Second Commitee (High Seas: General Regime): A/CONF. 13/C. 2/SRI–SR 37.

– UN Conference Documents: Draft Articles on Straits and the Territorial Sea.
– US Draft Articles on the Breadth of the Territorial Sea, Straits and Fisheries, UN Doc. A/AC 138/SC II/L9, 30th July 1971.
– USSR Draft Articles on Straits Used for International Navigation, UN Doc. A/
AC 138/SC II/L9, 30th July 1971.
– UK Draft Articles on the Territorial Sea and Straits, UN Doc. A/CONF/62/C.2/L3, 3rd July 1974 (Third UN Conference on the Law of the Sea, Official Records, vol. III).
– Fiji Draft Articles Relating to Passage Through the Territorial Sea, UN Doc. A/CONF. 62/C.2/L19, 23rd July 1974 (Third UN Conference on the Law of the Sea, Official Records, vol. III).
– Malaysia, Morocco, Oman and Yemen: Draft Articles on Navigation Through the Territorial Sea Including Straits Used for International Navigation.
UN Doc. A/CONF. 62/C.2/L16, 22nd July 1974. Third UNCLOS, Official Records, vol. III.

B. The International Law Commission Yearbooks

(i) Regime of the Territorial Sea: Report of J.P.A. François: Doc. A/CN. 4/53, Yearbook of the ILC, 1952, vol. II, pp. 25–43.
(ii) Regime of the Territorial Sea: Second Report of J.P.A. François: Doc. A/CN. 4/61, Yearbook of the ILC, 1953, vol. 2, pp. 55–75.
(iii) Doc. A/CN. 4/61ADD. I. Amendments and Additions to the Second Report-Annex-Report of the Committee of Experts on Certain Technical Questions Concerning the Territorial Sea, Yearbook of the ILC, 1953, vol. 2, pp. 76–9.
(iv) Regime of the Territorial Sea: Limits; Dicussions in the 254th–258th Meetings, Baselines. 263rd–264th Meetings, Rights of Passage; and Proposed New Articles on Freedom of Passage in Certain Internal Waters: Discussions in the 264th–265th Meetings. Yearbook of the ILC, 1954, vol. 1, pp. 64–85, 91–4, 108–13, 117–19, 159–62.
(v) Regime of the Territorial Sea: Third Report of J.P.A. François, Doc. A/CN. 4/77, Yearbook of the ILC, 1954, vol. 2, pp. 1–6, 152–63.
(vi) Regime of the Territorial Sea: Discussions in the 316th–317th Meetings, Baselines; the 319th Meeting, Islands; 324th Meeting, Baselines. Yearbook of the ILC, 1955, vol. I, pp. 195–205, 216–18, 249–51.
(vii) Comments by Governments on the Provisional Articles Concerning the Regime of the Territorial Sea, Yearbook of the ILC, 1955, vol. 2 pp. 43–62.
(viii) Regime of the High Seas and the Territorial Sea: Report of J.P.A. François; Doc. A/CN. 4/97, Yearbook of the ILC, 1956, vol. 2, pp. 1–25.

(ix) UN Documents on the 'Juridical Regime of Historic Waters, including Historic Bays'. Yearbook of the ILC, 1962, vol. 2, pp. 1–26.

C. The League of Nations

(i) League of Nations Committee of Experts for the Progressive Codification of International Law. Draft on Questionnaire No. 2 of January 29th, 1926 on Territorial Waters, Vol. 20, AJIL, 1926 (special supplement), pp. 62–147.
(ii) Amended Draft Convention Communicated to Various Governments by the League of Nations' Committee of Experts for the Progressive Development of International Law, with Questionnaire No. 2, January 29th, 1926, League of Nations, Doc. C.196., 1927.V.
(iii) Schedule of Points drawn up by the League of Nations Preparatory Committee, Febr. 15, 1928. League of Nations Doc. C. 44 M. 21, 1928.V.
(iv) Preliminary Documents of the Conference for the Codification of International Law, The Hague, March 13, 1930. Bases of Discussion drawn up by the Preparatory Committee II. Territorial Waters, League of Nations, Doc. C.74.17.39, 1939.V.
(v) Conference for the Codification of International Law, The Hague.
(vi) Conference for the Codification of International Law, The Hague, March–April, 1930, Report of the Second Committee (Territorial Sea). Annex I. Articles concerning the Legal Status of the Territorial Waters; Extracts from the Second Committee, April 3rd, 1930. League of Nations Documents C. 340, M. 117, 1930.V.

National laws and legislations

— National Legislation and Treaties Relating to the Law of the Sea: UN Legislative Series, New York, 1980, ST/LEG/SER. B/19.
— National Legislation and Treaties Relating to the Territorial Sea, the Contiguous Zone, the Continental Shelf, the High Seas and to Fishing and Conservation of the Living Resources of the Sea, UN Treaty Series, New York, 1980 ST/LEG/SER. B/15.

Other sources of national laws and legislations quoted

The United States of America

— US Federal Coastal Zone Management Act of 1972, *International Legal Materials*, 1973, pp. 108ff.
— Coastal Zone Management Act Amendments of 1976, *New Directions in the Law of the Sea*, vol. IX, pp. 133ff.
— Maritime Protection, Research and Sanctuaries Act of 1972, *International*

Legal Materials, 1972, pp. 1394ff.
– Particularly the United States Ports and Waterways Safety Act of 1972, *New Directions in the Law of the Sea*, vol. VII, pp. 440–48.
– Amendment Ports and Waterways Safety Act of 1978, *International Legal Materials*, 1979, pp. 204ff.

United Kingdom (Case law)

– Bernard Pianka and Another v. Reg. (Privy Council), *Weekly Law Reports*, vol. 3, 1977, pp. 859–98.
– Reg. v. Keyn, 2. Ex. Division, 1876, pp. 63ff.

The Soviet Union

– *The U.S.S.R., Eastern Europe and the Development of the Law of the Sea*, (ed.) W.E. Butler, New York, Oceana Publications Inc., 1983, p. 8ff.
– *New Directions in the Law of the Sea*, (ed.) Kenneth R. Simmonds, New York, Oceana Publications Inc., 1983, pp. 9–26.

India

– 'Territorial Waters, Continental Shelf, Exclusive Economic Zone and other Maritime Zones Act, 1976', *New Directions in the Law of the Sea*, vol. V, pp. 305–16.

Collections of documents

– Nordquist M., and Simmonds K. (eds), *New Directions in the Law of the Sea*, Dobbs Ferry, NY, Oceana Publications Inc., 11 volumes, 1973–1981.
– Platzöder Renate (ed.), *Third United Nations Conference on the Law of the Sea; Documents*, Dobbs Ferry, NY, Oceana Publications Inc., 7 volumes, 1982.
– Rosenne Shabtai (ed.), *League of Nations Conference for the Codification of International Law*; Dobbs Ferry, NY, Oceana Publications Inc., 4 volumes, 1975.

Publications of learned societies

International Law Association

– Report of the 56th Conference New Delhi, 1974, Law of the Sea, *ILA Report 1974*, Bouchez, L.J., 'Ocean Navigation: International Legal Aspects', pp. 330–55. See generally pp. 312–408.

Institut de Droit International

— Résolutions du 17 septembre 1957, session (d'Amsterdam) sur la distinction entre le régime de la mer territoriale et le régime des eaux intérieures, *Annuaire de l'IDI*, vol. 47–11, 1957, pp. 437 and 85.
— Délibérations de l'Institut sur le Projet de Règlement relatif à la mer territoriale (session de Lausanne) *Annuaire de l'IDI*, 1928, pp. 627–77.
— Définition et Régime de la Mer Territoriale: Questionnaire et Rapport de Thomas Barclay, 3e Commission, Session d'Hamburg, *Annuaire de l'IDI*, vol. 11/12, 1892–1894, pp. 103–47.

Harvard University

Harvard Research in International Law Draft Convention and Comments, April 1929 on Territorial Waters, *American Journal of International Law*, vol. 23, 1929 (Special Supplment No. 2), pp. 241–380.

Collective publications and opinions

Bardonnet, D. and Virally, M., *Le Nouveau Droit International de la mer*, Paris, Pedone, 1983.

Bettati, R. *et. al.*, *La Souveraineté au XXe siècle*, Paris, Armand Collin, 1971.

Dupuy, R.J. and Vignes, D. (eds), *Traité du nouveau droit de la mer*, Economica, Paris—Bruylant, Bruxelles, 1985.

Gamble, Jr., J.K. and Pontecorgo, G. (eds), *Law of the Sea: The Emerging Regime of the Oceans*, Cambridge, Mass., Ballinger, 1973.

Lucchini, L. and Voelckel, M. (eds), *Les Etats et la mer: Le Nationalisme maritime: Notes et etudes documentaires*, Paris, La Documentation française, 1977.

Société française pour le droit international, Colloque de Rouen, Perspectives du droit de la mer à l'issue de la 3e Conférence des Nations Unies, 1984, Paris, Pedone, 341 pp.

Zacklin, R. (ed.), *The Changing Law of the Sea*, Leiden, Sijhoff, Western Hemisphere Perspectives, 1974.

General works on international law

Brownlie, Ian, *Principles of Public International Law*, 2nd edn, Oxford, Clarendon Press, 1979, 743 pp.

Fauchille, P., *Traité de Droit International Public*, 8th edn, Henri Bonfils, Paris, Rouuseau & Cie, 1921–26, 2 vol., 1182 pp.

Hall, W.E., *A Treatise on International Law*, 8th edn, (A. Pearce Higgins), Oxford, Clarendon Presss, H. Millford, 1924, 952 pp.

Oppenheim, L., *International Law*, Vol. I, 8th edn, (H. Lauterpacht), London, Longmans, Green and Co., 1955, 1072 pp.

Rousseau, C., *Droit International Public*, Paris, Sirez, Vol. IV, 1980, pp. 358–77.
Scelle, G., *Manuel de Droit International Public*, Ed. Donat Montchrestian, Paris, 1948.

Monographs

Anand, R.P., *Origin and Development of the Law of the Sea. The History of International Law Revisited*, The Hague/Boston/London, Nijhoff, 1983, 249 pp.
Apollis, G., *L'Emprise maritime et l'Etat côtier*, Paris, Pedone, 1981, 293 pp.
Baxter, R.R., *The Law of International Waterways with Particular Regards to Interoceanic Canals*, Cambridge, Mass., Harvard University Press, 1964, 371 pp.
Bouchez, L.J., *The Regime of Bays in International Law*, Leiden, Sijthoff, 1964, 330 pp.
Brittin, B.H., *International Law for Seagoing Officers*, 4th edn, Annapolis, Md., Naval Institute Press, 1981, 483 pp.
Bustamante, A.S., *The Territorial Sea*, New York, Oxford University Press, 1930, 177 pp.
Butler, W.E., *The Law of Soviet Territorial Waters. A Case Study of Maritime Law and Practice*, New York/London, Praeger, 1967, 192 pp.
——, *The Soviet Union and the Law of the Sea*, Baltimore/London, Johns Hopkins Press, 1971, 250 pp.
——, *International Straits of the World: North-East Passage*, Leiden, Sijthoff and Noordhoff, 1978, 199 pp.
Chouraqui, G., *La Mer confisquée*, Paris, Seuil, 1979.
Chung, I.Y., *Legal Problems Involved in the Corfu Channel Incident*, Genève, Droz, 1959, 287 pp.
Clingan, T.A. and Alexander, L.M. (eds), *Hazards of Maritime Transit*, Cambridge, Mass., Ballinger, 1973, 133 pp.
Duvignaux, H.M., *Droits et devoirs de l'Etat sur la mer territoriale en temps de paix et en temps de guerre*, Marseille, 1899.
Dubner, B.H., *The Law of Territorial Waters of Mid-Ocean Archipelagos and Archipelagic States*, The Hague, Njihoff, 1976, 122 pp.
——, *The Law of International Sea Piracy*, The Hague, Nijhoff, 1980, 176 pp.
Dupuy, R.J., *The Law of the Sea: Current Problems*, Dobbs Ferry, NY, Oceana Publications, 1974, 210 pp.
——, *L'Océan partagé; Analyse d'une négociation (Troisième Conférence des Nations Unies sur le Droit de la Mer)*, Paris, Pedone, 1979, 287 pp.
Fattal, A., *Convention de Genève sur la mer territoriale et la zone contiguë*, Ed. Librairie du Liban, Beyrouth, 1968, 319 pp.
Fulton, T.W., *The Sovereignty of the Sea*, Milwood, NY, Kraus Reprint Co., 1976, 799 pp.
Geouffre de la Pradelle, A., *Le Droit de l'Etat sur la mer territoriale*, Paris, Pedone, 1898, 63 pp.
——, *La Mer*, Paris, Ed. Internal., 1934, 637 pp.

Gidel, G., *Le Droit international public de la mer. Le temps de paix*, 3 volumes (reprint), Vaduz/Liechtenstein, Topos Verlag, 1981.

Godey, P., *Régime internatonal de la mer territoriale*, Paris, 1896.

Gorshkov, S.G. (Amiral de la flotte soviétique), *Les Navires militaires dans la guerre et dans la paix*, 1974.

Grotius, H., *The Freedom of the Seas*, New York, Oxford University Press, 1916.

Gunnar, A., *International Straits of the World: The Baltic Straits*, The Hague, Martinus Nijhoff, 1982, 132 pp.

Janis, M.W., *Sea Power and the Law of the Sea*, Lexington, Mass., Lexington Books, 1976.

Jessup, J.C., *The Law of Territorial Waters and Maritime Jurisdiction*, New York, G.A. Jennings Co., 1927, 483 pp.

Khoshkish, A., *The Right of Innocent Passage. A Study in International Maritime Law*, Genève, Ed. Générales, IUHEI, 1954, 168 pp.

Koh, K.L., *Staits in International Navigation*, Dobbs Ferry, NY, Oceana Publications, 1982.

Masterson, W.E., *Jurisdiction in Marginal Sea*, New York, 1929, 401 pp.

Matte, M.N., *Deux frontières invisibles: de la mer territoriale à l'air 'territorial'*, Paris, Pedone, 1965, 294 pp.

Meyer, C.B.V., *The Extent of Jurisdiction in Coastal Waters*, Leiden, Sijthoff, 1937, 533 pp.

O'Connell, D.P., *The Influence of Law on Sea Power*, Manchester, Manchester University Press, 1975, 204 pp.

——, *International Law of the Sea*, Clarendon Press, Oxford, 1982, 634 pp.

Oudendijk, J.K., *Status and Extent of Adjacent Waters*, Leiden, Sijthoff, 1970, 160 pp.

Rao, C.P., *The New Law of Maritime Zones with Special Reference to India's Maritime Zones*, New Delhi (India), Milind Publications, 1983, 423 pp.

Smith, B.D., *State Responsibility and the Marine Environment: The Rules of Decision*, Oxford, Clarendon Press, 1988, 281 pp.

Solodovnikoff, P., *La Navigation maritime dans la doctrine et la pratique soviétique*, (Etude de droit international public), Paris, Libr. Générale de Droit et de Jurisprudence, 1980, 389 pp.

Swarztrauber, S.A., *The Three-Mile Limit of Territorial Seas*, Annapolis, Md., Naval Institute Press, 1972, 316 pp.

Symmons, C.R. *The Maritime Zones of Islands in International Law*, The Hague, Nijhoff, 1979, 307 pp.

Thommen, T.K., *Legal Status of Government Ships in International Law*, The Hague, Nijhoff, 1962, 177 pp.

Truver, S.C., *International Straits of the World: The Strait of Gibraltar and the Mediterranean*, Leiden, Sijthoff and Noordhoff, 1980, 272 pp.

Wetering, W. Van de, *Les Eaux territoriales et leur régime en temps de paix et en temps de guerre*, Genève, 1923.

Articles and contributions to collective works

Adede, A.D., 'Settlement of Disputes arising under the Law of the Sea Convention', *American Journal of International Law*, vol. 69, 1975, pp. 788–818.

Akinsanya, A., 'The Nigerian Territorial Waters Decrees of 1967 and of 1971 in International Law', *Revue égyptienne de droit international*, vol. 32, 1976, pp. 141-54.

Aldrich, G.H. *et al.*, 'The Pueblo Seizure: Facts, Law and Policy', *Proceedings of the American Society of International Law*, vol. 14, 1974, pp. 169–89.

Anand, R.P., 'Freedom of Navigation through Territorial Waters and International Straits', *Indian Journal of International Law*, vol. 14, 1974, pp. 169–89.

Baxter, R.R. 'Passage of ships through International Waters', *British Yearbook of International Law*, vol. 31, 1954, pp. 187–216.

Beckett, W.E., 'Criminal Jurisdiction over Foreigners (The "Franconia" and the "Lotus")', *British Yearbook of International Law*, vol. 8, 1927, 108–28.

Boggs, S.W., 'Delimitation of the Territorial Sea', *American Journal of International Law*, vol. 24, 1950, pp. 531–55.

——, 'Seaward Areas under National Jurisdiction', *American Journal of International Law*, vol. 45, 1951, pp. 240–66.

Bouchez, L.J., 'The Concept of Effectiveness as Applied to Territorial Sovereignty over Sea Areas, Air Space and Outer Space', *Netherlands International Law Review*, vol. 9, 1962, pp. 150–85.

——, 'Some Basic Problems of Coastal State Jurisdiction and the Failure of the Sea Conference', *Annals of International Studies*, vol. 4, 1973, pp. 143–81.

Brian, S., 'Innocent Passage as a Rule of Decision: Navigation v. Environmental Protection', *Columbia Journal of Transnational Law*, vol. 21, 1982, pp. 49–109.

Brown, P.M., 'Protective Jurisdiction of Maritime Water', *Proceedings of the American Society of International Law Review*, *AJIL*, vol. 17, 1923, pp. 89–95.

Brüel, E., 'Some observations on the statements concerning the legal position of international straits made by the International Court of Justice;, *Gegenwartsprobleme des Internationalen Reichts und Rechtsphilosophie*, Constantopulos and Wehberg (eds), Hamburg, Girardet, 1953, pp. 259–178.

Burke, W.T., 'Submerged Passage through Straits: Interpretation of Proposed Law of the Sea Treaty Test', *Washington Law Review*, vol. 54, 1977, p. 198.

Butler, W.E., 'Soviet Concepts of Innocent Passage', *Harvard International Law Journal*, vol. 7, 1965–66, pp. 113–20.

——, 'The Legal Regime of Russian Territorial Waters', *AJIL*, vol. 62, 1968, pp. 51–77.

——, 'Innocent Passage and the 1982 Convention: The Influence of Soviet Law and Policy', *AJIL*, vol. 81, 1987, pp. 331–47.

Caflisch, L., 'La révision du droit de la mer', *Annuaire Suisse de Droit International*, vol. 29, 1973, pp. 49–81.

Castberg, F., 'Distinction entre les eaux territoriales et les eaux intérieures',

Annuaire de l'Institut de Droit International, vol. 45, tome I, 1954, pp. 113–77.

Colliard, C.A., 'La Convention de Bruxelles relative à la responsabilité des exploitants de navires nucléaires', *AFDI*, 1962, pp. 41–64.

De Vries Reilingh, O.G., 'Warships in Territorial Waters, Their Right of Passage', vol. 2, *Netherlands Yearbook of International Law*, 1971, pp. 29–67.

Delupis, I., 'Foreign Warships and Immunity for Espionage', *AJIL*, vol. 78, 1984, pp. 53–75.

Dupuy, R.J., 'Droit de la mer ou droits sur la mer', *Revue Iranienne des Relations Inernationales*, No. 5 and 6, 1975–76.

Emmanueli, C., 'La pollution maritime et la notion de passage inoffensif', *Annuaire Canadien de Droit International*, vol. II, 1973, pp. 13–36.

Fenn, P.T., 'Origins of the Theory of Territorial Waters', *AJIL*, vol. 20, 1926, pp. 465–82.

Fitzmaurice, G., 'The Case of I'm Alone', *British Yearbook of International Law*, vol. 18, 1936, pp. 82–111.

____, 'Some Results of the Geneva Conference on the Law of the Sea: Part I. The Territorial Sea and Contiguous Zone and Related Topics', *International and Comparative Law Quarterly*, vol. 8, 1959, pp. 73–121.

Froman, D.F., 'Uncharted Waters; Non-Innocent Passage of Warships in the Territorial Sea', *San Diego Law Review*, vol. 21, 1984, pp. 625–89.

Ghost, S., 'The Legal Regime of Innocent Passage through the Territorial Sea', *Indian Journal of International Law*, vol. 20, 1980–82, pp. 216–42.

Hazou, L.L., 'Determining the extent of admissibility of reservations: some considerations with regard to the Third United Nations Conference on the Law of the Sea', *Denver Journal of International Law and Policy*, vol. 9, 1980, pp. 69–83.

Hill, C.A., 'U.S., Law of the Sea and its Effects on the Operating Navy: A Naval Officer's View', *Ocean Development and International Law Journal*, vol. 3, 1976, pp. 341–59.

Janis, M.W., 'Dispute Settlement in the Law of the Sea Convention: the military activities exception', *Ocean Development and International Law Journal*, no. 4, 1977, pp. 51–65.

Jennings, R.Y., 'The Limits of Continental Shelf Jurisdiction: Some Possible Implications of the North-Sea Cases Judgment', *International and Comparative Law Quarterly*, vol. 18, 1969, pp. 819–32.

Jessup, P.C., 'The International Law Commission's 1954 Report on the Regime of the Territorial Sea', *AJIL*, vol. 49, 1955, pp. 221–9.

____, 'The U.N. Conference on the Law of the Sea', *Columbia Law Review*, vol. 59, 1959, pp. 234–48.

Jones, J., 'The Corfu Channel Case: Merits', *British Yearbook of International Law*, vol. 26, 1952, pp. 447–53.

Klein, C.B., 'The Territorial Waters of Archipelagos', *Federal Bar Journal*, vol. 26, 1960, pp. 317–23.

Lucchini, L., 'Passage dans les eaux territoriales et séjour dans les ports du navire à propulsion nucléaire', Droit Nucléaire et Droit Océanique, *Economica*, 1977.

____, 'A propos de l'Amoco Cadiz—La lutte contre la pollution des mers:

Evolution ou révolution du Droit international', *Annuaire français de Droit international*, vol. 14, 1978, pp. 721–71.

McDorman, T.L., 'Reservations and the Law of the Sea Treaty', *Journal of Maritime Law and Commerce*, vol. 13, no. 4, 1982, pp. 481–591.

McDougal, M.S., Burke, W.T. and Vlasic, I.A., 'The Maintenance of Public Order at Sea and the Nationality of Ships', *The American Journal of International Law*, vol. 54, 1960, pp. 25–116.

McRae, D.M., 'The Legal Effect of Interpretative Declarations', *British Yearbook of International Law*, vol. 49, 1978, pp. 155–73.

Maduro, M.F., 'Passage through International Straits—The Prospects Emerging from the Third U.N. Conference on the Law of the Seas', *Journal of Maritime Law and Commerce*, vol. 12, 1980, I, pp. 65–95.

Manin, A., 'L'Echouement du Whisky, 137 et le Droit de la Mer', *Annuaire Français du Droit International*, vol. 27, 1981, pp. 689–750.

Martens, F. de, 'Le Tribunal d'arbitrage de Paris et la mer territoriale', Tome I, *Revue générale de Droit international public*, 1894, pp. 32–43.

Mor, Awad El, 'The Regime of Straits Used for International Navigation in the Light of the Third U.N. Conference on the Law of the Sea', *Revue égyptienne de droit international*, vol. 37, 1981, pp. 13–83.

Nakamura, K., 'The Passage through the Territorial Sea of Foreign Warships carrying Nuclear Weapons', *The Japanese Annual of International Law*, no. 25, 1982, pp. 1–10.

O'Connell, D.P., 'International Law and Contemporary Naval Operations', *British Yearbook of International Law*, vol. 44, 1970, pp. 19–85.

——, 'The Juridical Nature of the Territorial Sea', *British Yearbook of International Law*, vol. 45, 1971, pp. 303–83.

Oxman, B.H., 'Le Régime des navires de guerre dans le cadre de la Convention des Nations Unies sur le droit de la mer', *Annuaire Français de Droit International*, 1982, pp. 811–50.

Pharand, P.D., 'Innocent Passage in the Arctic', *Canadian Yearbook of International Law*, vol. 6, 1968, pp. 3–60.

Przetacznik, F., 'Freedom of Navigation through Territorial Sea and International Straits', *Revue de Droit International*, vol. 55, 1975, pp. 299.

Reeves, J.S., 'Submarines and Innocent Passage', *AJIL*, vol. II, 1971, pp. 147–53.

Richardson, E.L., 'Law of the Sea: Navigation and Other Traditional National Security Considerations', *San Diego Law Review*, vol. 19, no. 3, 1982, pp. 559–76.

Riphagen, W., 'The Jurisdiction of the Coastal State', *The Future of the Law of the Sea*, Bouchez, L.J. and Kaijen, L. (eds), Nijhoff, The Hague, 1973, pp. 154–62.

Robertson, H.B., 'Passage through International Straits: A Right Preserved in the Third U.N. Conference on the Law of the Sea', *Virginia Journal of International Law*, vol. 20, no. 4, 1980, pp. 801–57.

Ronzitti, N., 'Passage inoffensivo nel mare territoriale e la convenzione delle nazioni unite sul diritto del mare', *Rivista di Diritto Internationale*, vol. 68, 1985, Fasc. 1, pp. 32–53.

Rubin, A.P., 'The Impact of the Pueblo Incident in International Law (Incompatibility of Electronic Eavesdropping with Innocent Passage)', *Oregon Law Review*, vol. 49, 1969, pp. 1–12.

Selak, C.B., 'Fishing Vessels and the Principle of Innocent Passage', *AJIL*, vol. 48, 1954, pp. 627–35.

Sethu, R.R., 'The Right of Innocent Passage', *The Law Gazette*, no. 4, 1969, p. 138.

Shao, J., 'The Question of Innocent Passage of Warships: After UNCLOS III', *Marine Policy*, vol. 13, no. 1, 1982, pp. 56–67.

Slonim, S., 'The Freedom of Passage and the 1958 Conference on the Law of the Sea', *Columbia Journal of Transnational Law*, vol. 5, 1966, pp. 96–122.

Sorensen, M., 'Law of the Sea', *International Conciliation*, no. 516, 1958, pp. 193–256.

——, 'The Territorial Sea of Archipelagos', *Varia Juris Gentium Liber Anicorium dedicated to J.P.A. François*, Leiden, Sijthoff, 1959, pp. 315–31.

Tache, S.W., 'The Nationality of Ships: The Definition Controversy and Enforcement of Genuine Link', *The International Lawyer*, vol. 16, no. 2, 1982, pp. 301–12.

Tolentino, A.M., 'Philippine Position on Passage through Archipelagic Waters', *Philippine Yearbook of International Law*, vol. 4, 1974, pp. ??.

Vries, R.V. de, 'Warships in Territorial Waters, Their Right of Innocent Passage', *Netherlands Yearbook of International Law*, vol. 2, 1972, pp. 29–67.

Walker, W.L., 'Territorial Waters: The Cannon Shot Rule', *British Yearbook of International Law*, vol. 22, 1945, pp. 210–31.

Ward, R.E., 'The Right of Innocent Passage and the Legality of Reprisals', *San Diego Law Review*, vol. 13, 1975–76, pp. 765–78.

Williams, G.L., 'The Juridical Basis of Hot Pursuit', *British Yearbook of International Law*, vol. 20, 1939, pp. 83–97.

Young, E., 'New Laws for Old Navies: Military Implications of the Sea', *Survival*, no. 6, 1974, pp. 262–7.

Zwanenberg, A.V., 'Interference with Ships on the High Seas', *International and Comparative Law Quarterly*, vol. 10, 1961, pp. 785–817.

Courses at the Hague Academy of International Law

Baldoni, C., 'Les navires de guerre dans les eaux territoriales étrangères', *Recueil*, vol. 65, 1938, pp. 185–303.

Bernhardt, R., 'Custom and Treaty in the Law of the Sea', (Recueil des cours) *Hague Academy of International Law*, vol. V, 1987, pp. 251–330, particularly p. 329.

Brüel, E., 'Les détroits danois au point de vue du droit international', *Recueil*, vol. 55, 1936–I, pp. 599–695.

Caminos, H., 'Legal Regime of Straits in the 1982 Convention on the Law of the Sea' (Recueil des cours) *Hague Academy of International Law*, vol. V, 1987, pp. 13–245.

Gidel, G., 'La mer territoriale et la zone contiguë', *Recueil*, vol. 48, 1934–II, pp. 137–277.

Scerni, M., 'Les espaces maritimes et le pouvoir des Etats', *Recueil*, vol. 122, 1967–III, pp. 107–72.

Wilson, G.G., 'Les eaux adjacentes au territoire des Etats', *Recueil*, vol. I, 1923, pp. 127–75.

Index

Arrangement is word by word.